Adobe® InDesign® CS6

ILLUSTRATED

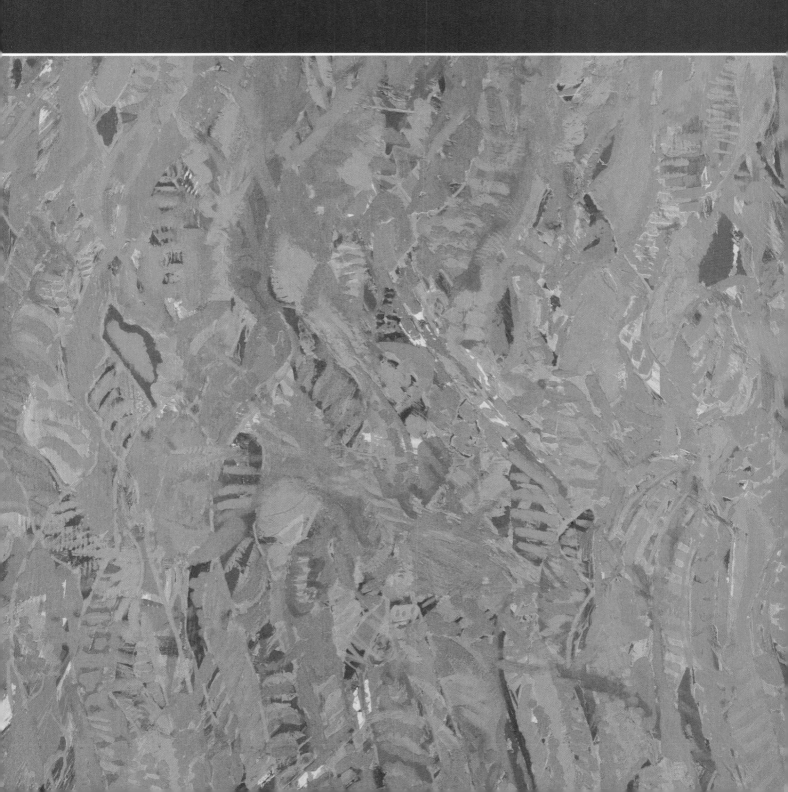

Adobe® InDesign® CS6

ILLUSTRATED

Ann Fisher

COURSE TECHNOLOGY
CENGAGE Learning®

Australia • Brazil • Japan • Korea • Mexico • Singapore • Spain • United Kingdom • United States

COURSE TECHNOLOGY
CENGAGE Learning·

Adobe® InDesign® CS6—Illustrated
Ann Fisher

Editor-in-Chief: Marie Lee

Executive Editor: Marjorie Hunt

Associate Acquisitions Editor: Amanda Lyons

Senior Product Manager: Christina Kling-Garrett

Product Manager: Kim Klasner

Editorial Assistant: Brandelynn Perry

Director of Marketing: Cheryl Costantini

Developmental Editor: Barbara Waxer

Senior Content Project Manager: Cathie DiMassa

Art Director: GEX Publishing Services

Print Buyer: Fola Orekoya

Text Designer: GEX Publishing Services

Proofreader: Kim Kosmatka

Indexer: BIM Indexing

QA Reviewers: Jeff Schwartz, Danielle Shaw,
   John Freitas, Susan Whalen

Cover Designer: GEX Publishing Services

Cover Artist: Mark Hunt

Composition: GEX Publishing Services

For product information and technology assistance, contact us at
Cengage Learning Customer & Sales Support, 1-800-354-9706

For permission to use material from this text or product, submit all requests online at **www.cengage.com/permissions**
Further permissions questions can be emailed to
permissionrequest@cengage.com

Library of Congress Control Number: 2012943492

ISBN-13: 978-1-133-18758-5

ISBN-10: 1-133-18758-7

Cengage Learning
20 Channel Center Street
Boston, MA 02210
USA

Cengage Learning is a leading provider of customized learning solutions with office locations around the globe, including Singapore, the United Kingdom, Australia, Mexico, Brazil, and Japan. Locate your local office at:
international.cengage.com/region

Cengage Learning products are represented in Canada by Nelson Education, Ltd.

To learn more about Course Technology, visit **www.cengage.com/coursetechnology**

To learn more about Cengage Learning, visit **www.cengage.com**

Purchase any of our products at your local college store or at our preferred online store **www.cengagebrain.com**

Printed in the United States of America
1 2 3 4 5 6 7 18 17 16 15 14 13 12

Brief Contents

Contents

Integration

Preface

Welcome to *Adobe® InDesign® CS6— Illustrated*. The unique page design of the book makes it a great learning tool for both new and experienced users. Each skill is presented on two facing pages so that you don't have to turn the page to find a screen shot or finish a paragraph. See the illustration on the right to learn more about the pedagogical and design elements of a typical lesson.

This book is an ideal learning tool for a wide range of learners—the "rookies" will find the clean design easy to follow and focused with only essential information presented, and the "hot shots" will appreciate being able to move quickly through the lessons to find the information they need without reading a lot of text. The design also makes this a great reference after the course is over!

Coverage

This text is organized into eight units. In these units, students learn how to work with the InDesign interface, along with objects, text, vector and bitmap graphics. They will also use the Links, Pages, and Layers panels to organize their publications. In addition, students will learn about color options in InDesign, and create tables and interactive documents.

Each two-page spread focuses on a single skill.

Introduction briefly explains why the lesson skill is important.

A case scenario motivates the steps and puts learning in context.

UNIT
D
InDesign CS6

Understanding Bitmap and Vector Graphics

Graphic files come in many formats. Two formats that are commonly placed into InDesign documents are bitmap and vector. A **bitmap graphic** is a graphic that is made up of **pixels**: tiny color squares arranged in a grid that are used to display graphics shown on a monitor or television screen. Scanned photographs and photographs taken from a digital camera are bitmap graphics. Files created in an image-editing software program, such as Adobe Photoshop, are another example of bitmap graphics. If you zoom in on a bitmap graphic or greatly increase its size, you can see its pixels. A **vector graphic** is a graphic that is made up of **vectors**, which are straight or curved line segments connected by **anchor points** (small dots), much like a completed connect-the-dots drawing. Vector graphics are created in drawing programs such as Adobe Illustrator. They are an ideal format for illustrations and logos because they can be resized in page layouts without losing image quality. Vector graphics can be manipulated in InDesign using the Pen tool and the Direct Selection tool. You can add, move, and delete anchor points and line segments to change the shape of the vector. Before working with the images you'll use in the advertisement, you review the properties of bitmap and vector graphics.

STEPS

1. **Start InDesign, open ID D-1.indd from the drive and folder where you store your Data Files, then save it as** graphics_ID-D
   The file includes one bitmap image of papayas and one vector image of an apple.

2. **Click the workspace switcher on the Menu bar, then click** Essentials

3. **Click the Zoom tool** **on the Tools panel**
   You use the Zoom tool to enlarge your view of the bitmap image to view the pixels.

4. **Drag a small rectangle with the Zoom tool pointer** ⊕ **over the papayas image in the approximate location shown in Figure D-1, then release the mouse button**
   The dotted rectangle that appears as you drag the Zoom tool pointer is called a **marquee**. Everything inside the marquee will be enlarged on the screen when you release the mouse pointer. At a high zoom percentage, you can easily see the pixels that make up the image.

5. **Click View on the Menu bar, then click** Fit Page in Window

6. **Click the Direct Selection tool** ⍅ **on the Tools panel, then position the Direct Selection tool pointer** ⍅ **near the upper-right edge of the apple until it appears with a small line segment next to it** ⍅
   When the Direct Selection tool pointer is positioned over the edge of an unselected vector graphic, the anchor points and line segments become visible. As shown in Figure D-2, the pointer is over a line segment, indicated by the tiny line segment icon next to the arrow pointer.

QUICK TIP
In order to manipulate a vector graphic's anchor points and line segments in InDesign, you must copy and paste it from Illustrator to InDesign. If you use the Place command, the vector graphic will not be editable.

7. **Click any one of the anchor points on either side of the line segment, then drag slowly in any direction to change the location of the anchor point and the shape of the apple, as shown in Figure D-3**
   Most vector graphics are created in Adobe Illustrator, but they can be manipulated in Adobe InDesign using the similar tools.

8. **Save your work, then close** graphics_ID-D.indd

InDesign 78   Working with Graphics

Tips and troubleshooting advice, right where you need it—next to the step itself.

Assignments

The lessons use MegaPixel, a design agency, as the case study. MegaPixel has many clients including The Happy Apple, an organic supermarket, and BreakTime, a student-travel company. The assignments on the light yellow pages at the end of each unit increase in difficulty. Additional case studies provide a variety of interesting and relevant exercises for students to practice skills.

Assignments include:

- **Concepts Reviews** consist of multiple choice, matching, and screen identification questions.

- **Skills Reviews** provide additional hands-on, step-by-step reinforcement.

- **Independent Challenges** are case projects requiring critical thinking and application of the unit skills. The Independent Challenges increase in difficulty, with the first one in each unit being the easiest. Independent Challenges 2 and 3 become increasingly open-ended, requiring more independent problem solving.

- **Real Life Independent Challenges** are practical exercises to help students with their everyday lives by focusing on important and useful essential skills, including creating business cards, greeting cards, schedules, and booklets.

- **Advanced Challenge Exercises** set within the Independent Challenges provide optional steps for more advanced students.

- **Visual Workshops** are practical, self-graded capstone projects that require independent problem solving.

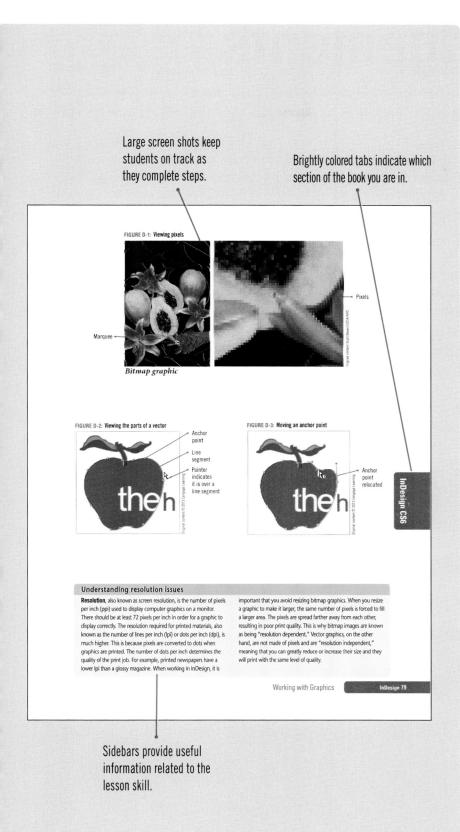

Large screen shots keep students on track as they complete steps.

Brightly colored tabs indicate which section of the book you are in.

Sidebars provide useful information related to the lesson skill.

Acknowledgements

Author Acknowledgements

I very much enjoyed writing this book, mostly because of the great team that I had to work with. I would like to thank Marie Lee, Editor-in-Chief at Course Technology; Marjorie Hunt, Executive Editor; and Amanda Lyons, Associate Acquisitions Editor for giving me this opportunity. I would also like to thank my Senior Product Manager, Christina Kling-Garrett, and my Senior Content Project Manager, Cathie DiMassa. These two women are fun, smart, and know how to get the job done. Barbara Waxer, both my friend and developmental editor, brought ideas and energy into this project. Her wonderful karma was transmitted from New Mexico to Boston and into the pages of this book. Barbara also provided me with beautiful images to use in the book. Thank you too, to Anita Quintana of Media Mantis Designs and Santa Fe Community College. Anita designed the Happy Apple logo and the Newsletter document found in Unit A. I would also like to thank Charles Cooper for providing me with beautiful images of Sun Valley, Idaho which are used in some of the end-of-unit exercises.

And of course, thank you to our wonderful QA reviewers, Jeff Schwartz, John Freitas, Susan Whalen, and Danielle Shaw who all were instrumental in making sure the exercises flowed perfectly.

Finally, I would like to dedicate this book to my husband, Douglas Fisher, who made it possible for me to find the time to write, my children, and of course my dog, Panda, who was great company during the writing and editing process.

– Ann Fisher

Advisory Board Acknowledgements

We would like to thank our Advisory Board for their honest feedback and suggestions that helped guide our development decisions for this edition. They are as follows:

Rich Barnett, Wadsworth High School

Lisa Cogley, James A. Rhodes State College

Trudy Lund, Smoke Valley School District

Diane Miller, James A. Rhodes State College

Charles Schneider, Red Clay Consolidated School District

Read This Before You Begin

This book assumes the following:

1. The software has been registered properly. If the product is not registered, students must respond to registration and dialog boxes each time they start the software.
2. Default tools in the Tools panel might differ, but tool options and other settings do not carry over to the End-of-Unit exercises or between units.
3. Students know how to create a folder using a file management utility.
4. After introduction and reinforcement in initial units, the student will be able to respond to the dialog boxes that open when saving a file. Later units do not provide step-by-step guidance.
5. Panels, windows, and dialog boxes have default settings when opened. Exceptions may occur when students open these elements repeatedly in a lesson or in the unit.
6. Students will be instructed in the early units on how to update missing links. Later units do not provide step-by-step guidance.
7. The few exercises that do contain live type were created using commonly available fonts. Nevertheless, it is possible that students may run into a missing font issue when opening a data file. In that case, students should use an available font that is similar to the size and weight of the type shown in the lesson.

Frequently Asked Questions

What are the Minimum System Requirements (Windows)?

- Intel® Pentium® 4 or AMD Athlon® 64 or faster processor with 1GB RAM (2GB recommended)

- Microsoft® Windows Vista or Windows 7

- 1.6GB of available hard disk space (2 GB recommended)

- Color monitor with 16-bit color video card

- DVD-ROM

- Adobe Flash Player 10 (for exporting SWF files)

What are Data Files and where are they located?

Your instructor will provide the Data Files to you or direct you to a location on a network drive from which you can download them. As you download the files, select where to store them, such as a hard drive, a network server, or a USB drive. The instructions in the lessons refer to "the drive and folder where your Data Files are stored" when referring to the Data Files for the book.

What software was used to write and test this book?

This book was written and tested with Adobe InDesign CS6 using a typical installation of Microsoft Windows 7 with Aero turned on.

Do I need to be connected to the Internet to complete the steps and exercises in this book?

Some of the exercises in this book assume that your computer is connected to the Internet. If you are not connected to the Internet, see your instructor for information on how to complete the exercises.

What do I do if my screen is different from the figures shown in this book?

This book was written and tested on computers with monitors set at a resolution of 1280 × 1024. If your screen shows more or less information than the figures in the book, your monitor is probably set at a higher or lower resolution. If you don't see something on your screen, you might have to scroll down or up to see the object identified in the figures.

CourseMate

ENGAGING. TRACKABLE. AFFORDABLE

Cengage Learning's CourseMate for Adobe InDesign CS6 Illustrated brings course concepts to life with interactive learning, study, and exam preparation tools that support the printed textbook. Watch student comprehension soar as your class works with the printed textbook and the textbook-specific website. CourseMate goes beyond the book to deliver what you need!

FOR STUDENTS:

Interactive eBook that you can read, highlight, or annotate on your computer.

Total Training videos with audio-visual, step-by-step instructions reinforce concepts you learn about Adobe InDesign.

Glossary and Flashcards to help you master key terms.

Interactive exercises give you immediate feedback to help you learn.

FOR INSTRUCTORS:

Engagement Tracker, a first-of-its-kind tool that monitors student engagement in the course.

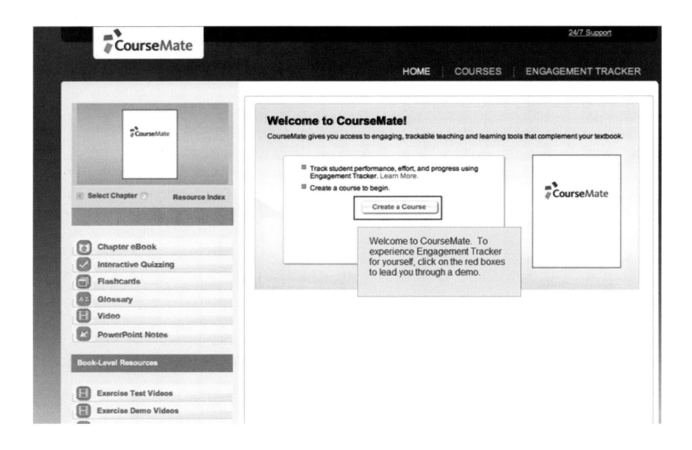

Instructor Resources

The Instructor Resources CD is Course Technology's way of putting the resources and information needed to teach and learn effectively into your hands. With an integrated array of teaching and learning tools that offer you and your students a broad range of technology-based instructional options, we believe this CD represents the highest quality and most cutting edge resources available to instructors today. The resources available with this book are:

• **Instructor's Manual**—Available as an electronic file, the Instructor's Manual includes detailed lecture topics with teaching tips for each unit.

• **Sample Syllabus**—Prepare and customize your course easily using this sample course outline.

• **PowerPoint Presentations**—Each unit has a corresponding PowerPoint presentation that you can use in lecture, distribute to your students, or customize to suit your course.

• **Figure Files**—The figures in the text are provided on the Instructor Resources CD to help you illustrate key topics or concepts. You can create traditional overhead transparencies by printing the figure files. Or you can create electronic slide shows by using the figures in a presentation program such as PowerPoint.

• **Solutions to Exercises**—Solutions to Exercises contains files students are asked to create or modify in the lessons and end-of-unit material. Also provided in this section is a document outlining the solutions for the end-of-unit Concepts Review, Skills Review, and Independent Challenges.

• **Data Files for Students**—To complete the units in this book, your students will need Data Files. You can post the Data Files on a file server for students to copy. The Data Files are available on the Instructor Resources CD-ROM, the Review Pack, and can also be downloaded from cengagebrain.com. For more information on how to download the Data Files, see the inside front cover.

• **ExamView**—ExamView is a powerful testing software package that allows you to create and administer printed, computer (LAN-based), and Internet exams. ExamView includes hundreds of questions that correspond to the topics covered in this text, enabling students to generate detailed study guides that include page references for further review. The computer-based and Internet testing components allow students to take exams at their computers, and also save you time by grading each exam automatically.

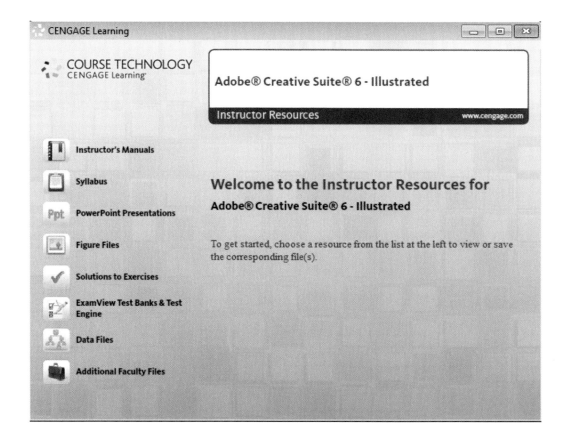

Other Adobe® CS6 Titles

Adobe® Dreamweaver® CS6—Illustrated
Sherry Bishop (9781133526025)

Eleven units provide essential training on using Dreamweaver CS6 to create websites. Coverage includes creating a web site, developing web pages, formatting text, using and managing images, creating links and navigation bars using CSS to lay out pages, and collecting data with forms.

Adobe® Flash® Professional CS6—Illustrated
Barbara M. Waxer (9781133526001)

Eight units provide essential training on using Adobe Flash Professional CS6, including creating graphics, text, and symbols, using the Timeline, creating animation, creating buttons and using media, adding interactivity, and integrating content with other CS6 programs.

Adobe® Illustrator® CS6—Illustrated
Chris Botello (9781133526407)

Eight units cover essential skills for working with Adobe Illustrator CS6 including drawing basic and complex shapes, using the Pen tool, working with blends, compound paths and clipping masks, creating pattern fills and gradient fills for objects, and designing stunning 3D effects.

Adobe® InDesign® CS6—Illustrated
Ann Fisher (9781133187585)

Eight units provide essential training on using Adobe InDesign CS6 for designing simple layouts, combining text, graphics, and color, as well as multi-page documents, layered documents, tables, and InDesign libraries.

Adobe® Photoshop® CS6—Illustrated
Chris Botello (9781133190394)

Eight units offer thorough coverage of essential skills for working with Adobe Photoshop CS6 from both the design and production perspective, including creating and managing layer masks, creating color effects and improving images with adjustment layers, working with text and combining text and imagery, and using filters and layer styles to create eye-popping special effects.

Adobe® Creative Suite 6 Web Tools: Dreamweaver, Photoshop, and Flash Illustrated (9781133629740)

Covers essential skills for working with Adobe Dreamweaver® CS6, Adobe Photoshop® CS6, and Adobe Flash® CS6 with ten Dreamweaver units, one Bridge unit, four Photoshop units, five Flash units, and one unit on integration.

Adobe® Creative Suite 6 Design Tools: Photoshop, Illustrator, and InDesign Illustrated (9781133562580)

Covers essential skills for working with Adobe Photoshop® CS6, Adobe Illustrator® CS6, and Adobe InDesign® CS6 with seven Photoshop units, seven Illustrator units, six InDesign units, and one unit on integration.

For more information on the Illustrated Series, please visit:
www.cengage.com/ct/illustrated

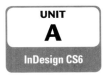

Getting Started with InDesign CS6

Files You Will Need:

To view a list of files needed for this unit, see the Data Files Grid in the back of the book.

Adobe InDesign CS6 is part of the Adobe Creative Suite 6 (CS6) family of software programs. InDesign is a page layout software program used to design and produce documents that can be printed or used on the web and mobile devices. You can create anything from a simple business card to a book. You can also export InDesign documents for use in Adobe Dreamweaver and Flash. If you are working toward a career as a graphic designer, knowledge of InDesign is a must. MegaPixel is a graphic arts service bureau and design agency. You work as a designer at MegaPixel and use Adobe InDesign to create documents for a number of clients.

OBJECTIVES

Understand page layout software

Start InDesign

Explore the InDesign workspace

Create a new document

Name and saving a document

Work with panels

Work with guides

Understand export options for InDesign

Understanding Page Layout Software

Adobe InDesign is a page layout software program. **Page layout software** includes tools that allow you to easily position text and graphics on document pages. For example, using InDesign, you could create a newsletter that includes articles and pictures on each page. To make a document interactive for the web or a mobile device, you can incorporate hyperlinks, buttons, animation, sounds, and video. If you have the idea, you can create it in InDesign as long as you are familiar with its tools and features.  MegaPixel has hired an assistant, Chris, to help you out. You demonstrate InDesign's features to Chris using a newsletter you created for The Happy Apple, an organic supermarket, shown in Figure A-1.

DETAILS

Using InDesign, you can accomplish the following:

- **Create and place text**

  You can create text in InDesign and then format it. In addition to choosing fonts and font sizes, you can change the color of text, control the spacing between each character, and even place it along a path. You can also place text from another source, such as Microsoft Word, in an InDesign document.

QUICK TIP

If you are familiar with the Pen tool in Illustrator or Photoshop, you will be ready to use the Pen tool in InDesign.

- **Create and place graphics**

  You can create simple graphics in InDesign with the shape tools and the Pen tool. You can also place illustrations and photographs from other programs, such as Illustrator and Photoshop, in InDesign documents.

- **Choose from many colors**

  InDesign contains many color samples, called **swatches**, to choose from. The Swatches panel includes the basic colors used for printed materials. There are also other color libraries to choose from for special purposes. For example, there is a web swatch library for documents that will be used on the web or published digitally.

- **Position objects easily**

  InDesign offers many features that help you position text and graphics with accuracy. You can snap objects to ruler guides or a grid. You can also use the Transform panel and the Control panel to define an object's width, height, rotation angle, and vertical and horizontal location. The Align panel allows you to align and distribute objects by their tops, bottoms, centers, or sides.

- **Store items**

  Libraries are storage containers for items that you use repeatedly and want easy access to when working in InDesign. Company logos, legal jargon or standard language, and contact information are good examples of items to store in a library. Libraries look just like panels, but they are actually InDesign documents that are saved with the .indl extension. Libraries are not linked to one InDesign document; you can open and use them with multiple InDesign documents.

- **Create interactive buttons and hyperlinks**

  In InDesign, you can use buttons and hyperlinks to design clickable areas in a document that link to a web page, another file, or another page in your document. Hyperlinks and buttons that are created in InDesign become usable (clickable) when you export an InDesign document as an Adobe PDF (Portable Document Format) document or as a web format.

- **Export documents**

  You can export an InDesign document as another file type so that it can be used in another program or as a standalone product, such as an ebook. For example, you can export an InDesign document as a Flash Player file (SWF), a Flash Professional CS6 file (FLA), an EPUB, or a PDF.

Text created and
formatted in
InDesign

Logo created
in Adobe
Illustrator

Text created in
Microsoft Word
and placed in
InDesign

Photographs
placed in
frames

Image optimized
in Photoshop

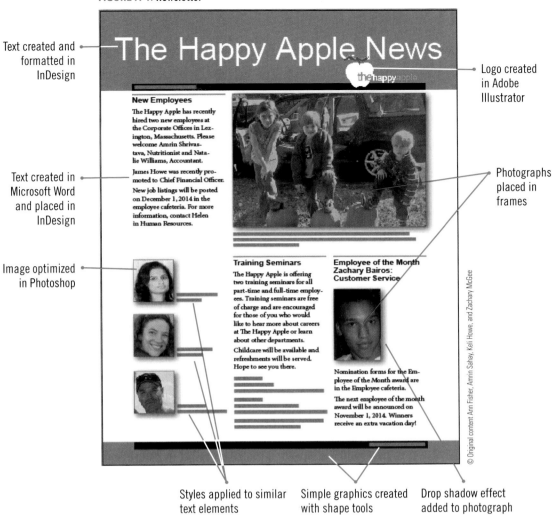

Styles applied to similar
text elements

Simple graphics created
with shape tools

Drop shadow effect
added to photograph

Starting InDesign

When you start InDesign for the first time, you will see the InDesign Welcome Screen. The Welcome Screen offers options for opening a recent document, creating a new document, or visiting one of Adobe's community websites. If you do not wish to view the Welcome Screen upon starting InDesign, you can click the Don't show again check box in the lower-left corner of the window. When you start InDesign without the Welcome Screen, the program opens without any documents open. You start InDesign and open a document so that you can familiarize Chris with the program.

STEPS

TROUBLE

Macintosh users: To open InDesign, double-click the hard drive icon on the desktop, double-click the Applications folder, double-click the Adobe InDesign CS6 folder, then double-click Adobe InDesign CS6. While performing the steps in this book, if you see the Missing Fonts dialog box, you can choose to use the substitute font supplied by InDesign or click Find Font, choose another font in the Font Family list, then click OK.

1. **Click the Start button ⊙ on the taskbar, point to All Programs, click Adobe (or the name of the Adobe folder in the Start menu) if necessary, then click Adobe InDesign CS6**

   The InDesign window opens, showing the default workspace, as shown in Figure A-2. You may see the Welcome Screen in the center of the window when InDesign opens. The Welcome Screen will not be used in this unit. To close the Welcome Screen, click the Don't show again check box in the lower-left corner, then click the Close button. At a lower screen resolution, your Menu bar may appear in two rows instead of one.

2. **Click File on the Menu bar, then click Open**

   The Open a File dialog box opens.

3. **Navigate to the location where you store your Data Files, click newsletter_ID-A.indd, then click Open**

   The newsletter_ID-A.indd file opens in InDesign, and a warning box appears stating that the document contains links to missing or modified files. You'll learn more about links in a later lesson, and you can explore the topic now by reading *Understanding more about links* below.

4. **Click Update Links in the warning box**

   The warning box closes, and the newsletter document opens with the Links panel open on the right side of the workspace, as shown in Figure A-3.

5. **Click the Collapse to Icons arrow ⏵⏵ to close the Links panel**

Understanding more about links

When you place a photo or a picture in InDesign, you are only placing a preview of it for viewing. Each preview is linked to the original artwork and its location on the hard drive. This helps to keep each InDesign document's size small and manageable. If you move the photos or pictures that you placed in InDesign to a new location or modify them after you placed them in InDesign, InDesign prompts you to find them by showing you a warning box stating that some files may be missing or modified. In many cases, the linked files are not missing, they have just been copied to a CD or copied onto a network. You need to navigate to the new location in order to open the document correctly.

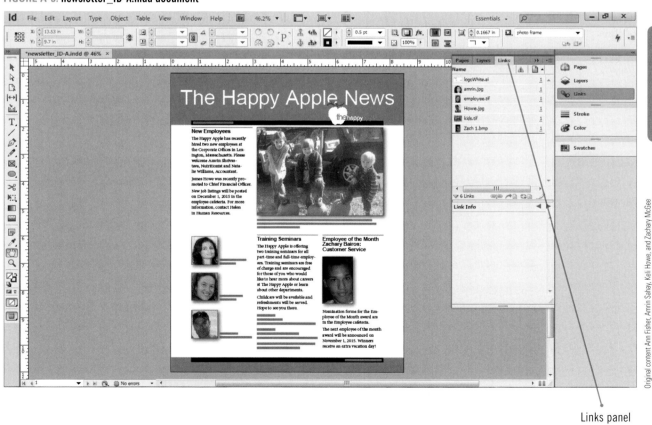

Links panel

Exploring the InDesign Workspace

A workspace is where you create your projects. Workspaces typically include an area designated for creating a finished product, much like a painter would use a canvas to create a painting. The InDesign workspace allows you to focus on your work without getting distracted by tools and panels. When you start InDesign for the first time, you see the default workspace, called "Essentials," with the Control panel and Tools panel along the top and left side of the InDesign window. You examine the workspace elements with Chris.

DETAILS

The InDesign workspace includes the following features, as shown in Figure A-4:

TROUBLE
The Menu bar appears at the top of the screen. The Minimize, Maximize, and Close buttons appear on the Document window. The document tab only appears if more than one document is open.

- The **document tab** appears just above the horizontal ruler and includes the document's name, its current magnification level, and a Close button. When more than one document is open, a tab appears for each document and the document tabs appear in a horizontal row. Click a document tab to view that document in the window. You can drag a document tab out of the group to open it in a stand-alone window.

- The **Menu bar** sits at the top of the workspace and includes several menus. To open a menu, click the menu name on the Menu bar. Each menu lists commands that relate to the menu category. To the right of the menu names are workspace and view options.

- The **Control panel** is located directly beneath the Menu bar and above the horizontal ruler. On a Macintosh, the Control panel appears above the Document window. When you select an object, the Control panel displays information about that object, such as its size and location on the page.

TROUBLE
Click the double arrow icon above the Tools panel to change the panel into two columns.

- The **Tools panel** contains the tools available in InDesign. There are tools for creating objects, such as the Rectangle tool, tools for transforming objects, such as the Rotate tool, and tools for changing the page view and navigating the workspace, such as the Zoom tool and the Hand tool. Some tools have a small black triangle in the lower-right corner. This indicates that additional tools are available beneath that tool. Click and hold the tool to see the hidden tools.

- **Panels** are small windows that contain options for working with selected objects. You make choices in panels by clicking buttons, choosing items from lists, or using a command on the panel menu. Panels are positioned on the right side of the workspace and are identified by a name and an icon.

QUICK TIP
The four sides of the document page are called **page guides**.

- The **Document window** is the central area that represents the open InDesign document. It resembles a piece of paper and is surrounded by a black border. The black border represents the page border. The default Document window size is 8.5" × 11". Notice the two red rectangles at the top and bottom of the publication. These elements extend to the page borders on one or more sides, a printing issue known as **bleeding**. To print this document correctly, making sure that red bleed elements are not trimmed too close, a special bleed guide is added to the document. Bleed elements are enlarged by .25" on each side that they touch the page border. The extra space allows for any margin of error that may occur when the document is trimmed.

- The **pasteboard** is the gray or white area surrounding the Document window. You can place items on the pasteboard before actually inserting them on the page. The pasteboard color is white when you view your Document window with guides and gray when you view the window without guides.

- The horizontal and vertical **rulers** run along the top and left sides of the Document window and pasteboard area. They are helpful for measuring and positioning objects.

- The **status bar** is at the bottom of the workspace. The status bar gives you the status of what is going on at the moment. For example, the status bar shows which page is active in a multipage document.

FIGURE A-4: Essentials workspace

Menu bar

Document tab

Click to change Tools panel layout

Rulers

Tools panel

Triangle indicates additional tools are available

Bleed element

Current workspace

Control panel

Panels (Iconic view)

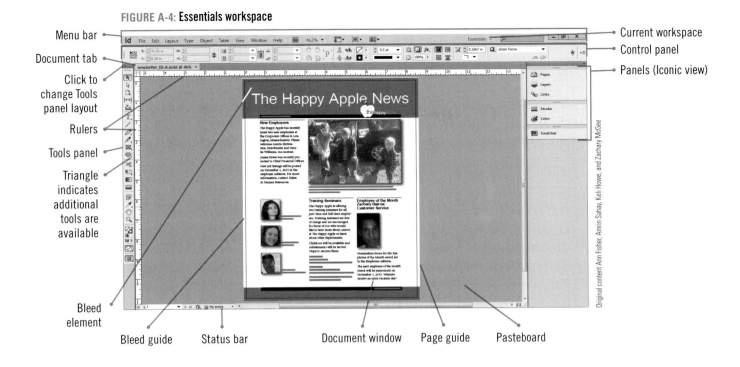

The Happy Apple News

Original content Ann Fisher, Amrin Sahay, Keli Howe, and Zachary McGee

Bleed guide   Status bar   Document window   Page guide   Pasteboard

Using custom workspaces

InDesign offers custom workspaces for specific types of InDesign projects. For example, the Interactive for PDF workspace displays the Buttons and Forms, Hyperlinks, and SWF Preview panels, all of which would be useful when creating an interactive document. To choose a custom workspace, click Window on the Menu bar, point to Workspace, and then click one of the eight workspace names. You can also create your own custom workspace with a unique name. For example, you may prefer to hide all of the panels in order to maximize your Document window, or you may want the Tools panel to be located closer to your layout. InDesign makes it very easy to create the workspace you want and then save it. Once the workspace is set up as you like it, click Window on the Menu bar, point to Workspace, then click New Workspace. In the New Workspace dialog box, name the workspace, choose whether you want the new workspace to capture panel locations and/or menu customization, and then click OK. Your custom workspace will be added to the list of custom workspaces. The name of the current workspace appears in the workspace switcher on the right side of the Menu bar. "Essentials" is the default workspace name. To switch to a different workspace, click the workspace switcher on the Menu bar, and then click the name of the workspace you want to use.

Creating a New Document

Before you create a new InDesign document, you should know what it is that you'd like to create. Planning helps you make the right choices in the New Document dialog box. To create a new document, click File on the Menu bar, point to New, then click Document to open the New Document dialog box. You can save your document settings in the New Document dialog box for future use. MegaPixel's client, The Happy Apple organic supermarket, is offering a new service for its customers: a low-interest Happy Apple credit card. You need to create an in-store flyer advertising the credit card. You show Chris how to create a new document.

STEPS

1. **With the newsletter_ID-A.indd document open, click** File **on the Menu bar, click** Close, **click** No **(Win) or** Don't Save **(Mac) to reject the changes to the newsletter_ID-A.indd document made when the links were fixed, click** Window **on the Menu bar, point to** Workspace, **then click** Reset Essentials

   The Essentials workspace is reset to display the Pages, Layers, Links, Stroke, Color, and Swatches panels in Iconic view.

2. **Click** Edit **(Win) or** InDesign **(Mac) on the Menu bar, point to** Preferences, **then click** General

   The Preferences dialog box opens with the options for the General category visible.

3. **Click** Units & Increments **on the left side of the dialog box, click the** Horizontal list arrow **under Ruler Units, click** Inches **if necessary, click the** Vertical list arrow, **click** Inches **if necessary, then click** OK **to close the dialog box**

   Inches will be used as the unit of measurement on the horizontal and vertical rulers.

4. **Click** File **on the Menu bar, point to** New, **then click** Document

   The New Document dialog box opens, as shown in Figure A-5, showing [Default] as the Document Preset. A **preset** is a collection of all of the settings in the New Document dialog box, saved and stored with a descriptive name and available for future use.

5. **Click the** Intent list arrow, **notice that you can choose between Print, Web, and Digital Publishing, then click** Print, **the default setting**

   The flyer you are creating will be printed. When you choose Web or Digital Publishing from the Intent list arrow, InDesign changes the unit of measurement to **pixels** (px), the unit of measure for on-screen resolution.

6. **Click the** Page Size list arrow **to view the standard sizes that are available**

   The default page size is Letter, which is 8.5" × 11". Other options include Legal, which is 8.5" × 14" and used for legal documents; Tabloid, which is 11" × 17" and used for small newspaper formats; and A4, which is the international standard paper size. Note that you can also create a custom size.

7. **Press** [Esc] **to close the list, then click the** Facing Pages check box **to remove the check mark**

   The New Document dialog box changes to display settings for a document that does not contain facing pages. Facing pages are used in multiple-page documents, such as magazines, that require left and right pages. **Facing pages** are also known as **spreads**. When you deselect the Facing Pages check box, the Document Preset changes from [Default] to [Custom] and the Inside and Outside Margins setting labels change to Left and Right.

8. **Double-click the** Top text box **of the Margins section, type** 1, **then press** [Tab]

   The three other Margins settings also change to 1 because the Make all settings the same button in the Margins section is currently selected.

9. **Click** OK **to close the New Document dialog box**

   A letter-sized document with 1-inch margins appears in the workspace, as shown in Figure A-6. The name of the document, "Untitled-1," appears on the document tab. The margins are indicated in the document by colored lines called **margin guides**.

FIGURE A-5: **New Document dialog box**

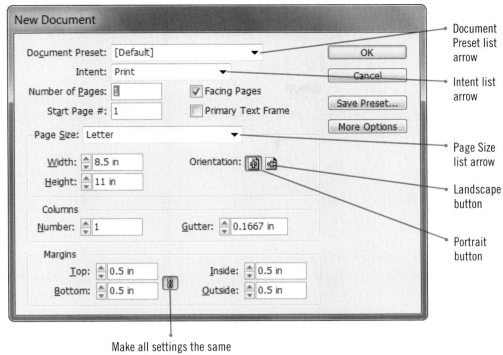

Document Preset list arrow

Intent list arrow

Page Size list arrow

Landscape button

Portrait button

Make all settings the same button (selected)

FIGURE A-6: **New document**

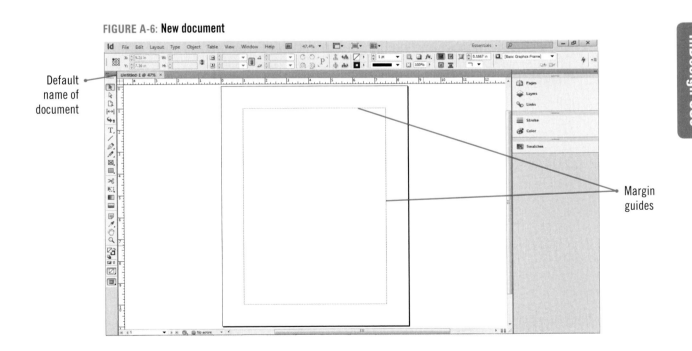

Default name of document

Margin guides

Naming and Saving a Document

Saving your work is very important so that you don't lose anything that you've created. To save a document, click File on the Menu bar, and then click Save. The first time that you save a new document, the Save As dialog box opens, asking you to name the document and to choose a location in which to store it. Once saved, the new filename, followed by the InDesign filename extension **.indd**, appears on the document tab. Once a document is named and saved, you should continue to save your work on a regular basis, such as every 10 minutes. ▓▓▓▓ You save the new document with a unique name.

STEPS

1. **Click** File **on the Menu bar, then click** Save As

   The Save As dialog box opens, as shown in Figure A-7. The default name of the file appears highlighted in the File name text box (Win) or the Save As text box (Mac). Below this text box is the Save as type list arrow (Win), or the Where up and down arrows and the Format up and down arrows (Mac). The default file type is InDesign CS6 document.

2. **Click the** Save in list arrow (Win) **or the** Save As down arrow (Mac), **then navigate to the location where you store your Data Files**

3. **Type** credit card flyer_ID-A **in the File name text box (Win) or the Save As text box (Mac), then click** Save

   The file's new name, credit card flyer_ID-A.indd, appears on the document tab.

TROUBLE

If your document is already a floating window, stop after Step 3.

4. **Drag the** document tab **down to the Document window, then release the mouse button**

   The document becomes a floating window without the document tab and the document name is incorporated into a title bar.

5. **Drag the** floating window **in the workspace so that you can see more of the pasteboard, as shown in Figure A-8**

   Working with floating windows is useful if you need to see artwork in another document while you work in the current one.

6. **Click the** title bar, **then slowly drag it in an upward direction until you see the blue border reappear, then release the mouse button**

   The document tab reappears.

Using Adobe InDesign Help

When working in InDesign, you can access information about the software using the help feature. Click Help on the Menu bar, then click InDesign Help. The InDesign Help page of the Adobe.com website opens in your browser. At the top of the page are help categories, including What's New, Layout and design, and Digital publications. Clicking a category brings you to that section of help and offers more specific topics within the chosen category. Clicking a topic opens a new web page with information about the chosen topic.

Your location
might differ

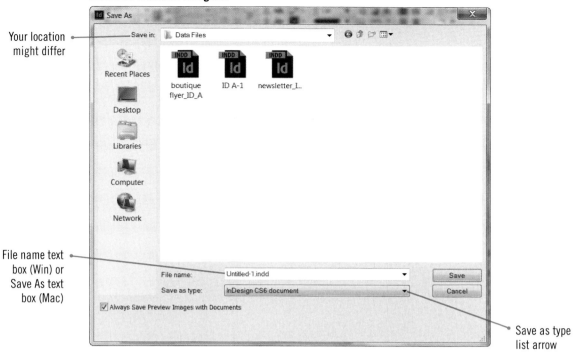

File name text
box (Win) or
Save As text
box (Mac)

Save as type
list arrow

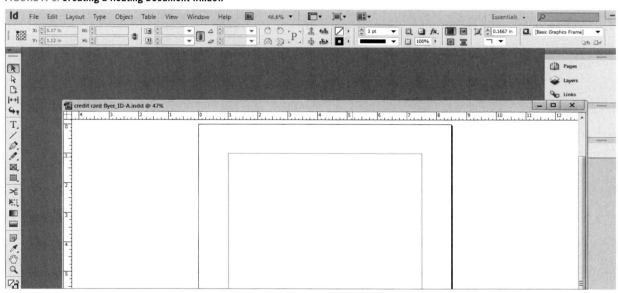

InDesign CS6

Understanding Adobe InDesign CS6 Preferences

You can make changes to InDesign based on your personal preferences. For example, you can choose to use an Italian dictionary instead of the default English dictionary to check the spelling in your document; you can have InDesign underline misspelled words in olive green instead of the default red; or you can change the default color of guides and margin guides. These settings and many more are available in the InDesign Preferences dialog box. To open the Preferences dialog box, click Edit (Win) or InDesign (Mac) on the Menu bar, point to Preferences, then click a preference category, such as Guides & Pasteboard, to open the dialog box. Click a different category on the left side of the dialog box to change categories. In order for the changes you make to stick to all future documents, no documents can be open while you make changes in the Preferences dialog box. If a document is open when you change preference settings, the changes will only affect the current open document.

Working with Panels

Panels are moveable objects in the workspace. Sometimes known as "floating panels," they can be dragged anywhere, even into the Document window. Panels contain buttons, check boxes, and menus you can use to work with and format InDesign objects. For example, the Swatches panel includes color swatches for applying colors to objects. To open a panel in the workspace, click the panel's name or icon. If you don't see the panel you need in the workspace, click Window on the Menu bar, then click the panel name. ▓▓▓▓▓ You demonstrate to Chris how he can customize the appearance of panels.

STEPS

1. **Click Window on the Menu bar, point to Workspace, then click Reset Essentials**

   If necessary, all default panel locations are restored. The most commonly used panels in InDesign appear in Iconic view on the right side of the default workspace: Pages, Layers, Links, Stroke, Color, and Swatches.

2. **Click Swatches on the right side of the workspace**

   As shown in Figure A-9, the Swatches panel opens and is displayed in full view.

3. **Click and hold the Swatches panel tab, then drag it to the Document window**

   The Swatches panel becomes a stand-alone panel. When you create a stand-alone panel, you can drag it wherever you need it in the workspace.

4. **Click the Panel menu button ▾☰ , then click Large Swatch**

   The color swatches on the Swatches panel are displayed in a larger size, making it easier to see them. Each panel has a panel menu button that opens a menu of commands that you can use to change the contents and display of the panel.

5. **Click ▾☰ , then click Name**

   The color swatches on the Swatches panel return to their default size, listed by name.

6. **Drag the Swatches panel tab to just below the Color panel on the right side of the workspace until a light blue line appears under the Color panel, then release the mouse button**

   The Swatches panel is collapsed and returned back to its original icon state and location.

> **QUICK TIP**
> Click the Expand Panels button ◄◄ in the upper-right corner above the panel groups to show all of the panel groups in full view. When all panels are expanded to full view, click the Collapse to Icons button ►► in the upper-right corner to close all of the panel groups.

Working in Normal and Preview modes

Normal mode is the default view when InDesign opens; it displays all of the non-printing elements, such as frame borders, guides, grids, margin guides, and column guides. **Preview mode** hides all of the non-printing elements so that you can focus on your layout without distraction. You can quickly switch from one mode to the other by pressing [W].

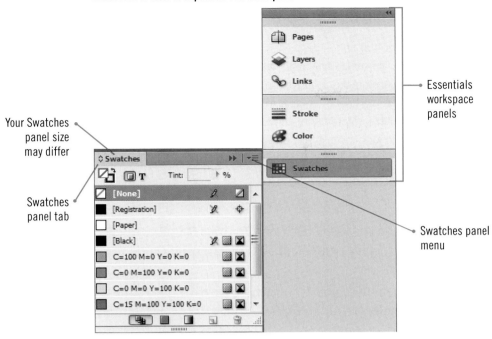

Your Swatches panel size may differ

Swatches panel tab

Essentials workspace panels

Swatches panel menu

Working with panels

Each workspace features different panels that are displayed on the right side of the workspace. Click a panel name to open it in full view. Some panels are part of a group, while others are not. Each group has a row of dotted lines at its top that you can click and drag to move the entire panel group to a new location. There are many ways to arrange panels. For example, you can drag a panel out of its group to make it stand alone. You can also add a panel to a group by dragging the panel on top of the group's dotted line. Finally, you can combine panel groups into one large group. This is known as **docking**. To dock a panel group to another group, drag the panel group to the bottom of the other group until the destination group's dotted lines turn blue, then release the mouse button. Docking panels is useful for grouping frequently used panels. To return panels to their default locations, click Window on the Menu bar, point to Workspace, then reset the workspace you are currently using. All panels are listed on the Window menu. To display a panel, click Window on the Menu bar, then click the name of the panel. If that panel is part of a group, the entire group is displayed in expanded view with the selected panel in front of the others.

InDesign CS6

Working with Guides

Guides are horizontal and vertical lines that you create and position in the Document window. Guides have what seems like a magnetic pull that causes objects such as text or graphics to **snap**, or exactly align, to them. This feature makes it easy to position objects precisely where you want them. You have many options for controlling how the guides in a document work for you: you can align them, lock them, group them, ungroup them, rotate them, and so on. Once you place guides, it is a good idea to group them into one unit and then lock them so you do not move them by accident. ▓▓▓▓ You create four guides on the flyer document to help you accurately position objects that you plan to include in the flyer.

STEPS

TROUBLE
If you see Show Guides instead of Hide Guides, click Show Guides to select it.

QUICK TIP
If the rulers are not visible, click View on the Menu bar, then click Show Rulers.

1. **Click the Selection tool ▶ on the Tools panel, if necessary**

2. **Click View on the Menu bar, point to Grids & Guides, then verify that the first menu item is Hide Guides instead of Show Guides, indicating that guides will show when you create them**

3. **Position the mouse pointer anywhere over the horizontal ruler between the 0-inch and 8.5-inch marks**

   The mouse pointer changes to ▷.

4. **Click the horizontal ruler, drag a guide down to approximately the 3-inch mark on the vertical ruler, as shown in Figure A-10, then release the mouse button**

   A new horizontal guide appears on the page, aligned with the 3-inch mark on the vertical ruler. The Y Location text box on the Control panel displays the vertical location of the guide on the page. You can change the value in the Y Location text box to move the guide to a new location.

5. **Click anywhere on the page to deselect the guide**

   The color of the guide, light blue, can be seen once the guide is no longer selected and the ruler guide icon disappears.

6. **Position the Selection tool pointer ▶ over the guide, then drag the guide to the 4-inch mark on the vertical ruler**

   The original guide is relocated to the 4-inch mark on the vertical ruler. Guides can be moved to new locations after they are created, unless they are locked.

7. **Click the horizontal ruler anywhere between the 0-inch and 8.5-inch marks, then drag a guide down to the 8-inch mark on the vertical ruler**

   A new horizontal guide appears on the page, aligned with the 8-inch mark on the vertical ruler. You can also insert guides by double-clicking the ruler.

8. **Double-click the 1.5-inch mark on the horizontal ruler**

   A new vertical guide appears, aligned with the 1.5-inch mark on the horizontal ruler. The X Location text box on the Control panel displays the horizontal location of the guide on the page. Notice that the new guide extends beyond the margins.

9. **Double-click the 7-inch mark on the horizontal ruler, then save your work**

   Compare your screen to Figure A-11. Notice that the guides created by dragging from the horizontal ruler are the same width as the document page (**page guides**). If you create a guide by double-clicking a ruler or by dragging from a point on the ruler that is outside of the width or height of the document, the created guide extends beyond the document margins and to all of the pages in the spread (**spread guides**).

10. **Click File on the Menu bar, then click Exit (Win) or click InDesign on the Menu bar, then click Quit InDesign (Mac) to exit InDesign**

FIGURE A-10: **New guide**

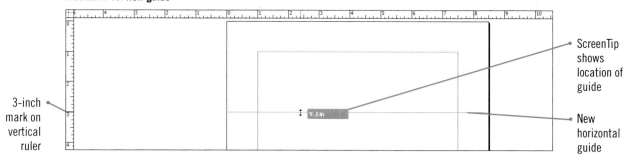

3-inch
mark on
vertical
ruler

ScreenTip
shows
location of
guide

New
horizontal
guide

FIGURE A-11: **Four new guides**

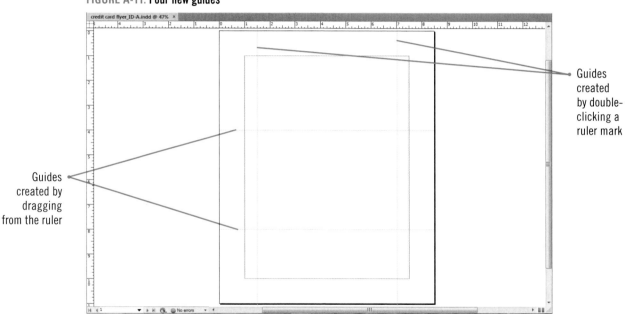

Guides
created
by double-
clicking a
ruler mark

Guides
created by
dragging
from the ruler

Using guides and grids

Liquid guides appear as dashed lines. They are used for InDesign layouts that will be used on the web. Objects that intersect a horizontal or vertical liquid guide will change in height or width if the web page size is changed. To align a guide exactly on a ruler mark, press and hold [Shift] as you drag to create the guide. To lock guides, click View on the Menu bar, point to Grids & Guides, then click Lock Guides. You can remove guides by dragging them off of the page. The **grid** is a preset group of vertical and horizontal lines equidistant from each other in the Document window, much like traditional grid paper. There are only two grids: the **baseline grid**, useful for working with columns of text, and the **document grid**, useful for aligning

objects. Grids are most useful when your design requires you to place multiple items the same distance from each other, such as a dozen check boxes that are part of a checklist. You can change the grid settings, such as its color and spacing, in the Grids section of the Preferences dialog box. To turn the grid on or off, click View on the Menu bar, point to Grids & Guides, then click either Show Baseline Grid or Show Document Grid. You can also choose to snap objects to the grid. To do so, click View on the Menu bar, point to Grids & Guides, then click Snap to Document Grid. As you drag an object toward a grid line, the snap feature pulls it, much like a magnetic pull, and aligns it with the gridline.

InDesign CS6

Understanding Export Options for InDesign

An InDesign CS6 document can be exported as a file format that can be placed in another software program, such as an EPS, a JPG, or a PNG format. It can also be exported as a different file type such as an SWF, XML, or a PDF. In addition, you can export an InDesign document to Flash Professional CS6, where you can apply additional interactive elements to it. It is also possible to export an InDesign document as a digital publication that can be presented on an iPad or similar device, or as an EPUB, which is an ebook or electronic book. 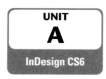 Ted explains to you that your job involves understanding several types of output. He asks you to become familiar with the many export options for InDesign documents.

To export a document, click File on the Menu bar, then click Export. The Export dialog box opens. Choose a file format from the Save as type list arrow (Win) or Format list arrow (Mac), as shown in Figure A-12, and then click Save. Another dialog box opens, offering you specific options for the file format you chose. For example, in Figure A-13, the file is being exported as an interactive PDF. The Export to Interactive PDF dialog box, shown in Figure A-13, allows you to keep the default settings or change them based on your needs. The export file formats are listed below.

- **Adobe PDF (Interactive) and Adobe PDF (Print)**, or **PDF** The file format used in the Adobe Reader and Adobe Acrobat programs that allows you to view documents created by other programs and saved in the PDF file format. An InDesign document exported as a PDF file can be opened and viewed by someone who does not have InDesign. You can export an InDesign document as an Adobe PDF (Print) format or as an Adobe PDF (Interactive) format.

- **EPS (Encapsulated PostScript)** An EPS is a file format which is ideal for print. It stands for encapsulated postscript. EPS files are saved with the CMYK color mode which is used in printing.

- **EPUB (Electronic Publication)** An electronic book file format for ebooks that can be optimized and read on a variety of devices.

- **FLA (Native Flash file type)** You can edit FLA files in Adobe Flash Professional CS6, a development program you can use to create animations that are used on websites and applications. An FLA file is an editable version of the file you originally created in InDesign.

- **HTML (Hypertext Markup Language)** A language web developers use to create web pages.

- **IDML (InDesign Markup)** A format that allows you to open InDesign files in another version of InDesign, such as CS5 or CS4.

- **JPEG (Joint Photographic Experts Group)** A JPEG is a compressed graphic file format that has a smaller file size than other graphic formats and is ideal for use on the web. You can export objects in an InDesign document page as JPEG files. You can also export one page, a range of pages, or an entire InDesign document as a JPEG.

- **PNG (Portable Network Graphics file)** PNG is an ideal file format for use on the web.

- **SWF (Shockwave Flash)** SWF is a very popular format for online animations and games. SWF files are scalable and compact, which makes them perfect for the web and mobile devices. SWF files can be viewed by anyone with Flash Player installed on his or her computer.

- **XML (eXtensible Markup Language)** XML is a file format that stores and transports data in a format accessible by other programs. The XML format allows others to build, modify, and collaborate on projects using shared files by adding **tags** that describe the data.

FIGURE A-12: Export file format options

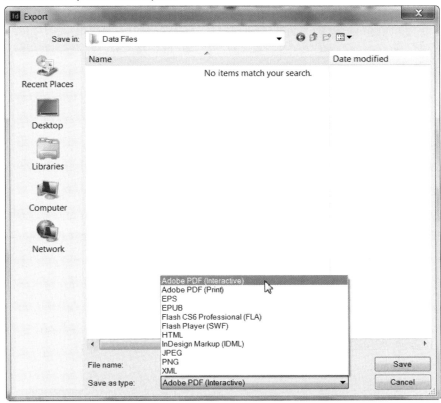

FIGURE A-13: Export to Interactive PDF dialog box

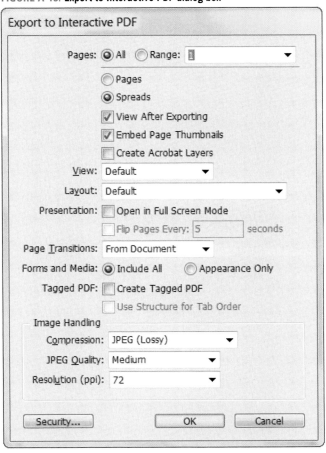

Practice

Concepts Review

Label the elements of the InDesign workspace shown in Figure A-14.

FIGURE A-14

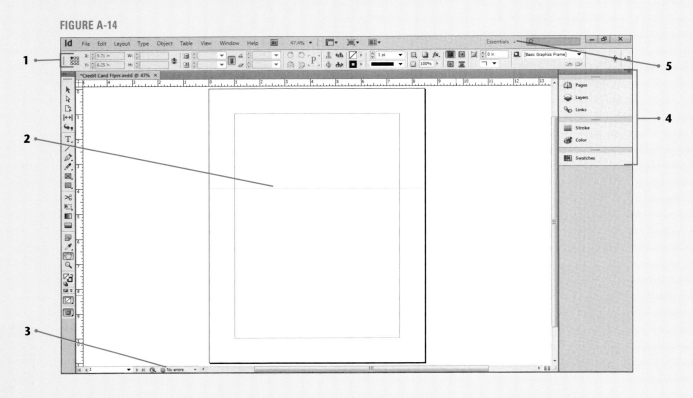

1. _____   4. _____
2. _____   5. _____
3. _____

Match each term with the statement that best describes it.

6. Pixel   **a.** Small floating windows that contain options for working with selected objects

7. Preset   **b.** Unit of measure used for onscreen resolution

8. [W]   **c.** Switches from Normal to Preview mode

9. Panel   **d.** Area where you can place objects before putting them on the page

10. Pasteboard   **e.** Collection of all of the settings in the New Document dialog box

Select the best answer from the list of choices.

11. Which of the following is found in the New Document dialog box?

   a. Intent list arrow

   b. Preferences

   c. Workspace switcher

   d. Panel list arrow

12. How can you create a guide without dragging the mouse pointer?

   a. Use the Guide dialog box

   b. Double-click a ruler mark on the ruler

   c. Click View on the Menu bar, then click Create Guide

   d. Double-click the Y Location value

13. What is the name of the default workspace?

   a. Print

   b. Preset

   c. Exploring

   d. Essentials

14. Which panel displays the vertical or horizontal location of a selected guide?

   a. Guides

   b. Control

   c. Essentials

   d. Location

Skills Review

1. Understand page layout software.

   a. List three types of documents you can create using InDesign.

   b. List four things you can do when working in InDesign.

2. Start InDesign.

   a. Start InDesign using the process appropriate for your operating system and computer.

   b. Open the document boutique flyer_ID-A.indd from the location where you store your Data Files.

   c. Click Update Links in the warning box, if necessary.

   d. Click OK to substitute missing fonts (Mac).

3. Explore the InDesign workspace.

   a. Locate the following items in the InDesign workspace.

     • Title tab (Win) or Title bar (Mac)

     • Menu bar

     • Control panel

     • Horizontal and vertical rulers

     • Tools panel

     • Status bar

     • Panels

     • Document window

     • Pasteboard

   b. Click File on the Menu bar, then click Close.

4. Create a new document.

   a. Open the New Document dialog box using a command on the File menu.

   b. Click the Document Preset list arrow, then click [Default], if necessary.

   c. Verify that the Intent list arrow is set to Print.

   d. Click the Page Size list arrow to view the standard sizes that are available, then click Compact Disc.

   e. Remove the check mark in the Facing Pages check box.

   f. Double-click 0.5 in the Top text box of the Margins section, type **1**, then press [Tab].

   g. Click OK to close the New Document dialog box.

5. Name and save a document.

   a. Click File on the Menu bar, then click Save As.

   b. Click the Save in list arrow (Win) or the Save As down arrow (Mac), then navigate to the location where you store your Data Files.

Skills Review (continued)

   c. Type **cd cover_ID-A** in the File name text box (Win) or the Save As text box (Mac), then click Save.

   d. Drag the document tab down to the Document window, then release the mouse button when the blue outline around the Document window disappears. (*Hint*: If your document is already a floating window, move to the steps in topic 6.)

   e. Click the title bar, then slowly drag it in an upward direction until you see the blue border reappear (Win) or until it is just below the Option bar (Mac), then release the mouse button.

6. Work with panels.

   a. Click Window on the Menu bar, point to Workspace, then click Reset Essentials.

   b. Click the Stroke icon to open the Stroke panel group and display the Stroke panel in full view.

   c. Drag the Stroke Panel tab to the Document window.

   d. Click the Panel menu button, click Stroke Styles, then click Cancel.

   e. Drag the Stroke panel tab on top of its original group so that the Stroke panel tab overlaps the Color panel tab.

   f. Click the double arrow icon in the upper-right corner of the Stroke panel group to collapse the group.

7. Work with guides.

   a. Click the horizontal ruler, drag to approximately the 1.5-inch mark on the vertical ruler to create a horizontal guide, then release the mouse button.

   b. Create another horizontal guide at the 2.5-inch mark on the vertical ruler.

   c. Create a vertical guide by double-clicking the .5-inch mark on the horizontal ruler.

   d. Save your work, compare your screen to Figure A-15.

8. Export an InDesign document.

   a. Click File on the Menu bar, then click Export.

   b. In the Export dialog box, click the Save as type list arrow (Win) or the Format list arrow (Mac), then click Adobe PDF (Print).

   c. Click Save.

   d. In the Export Adobe PDF dialog box, click Export.

   e. Close the PDF window.

   f. Click File on the Menu bar, then click Exit (Win), or click InDesign on the Menu bar, then click Quit InDesign (Mac) to exit InDesign.

FIGURE A-15

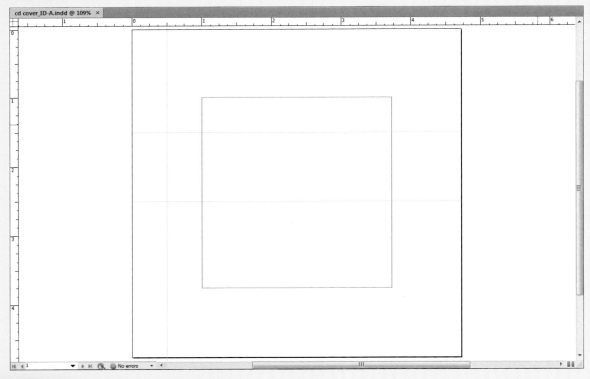

Independent Challenge 1

Your cousin wants to start creating her own greeting cards rather than buying them. She is looking for someone to create a greeting card template for her so that she can easily place her graphics when creating the cards in InDesign. You offer to help her by creating an InDesign document with the appropriate settings. She has requested a simple postcard style card that is 4 inches wide and 5 inches high.

a. Start InDesign.

b. Open the New Document dialog box to create a new document.

c. Change the Document Preset to [Custom], then verify that the Intent setting is set to Print.

d. Change the width of the new document to **4** inches and the height to **5** inches.

e. Change all four margin settings to **0.5** inches, if necessary.

f. Click the Portrait orientation button, if necessary.

g. Remove the check mark in the Facing Pages check box, if necessary.

h. Click OK to close the New Document dialog box, then save the document as **postcard_ID-A**.

i. Compare your screen to Figure A-16, close postcard_ID-A.indd, then exit InDesign.

FIGURE A-16

Independent Challenge 2

You have recently been promoted from stock room manager to customer service associate at The Software Depot. You need to get up to speed on new software programs so that you can answer customer questions. Your first assignment is to prepare yourself for answering customer inquiries about customizing InDesign.

a. Start InDesign.

b. Create a new document using the Default settings in the New Document dialog box, then save the new document as **sample_ID-A**.

c. Display the rulers, if necessary.

d. Click the Pages panel tab to open it in full view, then drag the Pages panel tab to the Document window, click the Links panel tab, then drag it to the Document window.

e. Click the Links panel tab, drag it to the bottom of the Pages panel, then release the mouse button when a blue line appears. (*Hint*: If the Links panel is too tall, click the Show/Hide Link Information button on the panel to collapse the lower half of the panel.)

f. Close the Layers panel, if necessary.

Independent Challenge 2 (continued)

g. Click Window on the Menu bar, then click Text Wrap.

h. Drag the Text Wrap panel below the Links panel to add it to the Pages and Links panel group.

i. Drag the new arrangement of docked panels from the top, dark gray bar to the left side of the Document window so that it is near the Tools panel, then compare your screen to Figure A-17.

Advanced Challenge Exercises

- Click Window on the Menu bar, point to Workspace, then click New Workspace.
- Save the workspace as **Custom Workspace**.
- Click Window on the Menu bar, point to Workspace, then click [Typography].
- Click Window on the Menu bar, point to Workspace, then click Custom Workspace.

j. Save your work, close sample_ID-A.indd, then exit InDesign.

FIGURE A-17

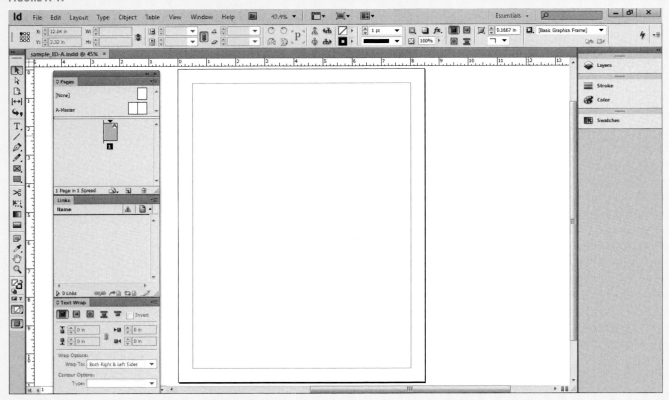

Independent Challenge 3

Your family decides to have a last-minute yard sale this weekend. You've made a flyer advertising the sale and decide to adjust some of the document settings so that you can use it again in the future.

a. Start InDesign, open ID A-1.indd, update the links in the document if necessary, then save it as **yard sale_ID-A**.

b. Click the Selection tool, select the top guide, which is at the 3.25-inch mark on the vertical ruler, then press [Delete].

c. Select the bottom guide, then drag it down until it snaps to the top of the text box at the bottom of the document.

d. Create a new horizontal guide anywhere on the page, and then change its Y Location value to 3 on the Control panel.

e. Press [W] to view your document in Preview mode.

Independent Challenge 3 (continued)

f. Compare your document to Figure A-18.

g. Press [W] to switch to Normal mode.

h. Click View on the Menu bar, point to Grids & Guides, then click Lock Guides.

Advanced Challenge Exercises

- Open the Guides & Pasteboard category in the Preferences dialog box.
- Click the Margins list arrow, then click Dark Green.
- Click the Columns list arrow, then click Red.
- Click the Preview Background list arrow, then click Sulphur.
- Click OK to close the Preferences dialog box.

i. Save yard sale_ID-A.indd, close it, then exit InDesign.

FIGURE A-18

Yard Sale
Saturday, August 29, 2015
34 Elm Road
9:00 am - 2:00 pm

Books, Clothing, Toys, Kitchen Appliances
and More!

Original content Paul McKinnon/Shutterstock.com

Real Life Independent Challenge

Your professor has provided a bonus question during the first week of your graphic arts class. If you get the answer right, you'll receive 10 points, so you're determined to find the answer. The question is:

"What is a character style?"

a. Start InDesign.

b. Access InDesign Help to find the answer to the above question.

c. Record your answer in a word-processing program or on paper.

d. Exit InDesign.

InDesign CS6

Visual Workshop

Create a new [Default] size document with 1-inch margins. Save the document as **guides_ID-A**, then create the guides shown in Figure A-19. Save the document and then exit InDesign.

FIGURE A-19

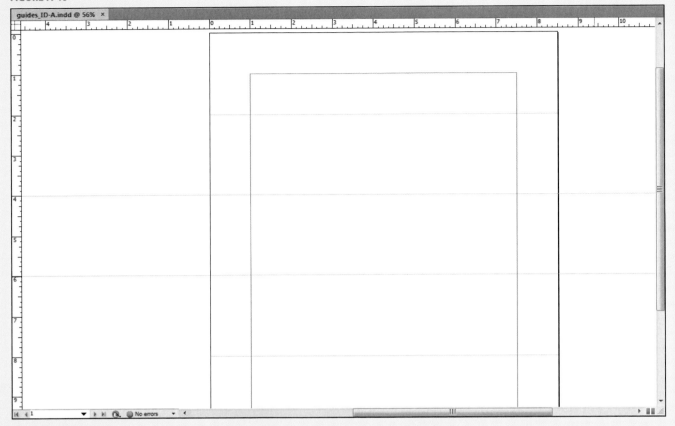

Getting Started with InDesign CS6

Working with Text

Files You Will Need:

To view a list of files needed for this unit, see the Data Files Grid in the back of the book.

Text is one of the most important features in InDesign. Even in a small amount, such as a title, text can greatly influence the overall design of a publication. The role of text is to grab its viewers' attention and deliver a message to them successfully. InDesign provides many text features that you can use to control how text appears in a document and to give text a personality all its own.  Each month, the President of The Happy Apple writes a customer newsletter and MegaPixel helps her format it attractively in InDesign.

OBJECTIVES

Create text boxes

Place and flow text

Format text

Format paragraphs

Create and apply paragraph styles

Modify a paragraph style

Create and apply character styles

Find and change text

Track changes

Creating Text Boxes

Text boxes, also referred to as text frames, are containers for text. When you create a text box, a flashing cursor appears in the upper-left corner of the box, indicating that you can start typing. Because text automatically wraps to the next line once it hits the right side of the text box, the amount of text you can fit horizontally in a text box depends on the size of the text box. You can copy and paste text from another source into InDesign or place a text file in an InDesign document using the Place command. ▓▓▓ You create a text box in the first column of the newsletter, then copy it to the second and third columns.

QUICK TIP
Update links if necessary.

1. **Start InDesign, open ID B-1.indd from the location where you store your Data Files, then save the document as november news_ID-B**

   The document opens with the standard newsletter elements already in place, such as the margin guides, the newsletter heading, and the Happy Apple logo.

2. **Click the workspace switcher on the Menu bar, then click Reset Essentials**

   The workspace is returned to the Essentials workspace. Any floating panels are restored to their default locations.

3. **Click the Type tool ⊤ on the Tools panel, then position the Type tool pointer 工 on the left margin guide**

QUICK TIP
If you do not want to see the transformation values that appear when creating margins or other InDesign objects, remove the check mark next to Show Transformation Values in the Interface section of the Preferences dialog box.

4. **Click and drag the Type tool pointer 工 to create a text box of any height that snaps to the left margin guide, the bottom margin guide and the guide that defines the right side of the first column, as shown in Figure B-1, then release the mouse**

   A text box is added to the page and the cursor is flashing in the upper-left corner of the text box. InDesign pages can have one or more columns. The space between two columns is called the **gutter**.

5. **Click the Selection tool ▶ on the Tools panel, then click the lower-left reference point on the Control panel**

   When you click the Selection tool, a bounding box appears around the text box to indicate it is selected. You can change the size and location of the selected text box using reference points on the Control panel. A **reference point** is one of nine tiny squares that represent the corners, midpoints, and center of a selected frame. Clicking the lower-left reference point on the Control panel selects the reference point as the fixed point for the object. When you resize the object, changes emanate from the fixed reference point.

6. **Double-click the Height (H) value on the Control panel, type 6, then press [Enter] (Win) or [return] (Mac)**

   The height of the text box is added to the top of it. The bottom of the text box remains affixed to the bottom margin guide.

7. **Press and hold [Alt] (Win) or [option] (Mac), then slowly drag the text box to the right, as shown in Figure B-2**

   The double-white arrow icon indicates that you are duplicating the selected object.

8. **Drag the copy of the text box so that it snaps to the second column margin guides and the bottom margin guide, then release the mouse**

   The document contains two text boxes.

QUICK TIP
To find out the width of the gutter, click Layout on the Menu bar, then click Margins and Columns to view the Gutter value in the Margins and Columns dialog box.

9. **Repeat Steps 7 and 8 using the middle text box to add a third text box to the third column, deselect all, then save your work**

   You created three text boxes into which you can place text for the newsletter.

10. **Click View on the Menu bar, point to Extras, click Show Frame Edges so that you can see the three text frames, then compare your screen to Figure B-3**

FIGURE B-1: Creating a text box

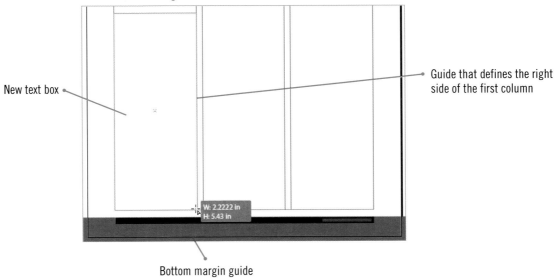

New text box

Guide that defines the right side of the first column

W: 2.2222 in
H: 5.43 in

Bottom margin guide

FIGURE B-2: Duplicating the text box

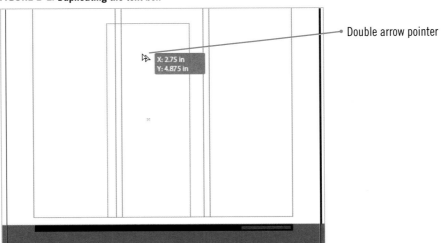

Double arrow pointer

X: 2.75 in
Y: 4.875 in

FIGURE B-3: The three new text frames

Three text frames

Placing and Flowing Text

In multipage documents, such as magazines or books, text usually comes from other sources like Microsoft Word. You can place all of the text contained in a file created in another source in InDesign using the Place command on the File menu. Once placed, you can flow text into many text boxes throughout the pages in an InDesign document. Flowing text (also known as **threading** text) into text boxes can be compared to pouring a pitcher of water into a series of water glasses until there is no more water to pour. Table B-1 details all of the methods that you can use to flow text. ◼◼◼◼◼ The Happy Apple's newsletter is in Microsoft Word format. You plan to place the text into the first text box and then flow it into the second and third.

STEPS

1. **Click View on the Menu bar, then click Zoom In**

   The magnification level increases and can be seen in the document name tab. Continue to zoom in for a better view, if necessary.

2. **Click the Hand tool 🖐 on the Tools panel, then drag the page into better view, if necessary**

   If you are working with a single-page document, double-clicking the Hand tool will fit the single page in the window. The command key for Fit Spread in Window is [Alt][Ctrl][0] (Win) or [option]⌘[0] (Mac). The command key for Fit Page in Window is [Ctrl][0] (Win) or ⌘[0] (Mac).

3. **Click the Type tool T. on the Tools panel, then click inside the first text box you created**

   The flashing cursor appears in the text box. The text you place will flow into this text box.

QUICK TIP

You can flow text into text boxes on pages that are not near each other. For example, you can place a text file in a text box on page 1 of a document and then flow some of it or the rest of it into another text box on page 7.

4. **Click File on the Menu bar, click Place, navigate to the location where you store your Data Files, click Letter.doc, then click Open**

   All of the text contained in the Letter file flows into the text box. The entire text box is filled and, as shown in Figure B-4, a red overset text icon appears at the bottom of the text box, indicating that there is more text available than this text box can display. The text is displayed with the formatting that was applied to it in Microsoft Word.

5. **Click the Selection tool ▶ on the Tools panel, then click the overset text icon ⊞**

   When you click the overset text icon, the pointer becomes a loaded text pointer with a link icon, indicating that the text that is about to be placed is part of the same text file that filled the previous text box.

6. **Click anywhere in the second text box**

   The overset text icon pointer appears with loaded text, and the remaining text fills the second text box. A link is established between the two text boxes. If you were to delete all of the text from these two text boxes and then place a new text file into the first text box, the overset text would automatically flow into the second text box because of the established link. Deleting flowed text from the text boxes does not delete the link.

7. **Click ⊞ in the second column, then click the third text box so that the text fills the three columns**

   Your columns should resemble the columns in Figure B-5.

QUICK TIP

To see text threads, the Selection tool must be selected.

8. **Click View on the Menu bar, point to Extras, then click Show Text Threads**

   The blue text thread shows the flow of text from the first text box to the second and from the second to the third. Viewing text threads is helpful if you are not sure how text boxes are linked and how text is flowing in a document.

9. **Click View on the Menu bar, point to Extras, click Hide Text Threads, click View on the Menu bar, point to Extras, click Hide Frame Edges, then save your work**

November 2015

Dear Customers,
While driving to work the other
day, I noticed how hungry I
was. I tried to remember what
I had for breakfast. And, then
I realized that I had rushed out
of the house with a travel mug
of coffee. Some breakfast! I
was trying to get a few errands
done before work—pick up the
antique linen tablecloth at the
dry cleaners and silver polish
at the department store. Many
of you can probably relate to
this type of running around as
you get ready for Thanksgiving
and of course, the December
holidays.
I'd like to give you some tips
and advice for staying healthy
during this time of year. If we
do not fuel our bodies, we
run the risk of becoming worn
down and more susceptible
to germs and viruses. Some
great on-the-go breakfast foods
include oatmeal bars, granola
bars, bananas, cheese, and
almonds. You may be surprised
that almonds would be a good
start to your day. Almonds are

— Overset text icon

FIGURE B-5: **Linked text**

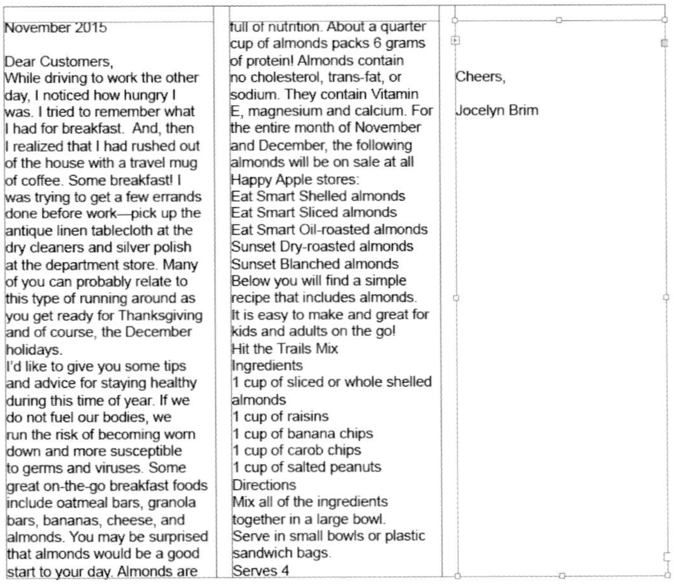

November 2015

Dear Customers,
While driving to work the other
day, I noticed how hungry I
was. I tried to remember what
I had for breakfast. And, then
I realized that I had rushed out
of the house with a travel mug
of coffee. Some breakfast! I
was trying to get a few errands
done before work—pick up the
antique linen tablecloth at the
dry cleaners and silver polish
at the department store. Many
of you can probably relate to
this type of running around as
you get ready for Thanksgiving
and of course, the December
holidays.
I'd like to give you some tips
and advice for staying healthy
during this time of year. If we
do not fuel our bodies, we
run the risk of becoming worn
down and more susceptible
to germs and viruses. Some
great on-the-go breakfast foods
include oatmeal bars, granola
bars, bananas, cheese, and
almonds. You may be surprised
that almonds would be a good
start to your day. Almonds are

full of nutrition. About a quarter
cup of almonds packs 6 grams
of protein! Almonds contain
no cholesterol, trans-fat, or
sodium. They contain Vitamin
E, magnesium and calcium. For
the entire month of November
and December, the following
almonds will be on sale at all
Happy Apple stores:
Eat Smart Shelled almonds
Eat Smart Sliced almonds
Eat Smart Oil-roasted almonds
Sunset Dry-roasted almonds
Sunset Blanched almonds
Below you will find a simple
recipe that includes almonds.
It is easy to make and great for
kids and adults on the go!
Hit the Trails Mix
Ingredients
1 cup of sliced or whole shelled
almonds
1 cup of raisins
1 cup of banana chips
1 cup of carob chips
1 cup of salted peanuts
Directions
Mix all of the ingredients
together in a large bowl.
Serve in small bowls or plastic
sandwich bags.
Serves 4

Cheers,

Jocelyn Brim

TABLE B-1: **Methods for flowing text**

method	steps	result
Manual text flow	Click the overset text icon, then click a page or a text box on a page to flow more text into it. Repeat steps as needed.	Text is added to one page or one text box at a time.
Semi-autoflow	Click the overset text icon, then press and hold [Alt] (Win) or [option]⌘ (Mac) each time you click the text boxes into which to flow the remaining text.	Each time a text box is filled, the pointer remains a loaded text icon and is ready to fill the next text frame. Unlike manual text flowing, you do not need to click the overset text icon again in order to keep flowing text from one text box to another.
Autoflow	Click the overset text icon, then press and hold [Shift] when you click another text box or another page.	Additional text boxes and pages are automatically created until all text is visible in the document.
Fixed-page autoflow	Click the overset text icon, then press and hold [Shift] [Alt] (Win) or [shift][option]⌘ (Mac) when you click a text box or page.	All text is flowed into the document without any new pages or text boxes created. Overset text must be set manually.

InDesign CS6

Formatting Text

Formatting text means changing the way that it looks without changing its meaning. In InDesign, there are many ways to change the look of your text. You can choose a typeface for your text. A **typeface** is a design created for a set of characters including the alphabet, numbers, and some symbols. A **font** is a set of characters based on a typeface using a specific size and style. For example, the Arial Narrow font is based on the typeface Arial. You can change the size, color, and style of text using the Control panel, the Character panel, and the Swatches panel. You magnify the text, which includes "A letter from the President" and then format it using the Control panel.

STEPS

1. **Click the Zoom tool on the Tools panel, then drag the Zoom tool pointer around "A letter from the President" at the top of the first column**
   The text fills the window.

2. **Click the Type tool on the Tools panel, then double-click the word letter**
   When you format text selected with the Type tool, the Formatting affects text button is highlighted on the Tools panel. The current fill and stroke will affect the text and not the text box.

3. **Triple-click the word letter to select the entire line**
   Text must be selected in order to change its appearance. When text is selected, the Control panel displays text formatting controls, as shown in Figure B-6. The Control panel identifies the current font and size, among other attributes, applied to the selected text.

4. **Click the Font list arrow on the Control panel, scroll down, then click Times New Roman (Win) or point to Times New Roman, then click Regular (Mac)**
   The text font changes to Times New Roman.

5. **Click the Font Size list arrow on the Control panel, then click 24 pt**
   The text font size increases to 24 pt.

6. **Double-click the Hand tool on the Tools panel to fit the page in the window**

7. **Click on the Tools panel, click anywhere in the word President, then compare your text to Figure B-7**
   The Control panel identifies the new font and font size applied to the text. If you click the cursor within a line or a paragraph, the character attributes of that text are displayed on the Control panel.

8. **Click the Selection tool on the Tools panel, click Object on the Menu bar, then click Text Frame Options**
   The Text Frame Options dialog box opens, where you can format the location of the text within the text box.

9. **Click the Align list arrow, click Center, click OK, then save your work**
   The text is vertically centered in the text box.

Using the Story Editor

InDesign provides a special window, called the Story Editor, for you to use to edit text that you have already placed in a document. It is much easier to see text in the Story Editor than on the InDesign page because it fills the entire screen, much like working in a word-processing program. To work in the Story Editor, click the Type tool on the Tools panel, click in the section of text that you wish to edit, click Edit on the Menu bar, then click Edit in Story Editor. The Story Editor opens and you'll see the cursor in the same place that you clicked in the text. You can access the Control panel from the Story Editor, and make formatting changes in addition to editing the text. Once you make changes to the text, simply click the Close button in the Story Editor window and you'll be back in the original text box in InDesign.

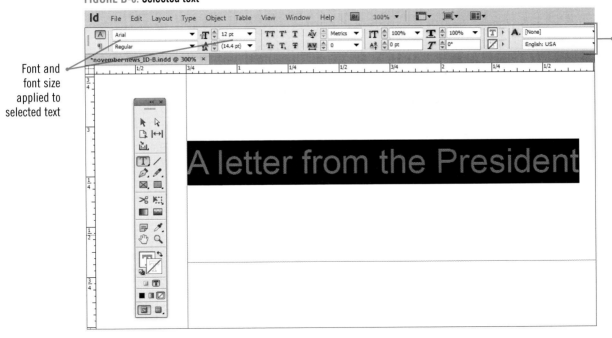

Font and font size applied to selected text

Text options on the Control panel

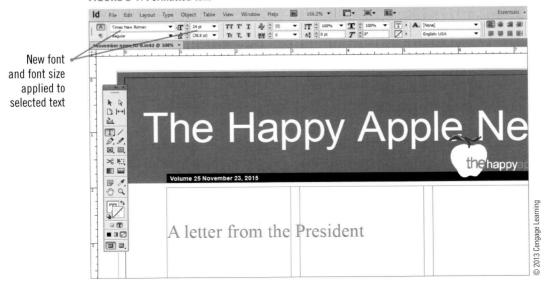

New font and font size applied to selected text

© 2013 Cengage Learning

InDesign CS6

Kerning and Tracking

On the Character panel, you can control the space between two or more characters using the Kerning and Tracking settings. **Kerning** means to change the space between just two characters. **Tracking** means to change the space between all characters in a selection of text, such as a headline or an entire paragraph. To kern a pair of characters, click the Type tool cursor between the two characters, then click the Kerning list arrow and choose a preset value or use the Kerning up and down arrows to change the value in increments of 1/1000 of an em space. An **em space** is a printing measurement and is represented by the size of a the letter m in the current font and font size. A negative kerning value decreases the space between two characters and a positive kerning value increases the space. To track text, highlight the text and then choose a preset value using the Tracking list arrow, or use the up and down arrows provided.

Formatting Paragraphs

Paragraphs are lines of text that are separated by the space created when you press [Enter] (Win) or [return] (Mac). For example, if you type *Monday*, press [Enter] (Win) or [return] (Mac), and then type *Tuesday*, you have created two paragraphs—one on each line. Like text, you can format paragraphs by changing paragraph properties such as leading and alignment. **Leading** (pronounced "LED-ing") is the amount of space between the baselines of two lines of type. **Alignment** refers to the way a paragraph is horizontally spread out between the left and right sides of a text box. Alignment options are available on the Control panel. ▒▒▒▒▒ You format the title paragraph that introduces the letter by aligning it in the center of the first column.

STEPS

1. Click the Zoom tool 🔍 on the Tools panel, then drag the Zoom tool pointer ⊕ around "A letter from the President"

2. Click Type on the Menu bar, then click Show Hidden Characters, if necessary

   A **hidden character** is a symbol that represents something else, such as a space between words. It does not print. Notice the pound sign (#) that follows "President." This pound sign is a hidden character that represents the end of a story. The term "story" refers to all of the text in one text box or all of the text in linked text boxes.

QUICK TIP

To force text onto a new line without creating a new paragraph, press [Shift] [Enter] (Win) or [shift][return] (Mac). This is known as creating a **soft return**.

3. Click the Type tool **T** on the Tools panel, click after "President," press [Enter] (Win) or [return] (Mac), then compare your screen to Figure B-8

   A paragraph end symbol (another hidden character) appears after "President," indicating that "A letter from the President" is one paragraph. If you were to type a new line, you would be creating a second paragraph. The pound sign indicates that the end of the story now appears on the second line. The blue dots indicate spaces between words and are hidden characters.

4. Click Edit on the Menu bar, then click Undo Paragraph Return (Win) or Undo Typing (Mac) to remove the new paragraph

QUICK TIP

If necessary, drag the Paragraph panel out of the way so that you have a good view of the paragraph you are formatting.

5. Click Type on the Menu bar, then click Paragraph to open the Paragraph panel

   The Paragraph panel appears in the workspace. The Paragraph panel has many settings for changing the structure of a paragraph. To change values in the Paragraph panel text boxes, you can double-click an existing value and then type a new value, or click the up and down arrows to the left of each text box to choose a preset value.

QUICK TIP

If you select a text box with the Selection tool and then make changes in the Paragraph panel, the changes will apply to all paragraphs in the text box.

6. Triple-click the "A letter from the President" paragraph

   The entire paragraph is selected.

7. Click the Align center button ▤ on the Paragraph panel

   The text is horizontally centered between the left and right edges of the text box.

8. Click View on the Menu bar, then click Fit Page in Window

9. Click Edit on the Menu bar, click Deselect All, then save your work

   Your centered "A letter from the President" paragraph should look similar to the paragraph in Figure B-9.

Formatting controls on the Control panel

The Control panel has two buttons that allow you to switch between formatting characters and formatting paragraphs. The two buttons are at the far left side of the panel. The Letter "A" button is the Character Formatting Controls button. Click this button to display options for formatting characters, such as Font Size, Superscript, and All Caps, on the left side of the Control panel. The ¶ button is the Paragraph Formatting Controls button. Click this button to display options for formatting paragraphs, such as alignment and indentation, on the left side of the Control panel.

FIGURE B-8: Hidden characters

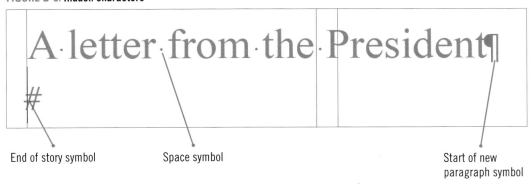

End of story symbol   Space symbol   Start of new
                                                    paragraph symbol

FIGURE B-9: Center-aligned text

Typing on a Path

The Type on a Path tool, part of the Type tool group, does just what its name implies. It allows you to type along a path, a wavy path, a diagonal path, a circular path, a zig-zaggy path—any type of path. A **path** is another name for a vector line. **Vectors** are types of graphics which are made up of anchor points and lines. You'll learn more about vectors in a later unit.

When you click the Type on a Path tool pointer on a path, the pointer begins flashing, as shown in Figure B-10. Begin to type and watch the text follow the path. When you finish typing, you can format the text using all the text features in InDesign. The figure shows a baseline shift of 10 points that has been applied to create some space between the text and the path. When you switch to the Selection tool, a bounding box appears around the path and a direction line appears within the text. To move the text along the path, drag the top of the direction line.

FIGURE B-10

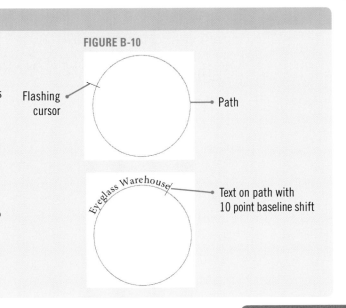

Flashing cursor   Path

          Text on path with
          10 point baseline shift

Creating and Applying Paragraph Styles

You have seen how to use the Paragraph panel to format an individual paragraph. **Paragraph styles** are useful when you want to format *several* paragraphs in a document. Paragraph styles work by lumping paragraph formatting options, such as indents, spacing before and after paragraphs, and alignment, into one named style. You simply apply the style to the paragraph and all of the formatting saved with the style is applied. Paragraph styles also enable you to control character formatting for paragraph text, such as font, size, style, and color. An **indent** is a blank space between text and its margin or frame border. ░░░░ You create a paragraph style in the New Paragraph Style dialog box named "Body," and then apply it to paragraphs in the newsletter using the Paragraph Styles panel.

STEPS

1. **Verify that none of the text boxes are selected, click** View **on the Menu bar, click** Hide Hidden Characters, **click** Type **on the Menu bar, then click** Paragraph Styles
   The Paragraph Styles panel opens, showing two available styles, [Basic Paragraph] and Normal. The [Basic Paragraph] style uses the Minion Pro font and 12 pt font size, which are the default text settings in InDesign. The Normal style was applied to the Letter document in Microsoft Word and was brought over to InDesign when you placed the Word document.

2. **Click the** Panel menu button ▾≡, **then click** New Paragraph Style
   The New Paragraph Style dialog box opens. It includes paragraph and character formatting categories.

3. **Type** Body **in the Style Name text box, then click** Basic Character Formats **on the left side of the dialog box**

4. **Click the** Font Family list arrow, **click** Arial, **click the** Font Style list arrow, **click** Regular **if necessary, then change the Font Size to 12 pt, if necessary**

5. **Click** Indents and Spacing **on the left side of the dialog box**

6. **Click the** Alignment list arrow, **click** Left **if necessary, double-click the value in the** Space Before **text box, type** .25, **press [Tab], type** .25 **in the Space After text box, press [Tab], compare your New Paragraph Style dialog box to Figure B-11, then click** OK
   When the Body style is applied to text, each paragraph will be left-aligned, the lines in each paragraph will not be indented, and there will be .25 inch of blank space before and after every paragraph. The text in the paragraphs will be Arial, 12-point, Regular.

7. **Click the** Type tool T. **on the Tools panel, if necessary, click the paragraph** While driving to work **four times, then click** Body **on the Paragraph Styles panel**
   The Body style is applied to the paragraph.

8. **Apply the** Body paragraph style **to the two paragraphs in the letter that begin with "I'd like to give you some tips" and "Below you will find"**

9. **Deselect all, compare your screen to Figure B-12, then save your work**

FIGURE B-11: New Paragraph Style dialog box

FIGURE B-11: New Paragraph Style dialog box

Basic Character Formats

Indents and Spacing

Space Before and Space After values

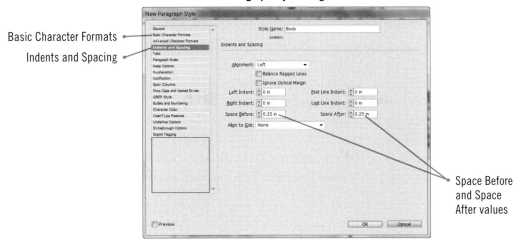

FIGURE B-12: Applied paragraph style

Body Style

Panel menu button

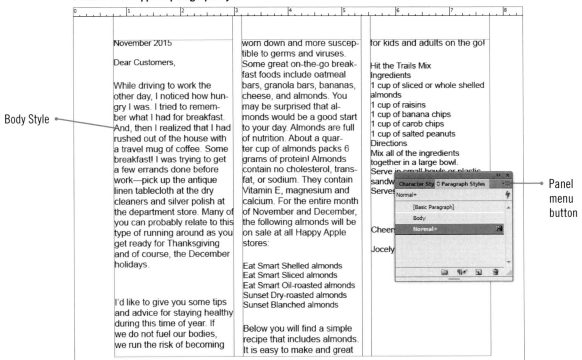

Understanding parent/child relationships with styles

You can create a new paragraph or character style from an existing paragraph or character style by basing one on the other. When you base one style on another, you pick up all of the formatting choices of one style and modify them to quickly make a new style. Doing so creates a parent/child relationship between the new style and the existing style. The original style becomes the parent and the new style based on the parent becomes the child. A link is formed between the two styles. The parent and child styles are identical at first, but you can further modify the child style to differentiate it from the parent. However, if you make a change to the parent style, that change will automatically be reflected in the child style. For example, if you change the font from Times New Roman to Calibri in the parent style, the font also changes to Calibri in the child style. Every paragraph that is formatted with both parent and child styles in the document will automatically change to the Calibri font. To create a child style based on a parent style, click the Based On list arrow in the General category of the New Paragraph Style or New Character Style dialog box, then choose the parent style that you want to base the new (child style) on. To base a style on an existing style without creating the parent/child relationship, select the style, click the Panel menu button, and then click Duplicate Style. The new style will be an unlinked duplicate that you can then modify to your needs.

InDesign CS6

Modifying a Paragraph Style

Once you've applied paragraph styles to the text in a document, you may need to make a change to one or more of the paragraph style settings. For example, you may not like the way the text is aligned or you may need to change the font size. You can make any necessary changes to a paragraph style by double-clicking the paragraph style on the Paragraph Styles panel. Doing so will open the Paragraph Style Options dialog box, which contains all of your original formatting choices. Once you make the necessary changes, close the dialog box. The text to which the style is applied in the document is automatically updated with the changes to the style. You decide to change the paragraph alignment to Left Justify to improve the look of the text in the columns and to decrease the space before and after each paragraph.

STEPS

1. **Double-click** Body **in the Paragraph Styles panel**

   The Paragraph Style Options dialog box opens. It includes all of the formatting choices made for the Body paragraph style.

2. **Click** Indents and Spacing **on the left side of the dialog box**

3. **Click the** Alignment list arrow, **then click** Left Justify

4. **Click the** down arrow **next to Space Before one time to change the value in the Space Before text box to** 0.1875

5. **Change the Space After value to** 0.1875, **then compare your Paragraph Style Options dialog box to Figure B-13**

6. **Click** OK **to close the dialog box, then compare your screen to Figure B-14**

   All of the paragraphs with the Body paragraph style applied are updated with the new settings.

Using the Fill with Placeholder Text feature

InDesign documents can contain lots of text. When you are using InDesign to create a book or a magazine, you may want to experiment with how text will look in your publication and how it will flow before the text is ready to be placed. For example, you may want to determine which font and size to use for text in order to make it spread over a certain number of pages. To fill text boxes with "fake text" while you await the "real text," click Type on the Menu bar, then click Fill with Placeholder Text. **Placeholder text** is made up of text that is divided into words of different lengths, often in Latin, to represent how real text will flow in your document. An example of placeholder text is: *Em ilit lummod tat. Ut ad ercil ecte magna adignibh et at.* When you are ready to replace the placeholder text with the real text, simply select all of the placeholder text and delete it. Any links between text boxes will be preserved so that the new text will automatically flow from one text box to another. You can also replace the provided placeholder text with your own placeholder text by saving a text document as Placeholder.txt in the InDesign application folder.

FIGURE B-13: Paragraph Style Options dialog box

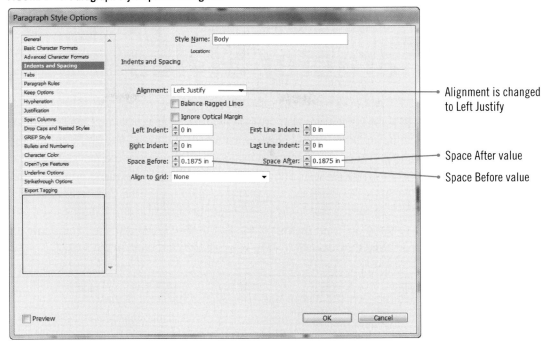

Alignment is changed to Left Justify

Space After value

Space Before value

FIGURE B-14: Updated paragraph styles

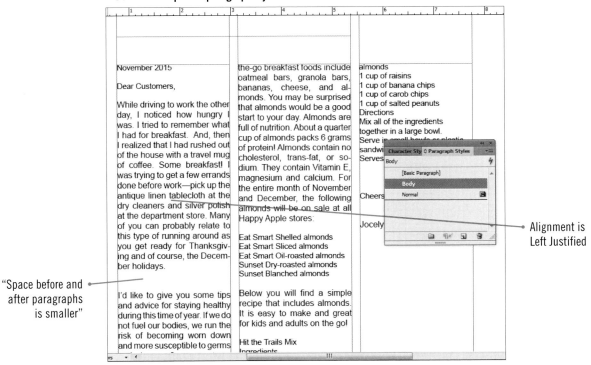

"Space before and after paragraphs is smaller"

Alignment is Left Justified

Creating and Applying Character Styles

Character styles work very much like paragraph styles, except that they are created just for characters. Character styles are perfect for short pieces of text, such as headings, labels, or titles. Imagine you have an InDesign document outlining your top five vacation choices, and you want to apply the same font, font size, and color to each vacation destination. You can choose the font, font size, and color; group them together as a character style; and save the style with a special name on the Character Styles panel. Then you could apply the character style to the vacation text in the document. You decide to create a character style for the Eat Smart brand name because it is The Happy Apple's in-house brand, and you want it to stand out from the rest of the text in the President's letter. You create a character style named "Eat Smart" and then apply it to each instance of "Eat Smart" in the letter.

STEPS

QUICK TIP
If necessary, drag the Character Styles panel out of the way so that you can easily see the text you are formatting.

1. **Click** Type **on the Menu bar, then click** Character Styles

   The Character Styles panel opens, showing one available style called "[None]." The pencil icon with a slash through it next to [None] indicates that this style cannot be changed or deleted.

2. **Click the** Character Styles panel button ▾≡ **, then click** New Character Style

   The New Character Style dialog box opens. On the left side of the dialog box are eight categories of possible formatting options for characters. The General category is where you name the character style. The Basic Character Formats and Character Color categories offer the most common formatting choices, such as font, style, font size, and color.

3. **Make sure the default style name in the Style Name text box is highlighted, then type** Eat Smart

   The default style name is replaced by "Eat Smart." This is the name of the style that will appear in the Character Styles panel.

4. **Click** Basic Character Formats **on the left side of the dialog box, click the** Font Family list arrow, **click** Arial, **click the** Font Style list arrow, **click** Italic, **click the** Size list arrow, **click** 11 pt, **then compare your New Character Style dialog box to Figure B-15**

5. **Click** Character Color **on the left side of the dialog box, scroll down, click the** C=15 M=100 Y=100 K=0 (red) swatch, **then click** OK

   The new style, Eat Smart, appears on the Character Styles panel.

6. **Use the** Zoom tool 🔍 **to zoom in on the five almond products listed in the second column**

7. **Click the** Type tool **T** **on the Tools panel, select the** first **instance of "Eat Smart" in the list, then click** Eat Smart **on the Character Styles panel**

   The Eat Smart style is applied to the Eat Smart text.

QUICK TIP
To modify an existing character style, double-click its name in the Character Styles panel, change settings as desired in the Character Style Options dialog box, then close the dialog box. The text to which the style is applied in the document is automatically updated with the changes to the style.

8. **Apply the Eat Smart character style to the other two instances of Eat Smart, deselect the text, compare your screen to Figure B-16, then save your work**

   The Eat Smart character style places emphasis on the Eat Smart brand.

9. **Reset the Essentials workspace, click** View **on the Menu bar, click** Fit Page in Window, **click** Edit **on the Menu bar, then click** Deselect All

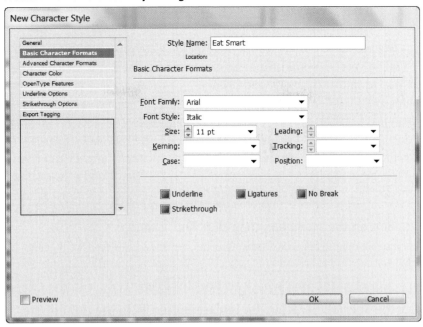

InDesign CS6

Finding and Changing Text

You may need to make changes to text in InDesign after you have typed it or placed it. In long documents, finding specific words or phrases can be time-consuming. The Find/Change dialog box offers a great way to find text quickly and change it, if necessary. For example, you could use the Find/Change dialog box to find and replace each instance of "Pacific" with the word "Atlantic." Using the Find/Change dialog box guarantees that you won't miss any instances of the word you want to change in the document. ▰▰▰▰ In the letter she submitted, the President mistakenly referred to the Sunrise brand as the Sunset brand. You need to find all instances of "Sunset" and change them to "Sunrise," and you also must add the registered trademark symbol after "Sunrise" each time it appears.

STEPS

1. Click Edit on the Menu bar, then click Find/Change

The Find/Change dialog box opens. You do not have to select text in order to use the Find/Change dialog box.

2. Type Sunset in the Find what text box, then type Sunrise in the Change to text box

QUICK TIP
To find and change fonts, click Type on the Menu bar, then click Find Font. The Find Font dialog box lets you replace one font with another.

3. Click the Special characters for replace button 🔳 to the right of the Change to text box, point to Symbols, then click Registered Trademark Symbol

In the Change to text box, "^r" appears next to "Sunrise," as shown in Figure B-17. The "^r" notation represents the registered trademark symbol (®) that will appear after "Sunrise" when it replaces "Sunset" in the document. A registered trademark symbol is a special symbol associated with the legal protections given a product whose name distinguishes it from other products.

4. Click Find

The first occurrence of the word "Sunset" is highlighted. You may need to drag the Find/Change dialog box out of the way to see the highlighted text.

5. Click Change

Sunrise® replaces Sunset in the text box in the document.

6. Click Change All

Clicking Change All replaces all instances of "Sunset" in the document with "Sunrise®," which in this case is just one additional change. A dialog box appears, telling you that one replacement was made when you clicked the Change All button.

7. Click OK, then click Done to close the Find/Change dialog box

8. Click the Type tool 🔳 if necessary, click before the B in "Below you will find" at the bottom of the second column, press [Enter] (Win) or [return] (Mac) three times to push the paragraph to the top of the third column, then save your work

9. Deselect all, press [W] to view your document in Preview mode, then compare your newsletter to Figure B-18

10. Click Window on the Menu bar, point to Workspace, click Reset Essentials, then close november news_ID-B

Find/Change dialog box options

There are many options that you can choose for your search in the Find/Change dialog box. You can search for text as whole words; for example, you can define a word like "pen" as a whole word so that the Find/Change feature will not alert you each time it finds "pen" in words such as "pencil" and "happen." To search for whole words, click the Whole Word button 🔳 in the Find/Change dialog box. You can have the Find/Change feature look for only upper- or lowercase versions of words by clicking the Case Sensitive button 🔳 in the dialog box. You can also choose to search the current document or all open documents for text.

FIGURE B-17: Find/Change dialog box

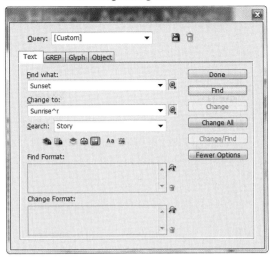

FIGURE B-18: Finished Newsletter

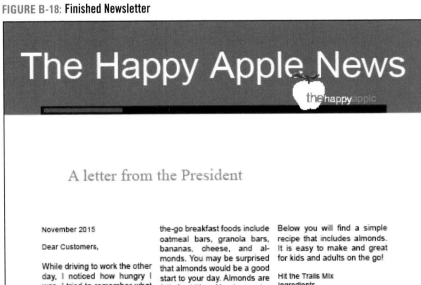

Tracking Changes

When two or more people collaborate on a document, it is helpful to be able to view the changes that each contributor has made. The Track Changes feature works by showing text edits highlighted in orange in the Story Editor window. Text that is marked for deletion has the strike through style applied to it. If you are OK with the changes made by your co-workers you can accept them or, if not, you can reject them using the Track Changes panel. Chris uses the November newsletter as a starting point for creating the December newsletter. He gives you the file to look at his edits to the Employee News section and then asks you to then edit the Seminar information.

1. Open the file ID B-2.indd, then save it as december news_ID-B

2. Click the Type tool T on the Tools panel, then click to the left of the "E" in Employee News in the first paragraph

3. Click Edit on the Menu bar, then click Edit in Story Editor

   The story opens in the Story Editor window. All of the edited text in the story is highlighted in orange to differentiate it from non-edited text.

4. Click Window on the Menu bar, point to Editorial, then click Track Changes

   The Track Changes panel opens. The changes made to the document will appear in the Story Editor Window. The Track Changes panel has buttons for viewing each change and for accepting or rejecting each change. It also has a field for you to enter a user name and a time field showing the time that the changes were made.

5. Click the Next Change button → on the Track Changes panel

   As shown in Figure B-19, the first change made by Chris is highlighted in blue. Chris changed the first paragraph New Employees to Employee News. You want to accept this change.

6. Click the Accept Change button ✔ on the Track Changes panel

   The blue highlighted text becomes highlighted in black in the Story Editor and the text updates in the document.

7. Click the Accept All Changes in Story button ✔ on the Track Changes panel, click OK to accept all changes in the story, then close the Story Editor window

   All of Chris's changes are accepted.

8. Click the Zoom tool 🔍 on the Tools panel, zoom in on the Seminar information at the bottom of the second column, click T, click anywhere in the text, then click the Enable Track Changes in Current Story button ⊚ on the Track Changes panel

   The Enable Track Changes in Current Story button must be pressed for the changes to appear in the Story Editor window.

9. Select the Flower Arranging text, type Yoga Classes, Tuesday evenings, delete November 7, 2015 so that only 7:00 pm – 8:30 pm remains, open the Story Editor window, then compare your screen to Figure B-20

10. Save your work, close december news_ID-B.indd, then exit InDesign

FIGURE B-19: Viewing changes in the Story Editor window

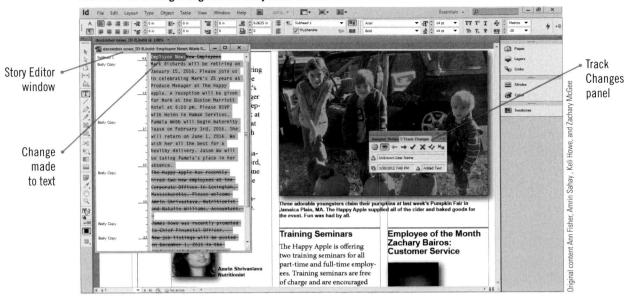

Story Editor window

Change made to text

Track Changes panel

Original content Ann Fisher, Amrin Sahay , Keil Howe, and Zachary McGee

FIGURE B-20: Making edits using Track Changes

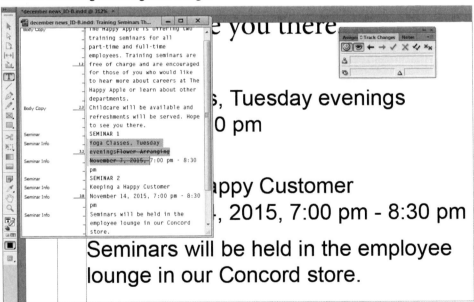

Practice

Concepts Review

Label the elements of the InDesign screen shown in Figure B-21.

FIGURE B-21

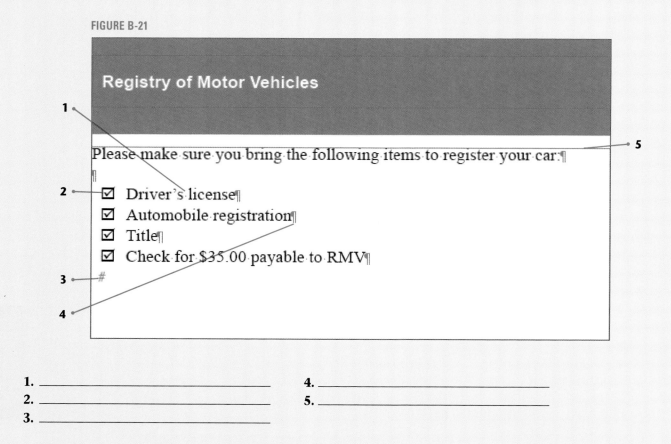

1. _____
2. _____
3. _____
4. _____
5. _____

Match each term with the statement that best describes it.

6. Threading
7. Gutter
8. Story Editor
9. Paragraphs
10. Leading

a. Space between two columns
b. Lines of text that are separated by the space created when you press [Enter] (Win) or [return] (Mac)
c. Vertical space from one baseline to the next
d. To flow text from one text box to another
e. Window where tracked changes can be seen

Select the best answer from the list of choices.

11. **What is all of the text in a text box, or all of the text in linked text boxes, called?**
    a. Type
    b. Story
    c. Book
    d. Document

12. **What style is applied to text that is marked for deletion using the Track Changes feature?**
    a. Bold
    b. Underline
    c. Strike through
    d. Highlighted

13. **What is the blank space between text and its margin or frame border called?**
    a. Indent
    b. Bullet
    c. Gutter
    d. Return

14. **How do you modify an existing paragraph style?**
    a. Click the Find/Change dialog box
    b. Select the text with the paragraph style applied, then make changes in the Control panel
    c. Double-click the paragraph style name in the Paragraph Styles panel
    d. Double-click the paragraph style name in the New Paragraph Style dialog box

Skills Review

1. **Create text boxes.**
   a. Start InDesign, open ID B-3.indd from the location where you store your Data Files, update the links if necessary, then save the document as **school news_ID-B**.
   b. Click the workspace switcher, click Reset Essentials, click Edit (Win) or InDesign (Mac) on the Menu bar, point to Preferences, then click Guides & Pasteboard.
   c. Click the Guides in Back check box to add a check mark if necessary, then click OK.
   d. Click the Type tool on the Tools panel if necessary, then position the Type tool on the left margin guide.
   e. Click and drag the Type tool to create a text box of any height that snaps to the bottom margin guide and the guide that defines the right side of the first column.
   f. Click the Selection tool, then click the lower-left reference point in the Control panel, if necessary.
   g. Double-click the Height (H) value on the Control panel, type **6.5**, then press [Enter] (Win) or [return] (Mac). (*Hint*: If the X Location value of the lower-left reference point is not 1 and/or the Y Location value is not 10, double-click the X Location value, type **1** if necessary, press [Tab], type **10** if necessary as the Y Location value, then press Enter (Win) or [return] (Mac).)
   h. Click the Type tool, position it on the right margin guide in the second column, then drag the Type tool pointer to create a text box above "READ" that snaps to the right margin guide and to the guide that defines the left side of the second column.
   i. Click the Selection tool, then verify that the bottom-left reference point is still selected on the Control panel.
   j. Change the Y Location value on the Control panel to 4.8 in, then change the Height (H) value to 2.5 in.

2. **Place and flow text.**
   a. Click the Type tool, then click inside the empty text box in the first column.
   b. Click File on the Menu bar, click Place, navigate to the location where you store your Data Files, click Book News.doc, then click Open.
   c. Click the Selection tool, click the overset text icon, then click anywhere in the second text box.
   d. Click View on the Menu bar, point to Extras, then click Show Text Threads.
   e. Click View on the Menu bar, point to Extras, then click Hide Text Threads.
   f. Save the document.

Skills Review (continued)

3. Format text.

   a. Click the Zoom tool, then drag the Zoom tool pointer around "A letter from the Principal", the date, and "Dear Parents" at the top of the first column.

   b. Click the Type tool, then double-click the word "Principal."

   c. Triple-click the word "Principal" to select the entire line.

   d. Click the Font list arrow on the Control panel, scroll up or down in the list if necessary, then click Segoe Script or another font if you do not have Segoe Script installed on your computer. (*Hint*: If the Paragraph Formatting Controls button is selected on the Control panel, the character formatting options appear on the right side of the Control panel.)

   e. Click the Font Size list arrow, then click 14 pt.

   f. Change the font of the date and "Dear Parents" to Times New Roman.

   g. Double-click the Hand tool to fit the page in the window.

   h. Click the Selection tool, then click the pasteboard to deselect the text box.

   i. Save your work.

4. Format paragraphs.

   a. Click the Zoom tool, then drag the Zoom tool pointer around "A letter from the Principal."

   b. Click Type on the Menu bar, then click Show Hidden Characters.

   c. Identify the end of the story by finding the pound sign hidden character.

   d. Click the Type tool, then triple-click the text.

   e. Click Type on the Menu bar, then click Paragraph.

   f. Click the Align center button on the Paragraph panel.

   g. Double-click the Hand tool to fit the page in the window.

   h. Click the Selection tool, then click the pasteboard to deselect the text box.

   i. Save your work.

5. Create and apply paragraph styles.

   a. Click Type on the Menu bar, then click Paragraph Styles.

   b. Click the Paragraph Styles Panel menu button, then click New Paragraph Style.

   c. Type **Paragraphs** in the Style Name text box.

   d. Click Basic Character Formats on the left, then change the font to Times New Roman and the font size to 11 pt.

   e. Click Indents and Spacing on the left side of the dialog box.

   f. Click the Alignment list arrow, then click Left.

   g. If necessary, change the First Line Indent value to 0, then change the Left Indent value to 0.

   h. Click the Space Before up arrow four times until you see 0.25 in the text box, change the Space After value to 0.25, then click OK.

   i. Click the Type tool if necessary, click the first paragraph after "Dear Parents," which starts with "While I was at the supermarket" four times, then click Paragraphs on the Paragraph Styles panel.

   j. Apply the Paragraphs paragraph style to the next paragraph starting with "Speaking of books."

   k. Save your work.

6. Modify a paragraph style.

   a. Double-click Paragraphs in the Paragraph Styles panel.

   b. Click Indents and Spacing on the left side of the dialog box.

   c. Click the Alignment list arrow, then click Left Justify.

   d. Change the Space After value to 0.125, change the Space Before value to 0.125, then click OK to close the dialog box.

Skills Review (continued)

   e. Click the Type tool, if necessary, click before the "O" in "Owen" at the bottom of the first column, then press [Enter] (Win) or [return] (Mac) to push the line of text to the beginning of the next column. (*Hint*: You may have to press [Enter] (Win) or [return] (Mac) twice.)

   f. Save your work.

7. Create and apply character styles.

   a. Click Type on the Menu bar, then click Character Styles.

   b. Click the Character Styles Panel menu button, then click New Character Style.

   c. Make sure the default style name in the Style Name text box is highlighted, then type **Popular Books**.

   d. Click Basic Character Formats on the left side of the dialog box, click the Font Family list arrow, scroll down if necessary and then click Calibri, click the Font Style list arrow, click Italic, click the Size list arrow, then click 11 pt.

   e. Click Character Color on the left side of the dialog box, scroll down and click the C=100 M=90 Y=10 K=0 (blue) swatch, then click OK.

   f. Use the Zoom tool to zoom in on the eight books listed at the top of the second column.

   g. Click the Type tool, select the name of the first book ("Owen Foote, Super Spy"), then click Popular Books on the Character Styles panel. (*Hint*: Do not select the author name or the comma.)

   h. Apply the Popular Books character style to the remaining seven books.

   i. Fit the document page in the window again, deselect all, then save your work.

8. Find and change text.

   a. Click Edit on the Menu bar, then click Find/Change.

   b. Type **our school librarian** in the Find what text box, type **Mrs. DiVito** in the Change to text box, then click Find.

   c. Click Change All, click OK, then click Done to close the Find/Change dialog box.

   d. Deselect all, press [W] to hide the frame borders, then compare your newsletter to Figure B-22.

   e. Click Window on the Menu bar, point to Workspace, then click Reset Essentials.

   f. Save your work, then close school news_ID-B.indd and exit InDesign.

9. Track changes.

   a. Open the file ID B-4.indd, update links, then save it as **library news_ID-B**.

   b. Click View on the Menu bar, then click Actual Size.

   c. Click the Type tool on the Tools panel, then click anywhere in the story in the first column.

   d. Click Edit on the Menu bar, then click Edit in Story Editor.

   e. Click Window on the Menu bar, point to Editorial, then click Track Changes.

   f. Click the Next Change button on the Track Changes panel.

FIGURE B-22

Cannon School News

A letter from the Principal

December 2015

Dear Parents,

While I was at the supermarket the other day I overheard two women discussing a book club. I, too, am in a book club and couldn't resist asking them what book their group was currently reading. At first they giggled and then explained to me that the book being read this month was *Gooney Bird and the Room Mother* by Lois Lowry for their second grade girls' book club. As an educator, I was so excited to hear that children were participating in book clubs. I did a little research of my own—on-line—and interviewing friends and family members, and found out that children's book clubs are a growing trend. What a great way for kids to get together socially and share their experiences about a book they've all read. I encourage you to see if this is something your child would like to do. Children take turns picking a book, the moms typically figure out the schedule and take turns hosting the meetings. Meetings can be every four to six weeks. Some book clubs have dinner together or a snack. If you are interested, I encourage you to contact the mothers of some of your child's friends. Most book clubs have between five and seven children. Keep me posted if you do start a book club. I'd love to hear about it.

Speaking of books, Mrs. DiVito has put together a list of popular books for children between the ages of 7 – 10. Books make wonderful gifts. I have included the following list of books.

Owen Foote, Super Spy by Stephanie Greene
Not My Dog by Colby F. Rodowsky
Matilda by Roald Dahl
The BFG by Roald Dahl
Dinotopia by James Gurney
I Like it Here at School by Jack Prelutsky
Clementine's Letter by Sara Pennypacker
My Father's Dragon by Ruth Stiles Gannett

Happy Reading!

Beverly McCann

READ!

Skills Review (continued)

g. Click the Accept All Changes in Story button on the Track Changes panel, then click OK.

h. Close the Story Editor window.

i. Click the Hand tool on the Tools panel, then move the page so that you can see the top of the second column.

j. Click the Enable Track Changes in Current Story button on the Track Changes panel.

k. Click the Type tool, then change *The BFG* by Roald Dahl to *The Borrowers* by Mary Norton.

l. Save your work, then close library news_ID-B.indd.

Independent Challenge 1

You work for an international foreign exchange student program. The company is celebrating 10 years in business. The owners are planning a special presentation and dinner in honor of this milestone and you are in charge of designing a postcard-style invitation. The details of the party are given to you as a text file. You use InDesign to format the text.

a. Start InDesign, then create a new document.

b. In the New Document dialog box, change the Width to **4** inches and the Height to **5** inches, change each of the four margin values to **0.5** inches if necessary, then close the New Document dialog box.

c. Save the new document as **party invitation_ID-B**.

d. Create a text box that snaps to the inside of all four margin guides. (*Hint*: The X Location of the bottom-left reference point should be .5, the Y Location should be 4.5, the Width of the text box should be 3, and the Height of the text box should be 4.)

e. Click File on the Menu bar, click Place, then place the Data File Invitation Text.doc into the text box.

FIGURE B-23

f. Show hidden characters.

g. Open the Paragraph panel.

h. Select all of the paragraphs in the text box, double-click the value in the Space After text box in the Paragraph panel, type **.25**, then press [Enter].

i. Click the Type tool, if necessary, click between the 7 and the comma (,) in the third line, then apply a Kerning value of –110.

j. Center-align all paragraphs.

k. Click in the first paragraph before the "t" in "ten," then press [Shift][Enter] (Win) or [shift][return] (Mac).

l. Change the font for all paragraphs to Edwardian Script ITC or to a similar font.

m. Change the font size of the first three paragraphs to **18** pt, then change the font of the last three paragraphs to **15** pt. (*Hint*: Type 15 in the Font Size text box because 15 pt is not an option on the Font Size list.)

n. Hide the hidden characters, deselect all, press [W], then compare your screen to Figure B-23.

o. Save the document, then exit InDesign.

Independent Challenge 2

Original content Ipatov/Shutterstock.com

You work for a magazine called *The Greater Outdoors*. Each month, one of your responsibilities is to design the type on the magazine cover. You try to use just the right fonts, sizes, colors, and styles so that the text on the cover helps deliver the message that is represented by the cover photo.

a. Start InDesign.

b. Open ID B-5.indd, then save it as **greater outdoors_ID-B**.

c. Using the character and paragraph formatting features in InDesign and any fonts installed on your computer, format the text in the five text boxes on the magazine cover. (Hint: You may need to resize text boxes if you change font sizes. Use the Selection tool to resize the text boxes.)

d. Create a paragraph style called **Date**, use Right as its Alignment value, then apply it to the February 2015 text.

e. Deselect all, press [W] to preview the page, then compare your screen to Figure B-24.

Advanced Challenge Exercise

- Display the Character panel if it is not already displayed.
- Zoom in on the magazine title, "The Greater Outdoors."
- Click the Type tool, then click between the "t" and the "d" in the word "Outdoors."
- In the Character panel, click the Kerning up arrow once to change the Kerning value to 10, then notice the new space between the two characters.
- Kern the space between the "a" and the "t" in the word "Greater" so that the new Kerning value is also 10.
- Triple-click "The Greater Outdoors," then change the Baseline Shift value to 6 pt on the Character panel.
- Deselect all, then fit the page in the window.

f. Save the document, then exit InDesign.

Independent Challenge 3

You are known in your family as the creative one. Your uncle is opening a new café and wants to create a unique menu template for the daily specials that will be offered. He is interested in seeing different samples of text options for the menu. You create four samples using placeholder text and the text formatting features in InDesign.

a. Start InDesign.

b. Open ID B-6.indd, then save it as **daily specials_ID-B**.

c. Click the Type tool in the first text box in the top-left corner.

d. Fill the text box with placeholder text using the Type menu.

e. Fill the remaining three text boxes with placeholder text.

InDesign CS6

Independent Challenge 3 (continued)

f. Create four paragraph styles for each text box and name them **Sample 1**, **Sample 2**, **Sample 3**, and **Sample 4**. Use any font, style, size, color, and indents and spacing options that you like. (*Hint*: Each time you create a new paragraph style, be sure that Based On is set to [No Paragraph Style].)

g. Modify any paragraph styles, as necessary. Do not worry if the overset text icon appears on one or more of the text boxes.

h. Save your work, deselect all, then compare your screen to Figure B-25.

Advanced Challenge Exercise

- Open the Paragraph Style Options dialog box for the Sample 1 paragraph style.
- Click the Preview check box to see changes that you make applied to the Sample 1 style.
- Click Basic Character Formats in the Paragraph Style Options dialog box.
- Change the Leading value, then change the Tracking value. Notice how the paragraph is affected.
- Click OK to close the Paragraph Style Options dialog box.

i. Save the document, then exit InDesign.

FIGURE B-25

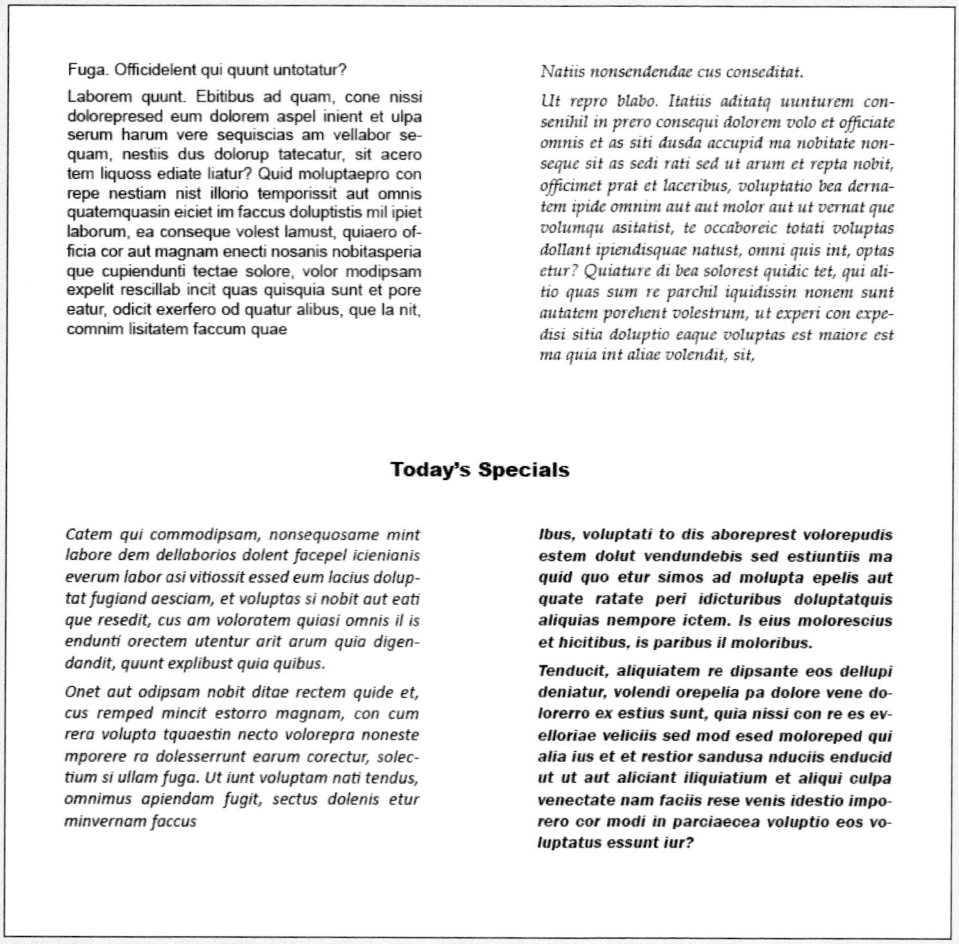

Fuga. Officidelent qui quunt untotatur?

Laborem quunt. Ebitibus ad quam, cone nissi dolorepresed eum dolorem aspel inient et ulpa serum harum vere sequiscias am vellabor sequam, nestiis dus dolorup tatecatur, sit acero tem liquoss ediate liatur? Quid moluptaepro con repe nestiam nist illorio temporissit aut omnis quatemquasin eiciet im faccus doluptistis mil ipiet laborum, ea conseque volest lamust, quiaero officia cor aut magnam enecti nosanis nobitasperia que cupiendunti tectae solore, volor modipsam expelit rescillab incit quas quisquia sunt et pore eatur, odicit exerfero od quatur alibus, que la nit, comnim lisitatem faccum quae

Natiis nonsendendae cus conseditat.

Ut repro blabo. Itatiis aditatq uunturem consenihil in prero consequi dolorem volo et officiate omnis et as siti dusda accupid ma nobitate nonseque sit as sedi rati sed ut arum et repta nobit, officimet prat et laceribus, voluptatio bea dernatem ipide omnim aut aut molor aut ut vernat que volumqu asitatist, te occaboreic totati voluptas dollant ipiendisquae natust, omni quis int, optas etur? Quiature di bea solorest quidic tet, qui alitio quas sum re parchil iquidissin nonem sunt autatem porehent volestrum, ut experi con expedisi sitia doluptio eaque voluptas est maiore est ma quia int aliae volendit, sit,

Today's Specials

Catem qui commodipsam, nonsequosame mint labore dem dellaborios dolent facepel icienianis everum labor asi vitiossit essed eum lacius doluptat fugiand aesciam, et voluptas si nobit aut eati que resedit, cus am voloratem quiasi omnis il is endunti orectem utentur arit arum quia digendandit, quunt explibust quia quibus.

Onet aut odipsam nobit ditae rectem quide et, cus remped mincit estorro magnam, con cum rera volupta tquaestin necto volorepra noneste mporere ra dolesserrunt earum corectur, solectium si ullam fuga. Ut iunt voluptam nati tendus, omnimus apiendam fugit, sectus dolenis etur minvernam faccus

Ibus, voluptati to dis aboreprest volorepudis estem dolut vendundebis sed estiuntiis ma quid quo etur simos ad molupta epelis aut quate ratate peri idicturibus doluptatquis aliquias nempore ictem. Is eius molorescius et hicitibus, is paribus il moloribus.

Tenducit, aliquiatem re dipsante eos dellupi deniatur, volendi orepelia pa dolore vene dolorerro ex estius sunt, quia nissi con re es evelloriae veliciis sed mod esed moloreped qui alia ius et et restior sandusa nduciis enducid ut ut aut aliciant iliquiatium et aliqui culpa venectate nam faciis rese venis idestio imporero cor modi in parciaecea voluptio eos voluptatus essunt iur?

Real Life Independent Challenge

You are moving out of state and need to sell some household items that you do not plan to take with you. Create a flyer in InDesign advertising three items that you would like to sell. (*Hint*: If you can't think of anything, use a dishwasher, computer table, and treadmill as the items in the flyer.) Include the item name, description, and price.

a. Start InDesign.

b. Open ID B-7.indd, then save it as **moving sale_ID-B**.

c. Click the Type tool after "Moving Sale," then press [Enter] (Win) or [return] (Mac) twice.

d. Type the first item you would like to sell (or use the items available in the Data File), then press [Enter] (Win) or [return] (Mac) to start a new paragraph.

e. Type a short description of the item, press [Enter] (Win) or [return] (Mac) to start a new paragraph, type the price, then press [Enter] (Win) or [return] (Mac).

f. Repeat Steps d and e to enter at least two more items for sale. (*Hint*: Do not insert extra paragraph returns between each price and the next item. You will use paragraph styles to insert space.)

g. Create a paragraph style named **Item**, using any formatting choices you like.

h. Create a paragraph style named **Description**, using any formatting choices you like, then do the same to create a paragraph style named **Price**. Include a Space After value for the Price style to create a space between the three items.

i. Apply the three styles to the three items, descriptions, and prices. You may want to modify one or more of the styles after you have applied them to the text to improve the appearance of the text.

j. Create a small text box at the bottom of the page listing your contact information, then format the Moving Sale text using any formatting you like.

k. Deselect all, press [W], save your work, then compare your screen to Figure B-26.

Advanced Challenge Exercise

- Create a new paragraph style named **Title**.
- In the New Paragraph Style dialog box, click the Based On list arrow, then click Item.
- Make formatting changes to the Title style, then close the dialog box.
- Apply the Title style to the Moving Sale text.

l. Save your work, then exit InDesign.

Moving Sale

Dishwasher
Less than one year old, great condition
$200.00

Computer Table
Good for small living space
$150.00

Treadmill
Folds up easily for storing
$400.00

Call Ann: 555-111-5555

InDesign CS6

Visual Workshop

Open ID B-8.indd, then save it as **gingerbread house_ID-B**. Format the text so that it resembles the text shown in Figure B-27. (*Hint*: The font used in the sample is Cambria, 22 point. The bullets used in the sample are Wingdings 2 GID:146.) Also, apply a .25-inch Space After value for the first paragraph to visually separate it from the list. Save the document and then exit InDesign.

Everything you need to make a gingerbread house:

◇ Small milk cartons
◇ Graham crackers
◇ Royal frosting
◇ Peppermint candies
◇ Gum drops
◇ Licorice sticks
◇ M&M's®
◇ Necco Wafers®
◇ Small candy canes
◇ Hershey's Kisses®
◇ Lemonheads®
◇ Red Hots®
◇ Mint leaves
◇ Plastic knives
◇ Paper plates
◇ Paper towels

Original content Hannamariah/Shutterstock

Working with Objects

When working with InDesign, there are many types of objects that you can add to your document pages. Graphics such as photos and illustrations are one type; other types include shapes, lines, text boxes, Microsoft Excel charts, and Microsoft Word tables. You can modify objects in InDesign using many tools, panels, and menu commands. For example, you can scale an object, rotate an object, or add color to it. You can group it with other objects, or change its transparency or location on the page. At MegaPixel, your boss has assigned you a new client, BreakTime, a company that organizes trips for high school students. The owner, Jennifer, asks you to help her with a "Save the Date" design for their website about an upcoming ski trip to Idaho. She has supplied you with an InDesign file containing basic details and a photo, and asks you to show her how to improve it by adding some simple graphics.

OBJECTIVES

Create an object

Transform an object

Arrange and lock an object

Step and repeat an object

Use Live Distribute

Use the Direct Selection tool

Modify corners and strokes

Create a multi-state object

Creating an Object

Sometimes the only type of object you need for a publication is a simple shape. Shapes can add visual interest to a document and serve as a background for text. The tools for creating shapes include the Rectangle, Ellipse, and Polygon tools. To select a shape tool, click and hold down the mouse button on the Rectangle tool (or currently selected shape tool) on the Tools panel, and then select the shape tool you want to use. With a shape tool selected, you can create a shape manually by dragging in the document, or you can click in the document to open the shape's dialog box and define its settings. You use the Swatches panel to add color to the fill and stroke (border) of the shape, and the Stroke panel to change the weight (thickness) and style of the stroke. You open the InDesign file from Jennifer and decide to create a background color for the image. You start by first making a rectangle and then format its fill and stroke.

STEPS

1. **Open the file ID C-1.indd, save it as ski trip_ID-C, then update links if necessary**

   Jennifer has given you a file intended for the web. Notice the ruler units are in pixels.

2. **Click the Rectangle tool 🔲 on the Tools panel**

QUICK TIP
You can also create a rectangle by clicking the Rectangle tool, clicking the page, and then entering width and height values in the Rectangle dialog box.

3. **Position the Rectangle tool pointer -¦- on the left side of the page**

4. **Drag to create a rectangle that is in the approximate size and location of the one shown in Figure C-1, then release the mouse button**

   The rectangle is selected, indicated by the **bounding box**. A bounding box is a rectangle whose size matches the width and height of the selected object. The bounding box includes eight selection handles that you can use to resize the object. The bounding box appears when an object is selected and then disappears when the object is deselected.

TROUBLE
If the rectangle is not selected, click the Selection tool ▶ on the Tools panel, then click the edge of the rectangle to select it.

5. **Verify that the rectangle is still selected, then click the Swatches panel icon 🎛 on the right to open the Swatches panel**

   The Swatches panel opens displaying the web palette. RGB stands for Red, Green, and Blue; the color mode used for web graphics. The rectangle has a black stroke that is 1-point wide applied to it by default.

QUICK TIP
You can change the tint (amount) of a color by dragging the Tint slider on the Swatches panel, then choosing a new value. For example, you can fill or stroke an object with 50% of a color for a lighter shade.

6. **Click the Fill button ◻ on the Tools panel, if necessary, then scroll to and click RGB Blue on the Swatches panel**

   To apply a fill color to an object, the Fill button must be in front of the Stroke icon on the Tools panel. The rectangle is filled with blue, as shown in Figure C-2. To apply a new stroke color to an object, click the Stroke button to bring it in front of the Fill button. You can create new colors on the Color panel by dragging the R, G, and B sliders. When you create a color, right-click the Swatch button on the Color panel, and then click Add to Swatches.

7. **Click the Stroke button 🔳 on the Tools panel, then scroll to and click [None] on the Swatches panel**

   The stroke is removed from the rectangle.

8. **Close the Swatches panel, then save your work**

Converting shapes

You can convert an existing shape into a different shape using the Convert Shape command on the Object menu. Click a shape in the document window, click Object on the Menu bar, point to Convert Shape, then click one of the available shapes in the list. You can choose from Rectangle, Rounded Rectangle, Beveled Rectangle, Inverse Rounded Rectangle, Ellipse, Triangle, Polygon, Line, and Orthogonal Line.

FIGURE C-1: **Creating a rectangle**

Rectangle with
bounding box

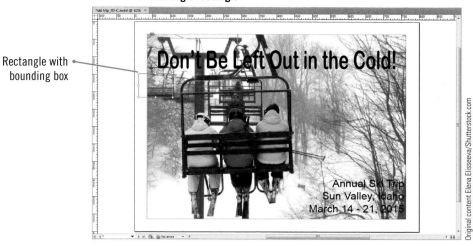

FIGURE C-2: **Filling the rectangle with RGB Blue**

Rectangle filled
with RGB Blue

Fill button

Stroke button

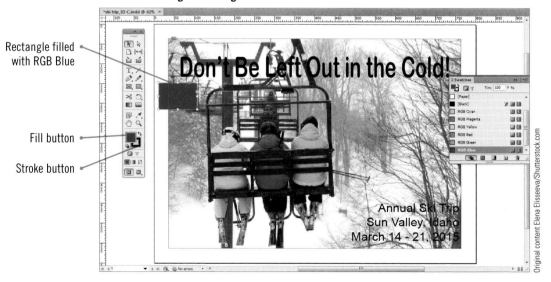

Transforming an Object

When you transform an object, you change its appearance. For example, you can rotate an object 45° or scale an object 50% to make it half its original size. The Transform commands in InDesign include Move, Scale, Rotate, Shear, and Flip. You can also transform objects using buttons on the Transform panel or the Control panel. You can change the width and height of an object and its location on the page. Before you transform an object, you choose a reference point from which to transform it. This point is called the **point of origin**, and it is the point of the selected object that remains fixed during the transformation. You show Jennifer how to use the Control panel to change the location of the rectangle and to change its width and height.

STEPS

1. **Click the Selection tool** ▶ **on the Tools panel, if necessary, then click the blue rectangle to select it**

2. **Locate the current value in the X Location text box on the Control panel, as shown in Figure C-3**

   The X Location value is the horizontal location of one of nine possible reference points on the selected rectangle. The nine reference points match the locations of the nine selection handles on the bounding box. In Figure C-3, the X Location value is 12 px and the upper-left reference point is selected. This means that the horizontal location of the upper-left point of the rectangle is 12 pixels from the left margin. There are 72 pixels in one inch. (Your selected reference point and your X Location value might be different.)

3. **Click the upper-left reference point on the Control panel if necessary, double-click the X Location value, type 0, then press [Tab]**

   The upper-left corner of the rectangle frame jumps to the new X location, aligned with the 0" mark on the horizontal ruler. On the Control panel, the value in the Y Location box is now selected.

4. **Type 0 in the Y Location box, then press [Enter] (Win) or [return] (Mac)**

   The upper-left corner of the rectangle frame moves to the upper-left corner of the page, aligned with the 0" mark on both the horizontal and vertical rulers, as shown in Figure C-4.

5. **Double-click the value in the W (Width) text box on the Control panel, type 800, then press [Tab]**

   The width of the rectangle increases to 800 pixels, which is approximately 11 inches. On the Control panel, the value in the H (Height) text box is selected.

6. **Type 600 in the H (Height) text box, then press [Enter] (Win) or [return] (Mac)**

   The height of the rectangle increases to 600 pixels (approximately 8.25 inches), the same height as the page. The new size, 800 px × 600 px, is standard size for web documents. The rectangle fills the page and covers the text and photo. You will send it behind the text and photo to be a background image in the next lesson.

7. **Click the Fill button** ▱ **on the Tools panel**

8. **Show the Swatches panel, click the Tint arrow, drag the Tint slider to 50% to change the fill color to 50% RGB Blue, close the panel, then save your work**

The Transform Again command

Once you transform an object, you can reapply the same transformation if you choose the Transform Again command on the Object menu. For example, if you want to rotate an object incrementally, you can rotate it once—say 5°—click Object on the Menu bar, point to Transform Again, and then click Transform Again to rotate it another 5°.

FIGURE C-3: Identifying the reference point

X Location
text box

Top-left
reference point

Top left point
on rectangle

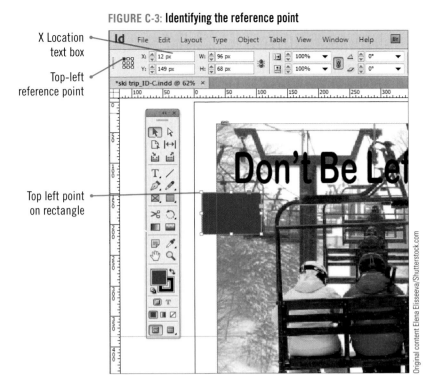

Original content Elena Elisseeva/Shutterstock.com

FIGURE C-4: Aligning the rectangle with the upper-left corner of the page

Your W and H
values may
differ

Upper-left corner
of rectangle is
aligned with
upper-left corner
of page

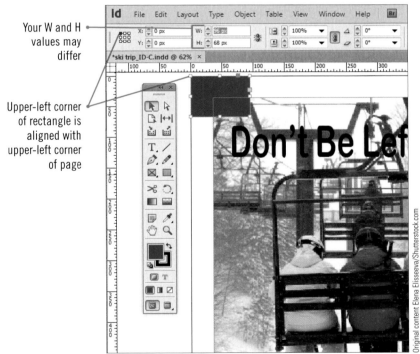

Original content Elena Elisseeva/Shutterstock.com

Editing corners

When you select an object with the Selection tool, a small yellow square appears on the right side of the bounding box. You can click this square to edit all corners of the object. When you click the square, it disappears and is replaced by four yellow diamonds on each corner of the bounding box. Clicking and dragging a diamond allows you to set the corner size. As you drag, you will see the value of the roundness of each corner. When you drag one corner, all of the corners change in the same amount. Press and hold [Shift] to manipulate only one corner. This can give way to some very interesting shapes. Press and hold [Alt] (Win) or [option] (Mac) while clicking a yellow diamond to change the shape into a new one.

Arranging and Locking an Object

InDesign objects are vertically stacked in a document, like a pile of papers, from bottom to top in the order that they are created or placed. For example, if you create a red circle and then a blue circle, the blue circle is "above" the red circle because it was the most recently created object. If the circles are side by side, they look like they are on the same level; but if you drag the blue circle over the red circle, the blue circle overlaps the red circle and hides part of it. You can easily change the stacking order of InDesign objects using the Arrange commands on the Object menu. Once an object is on the correct level in the stack and you no longer need to modify it, you may want to lock it. Locking an object ensures its location on the page will not be disrupted. It is also easier to select an item on top of a locked item because you won't select the locked item by mistake. You show Jennifer how to send the blue rectangle behind the text and the photo, and then lock it.

STEPS

1. **Verify that the blue rectangle is still selected**

2. **Click Object on the Menu bar, point to Arrange, then click Send Backward**

   The Send Backward command sends the selected object or objects back one level only in the document. The Send to Back command sends the selected object or objects to the back-most level of the document. The rectangle moves back one level behind the text box. The text box was the last object created before the rectangle was created.

3. **Click Object on the Menu bar, point to Arrange, then click Send Backward**

   The blue rectangle moves back one more level behind the photo, as shown in Figure C-5. It is now underneath all other objects in the document. The blue rectangle serves as a background image. Since it no longer needs to be modified, it is a good idea to lock it.

4. **Verify that the blue rectangle is still selected, click Object on the Menu bar, then click Lock**

   The blue rectangle is locked, indicated by the padlock icon shown in Figure C-6. Locked items cannot be selected or modified. To unlock an item, click Object on the Menu bar, then click Unlock All on Spread.

5. **Click the photo to select it, then repeat Step 4 to lock it**

   Having the blue rectangle and the photo locked will make it easier to work with new objects you create on top of them.

6. **Click the pasteboard to deselect all, press [W] to view your work in Preview mode, then save your work**

7. **Press [W] to return to Normal view**

Smart guides

Smart guides are guides that appear automatically as you position objects on a page. Smart guides are visual clues that let you know when the object you are positioning is touching a side or the center of another object, a margin guide, or the center of the page.

To use smart guides, select the Smart Guides command on the View, Grids & Guides menu. You can change the color of smart guides in the Guides & Pasteboard section of the Preferences dialog box.

FIGURE C-5: Moving the rectangle to the back

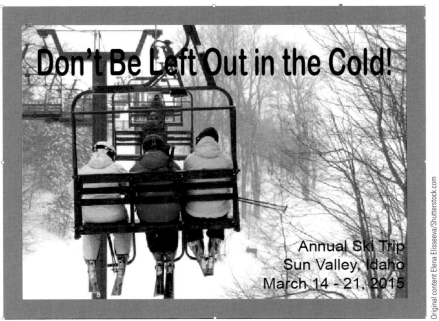

Original content Elena Elisseeva/Shutterstock.com

FIGURE C-6: Locking the blue rectangle

Padlock icon

Original content Elena Elisseeva/Shutterstock.com

Selecting objects

The Select commands on the Object menu allow you to select an object in a document regardless of which level it is on. For example, if a text box is hidden by a large frame and you cannot click it without moving the large frame out of the way, you can click the large frame, click Object on the Menu bar, point to Select, then click Next Object Below to select the text box. Once the text box is selected, you could click Object on the Menu bar, point to Arrange, and then click Bring to Front to bring the text box on top of the large frame. The placement of the large frame would not be affected. Another way to find and select a hidden object is to press [Ctrl] (Win) or [⌘] (Mac) and click continuously where you believe the object is hidden until you see the bounding box for the hidden object appear.

Stepping and Repeating an Object

The Step and Repeat feature in InDesign offers a quick solution for creating multiple identical objects spaced evenly apart from each other. Using Step and Repeat, you first select the object or objects that you would like to duplicate. Next, enter the number of objects you wish to create and the vertical and/or horizontal offset for the new objects. Vertical and horizontal offset values determine how far the copies will be offset from the original. After using Step and Repeat, it is a good idea to group objects together. To **group** objects means to select two or more objects, then make them into one selectable object by clicking Group on the Object menu. When objects are grouped, it is impossible to disrupt their alignment and distribution unless you ungroup the objects first. ▰▰▰▰ Jennifer would like you to create a design element for the flyer. You create a small oval using the Ellipse tool, and then use the Step and Repeat feature to create three more copies.

STEPS

1. **Click and hold the Rectangle tool** 🔲 **on the Tools panel, click the Ellipse tool** 🔘 **click in the approximate location shown in Figure C-7, then release the mouse button**
   The Ellipse dialog box opens.

2. **Type 30 in the Width text box, press [Tab], type 20 in the Height text box, then click OK**
   A small oval appears on the page.

3. **Open the Swatches panel, change the fill color of the oval to [Paper], then keep the default black stroke color**

4. **Verify that the oval is still selected, click Edit on the Menu bar, then click Step and Repeat**
   The Step and Repeat dialog box opens.

5. **Click the Preview check box to select it in the Step and Repeat dialog box**
   The Preview feature lets you see the results of what you enter in the Step and Repeat dialog box before you close the dialog box.

6. **Type 9 in the Count text box, press [Tab] until the Vertical Offset text box is highlighted, type 25, press [Tab], then type 0 in the Horizontal Offset text box, as shown in Figure C-8**
   Nine ovals appear selected below the original oval each one 25 pixels away from the other.

7. **Click OK to close the Step and Repeat dialog box, click the Selection tool** 🔼 **on the Tools panel, press and hold [Shift], then select the top oval so that all ten ovals are selected**

8. **Click Object on the Menu bar, then click Group**
   A dashed line appears around the ovals, indicating they are one group. The ten ovals are now editable as one selectable object.

9. **Deselect the grouped ovals then compare your screen to Figure C-9**
   You quickly created a simple pattern starting out with just one oval.

> **TROUBLE**
> If you get a warning dialog box after entering 9 in the Count text box, change the Vertical and/or Horizontal text boxes to 0 first, then go back and enter the Count value.

FIGURE C-7: Location for creating ellipse

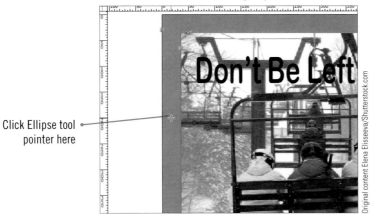

Click Ellipse tool
pointer here

Original content Elena Elisseeva/Shutterstock.com

FIGURE C-8: Step and Repeat dialog box

Count text box

Preview check box

FIGURE C-9: A simple pattern created using Step and Repeat

Newly created
oval group

Original content Elena Elisseeva/Shutterstock.com

InDesign CS6

Using the Move command

In InDesign, you can move an object using a specific vertical and/or horizontal offset. You can also move and copy the selected object. The Move command in InDesign is similar to the Step and Repeat command, but is more practical when you are moving one item and do not need to create multiple copies or a pattern. You move objects using the Move dialog box. First, make sure to select the object or objects you wish to move. Click Object on the Menu bar, point to Transform, then click Move or simply press [Shift][Ctrl][M] (Win) or [Shift] ⌘ [M] (Mac).

Entering a positive value in the Horizontal text box in the Move dialog box moves an item to the right of its original location. Entering a negative number moves an object to the left of its original location. Entering a positive value in the Vertical text box moves an item below its original location. Entering a negative value in the Vertical text box moves an item above its original location.

Using Live Distribute

To **distribute** objects is to place equal space between three or more objects. You can distribute objects using options on the Align panel or using the Live Distribute feature. The distribute options on the Align panel are useful when you want to distribute objects using a specific value. The Live Distribute feature is a better choice when you want to manually distribute objects until you achieve the exact result you are looking for. To use the Live Distribute feature, you select three or more objects, then press and hold the Spacebar while you drag a bounding box handle. As you drag, the space between the objects continually changes proportionally to reflect the amount and direction that you drag the mouse pointer. You show Jennifer how easy it is to modify the oval pattern using the Live Distribute feature.

STEPS

1. Select the group of ovals, click Edit on the Menu bar, then click Step and Repeat

2. Type 2 in the Count text box, press [Tab] twice, type 12 in the Vertical text box, press [Tab], type 16 in the Horizontal text box, then click OK

3. Make sure the Selection tool ▶ is selected on the Tools panel

4. Click the first group of ovals, press and hold [Shift], then click the second and third groups of ovals so that all three groups are selected, as shown in Figure C-10
   One bounding box surrounds the three selected groups.

5. Position the mouse pointer over the lower-right selection handle of the bounding box
   As shown in Figure C-11, the mouse pointer becomes a resize pointer.

TROUBLE
If you start to drag the selection handle before pressing [Spacebar], you will resize the objects instead of distributing them. Undo your last step and then try again.

6. Click the selection handle, press [Spacebar], drag the pointer slowly to the right, then drag to the left until the distribution of the three groups resembles the configuration shown in Figure C-12

7. Release the mouse button, then release [Spacebar]
   Overlapping the three groups has created a new pattern.

8. Verify that the three groups are still selected, click Object on the Menu bar, then click Group
   Grouping the three objects will ensure that the distribution among them will not be altered.

9. Save your work

Rotating an object

To **rotate** an object means to turn it around an axis or center point. In InDesign, there are multiple ways to rotate an object. You can manually rotate an object by placing the pointer outside of the bounding box. The pointer becomes a rounded arrow that you can drag to rotate the selected object. You can also use the Rotate commands on the Object menu. For example, you can choose to rotate an object 90° Clockwise. Finally, you can choose to use the Rotate dialog box by clicking the Rotate tool, located in the Transform tool group, pressing and holding [Alt] (Win) or

[option] (Mac), and then clicking the page. Enter a value in the Rotate dialog box and then click OK or Copy to rotate and copy the object. Double-clicking the Rotate tool rotates the selected object around the selected reference point on the Control panel. Or, you can select an object, click the Rotate tool, and press and hold [Alt] (Win) or [option] (Mac) while you click a specific point on the object. The Rotate dialog box opens and the rotation angle that you enter will take effect from the point that you clicked.

FIGURE C-10: Selecting the three groups

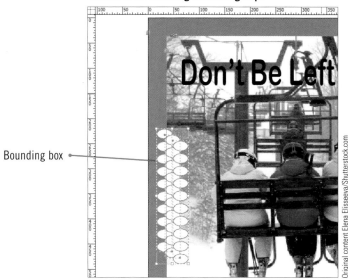

Bounding box

Original content Elena Elisseeva/Shutterstock.com

FIGURE C-11: Locating the resize pointer

Resize pointer

Original content Elena Elisseeva/Shutterstock.com

FIGURE C-12: Creating a new pattern

W: 67 px
H: 284 px

Original content Elena Elisseeva/Shutterstock.com

Using the Direct Selection Tool

You can use the Direct Selection tool to select just one of the items in a set of objects that are grouped together. You may want to do this in order to make a small change to one of the items in the group without ungrouping the group of items. To select one item in a group, make sure that the grouped object is not selected, then click the item you wish to select with the Direct Selection tool. Make changes as necessary to the item, then deselect it. ░░░░░ You use the Direct Selection tool to change the stroke color and stroke weights of some of the individual ovals in the pattern.

STEPS

1. **Click the Selection tool** ▶ **on the Tools panel, then drag the group of ovals about one-half inch to the right so that it is not overlapping the blue background frame**

2. **Click in the pasteboard to deselect all**

3. **Click the Direct Selection tool** ▷ **on the Tools panel, then click the** second oval **from the top in the first column of grouped ovals**

   The one oval is selected and can be changed without having to ungroup the group it is part of.

4. **Show the Swatches panel, if necessary, click the** Fill button ▱ **on the Swatches panel, then click** [None]

5. **Click the** Stroke button ▣ **on the Swatches panel, then click** RGB Green

6. **Click the** Stroke panel icon ▤ **to open the Stroke panel, click the** Weight list arrow, **click 3 pt, then deselect the oval**

   As shown in Figure C-13, the oval has a new fill and stroke applied.

7. **Using Figure C-14 as a guide, repeat Steps 3–5 to change the fill and stroke colors and stroke weight of the ovals**

8. **Save your work**

> **QUICK TIP**
> You can also manipulate one object in a group by double-clicking the object with the Selection tool. After modifying the object, deselect; when you click the object again, the entire group is selected.

Creating stroke styles

The Stroke panel has many options for creating interesting strokes. Once a stroke is applied to a line or a frame, you can create a simple style using options on the Stroke panel. The Type list offers a number of styles, such as Wavy or Dotted. You can also choose a style for the beginning and end of the stroke. The Start and End menus have many arrowhead styles. To create more advanced custom strokes which can be named, saved and loaded into other InDesign documents, you use the Stroke Styles dialog box. Click the Stroke panel menu button ▤ , then click Stroke Styles.

The Stroke Styles dialog box opens displaying seven stroke style options; each is a double or triple line style. You select one of the seven as a starting point, then click New to modify the stroke style in the New Stroke Style dialog box. Choose Stripe, Dotted or Dash from the Type list arrow, then modify the stripe in the Stripe preview window. When you're complete, click Add, then click Done. The new stroke style is added to the Stroke Styles dialog box. You can edit and delete stroke styles as needed.

FIGURE C-13: **Viewing the oval with a new fill and stroke**

Original content Elena Elisseeva/Shutterstock.com

FIGURE C-14: **Making changes to individual ovals**

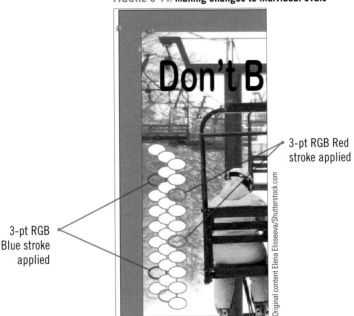

3-pt RGB Red
stroke applied

3-pt RGB
Blue stroke
applied

Original content Elena Elisseeva/Shutterstock.com

InDesign CS6

Using the Align panel

To **align** objects means to position one or more selected objects in relation to each other, in relation to the margins of a document, or in relation to the boundaries of the page or spread. When you align multiple objects with each other, you can align them by their edges or by their center points. You use the Align panel to align objects. The Align panel has three rows of buttons: the top row includes align buttons, the second row includes distribute buttons, and the bottom row includes distribute spacing buttons. When Align to Selection is chosen, items are aligned with each other according to the location of the outermost of the aligned edges in the selection. The Align to Page command aligns selected items using the boundaries of the page. The Align to Spread command aligns selected items using the boundaries of the left and right pages in the spread. The Align to Margins command aligns selected items within the margins.

Modifying Corners and Strokes

In InDesign, you can modify the corners of a rectangular shape using the Corner Options dialog box, which offers five types of corners, such as Rounded and Beveled. Like most dialog boxes, you can preview the settings applied to the selected object before closing the dialog box. To better see the changes made to corners, a thick stroke is recommended. You change the weight of a stroke on the Stroke panel. Jennifer asks if you can place an interesting border around the photo. You place a 4-point black stroke on the photo and then change its corners to Inverse Rounded.

STEPS

1. Click Window on the Menu bar, point to Workspace, then click Reset Essentials

2. Click the Stroke panel icon ▤ to open the Stroke panel

3. Click Object on the Menu bar, then click Unlock All on Spread

   The blue background rectangle and the photo are unlocked. The photo needs to be unlocked so that you can add a border to it.

4. Click the Selection tool ▶ on the Tools panel, click the pasteboard to deselect all, then click the text Don't Be Left out in the Cold to select the text box

5. Click Object on the Menu bar, then click Lock

   Locking the text frame will make it easier to select the photo.

6. Click the photo, click the Stroke button ▣ on the Tools panel, then click Black on the Swatches panel

7. On the Stroke panel, click the Weight list arrow, then click 4 pt

   As shown in Figure C-15, a 4-point stroke is added to the photo, creating a frame. The stroke is aligned to the center of the frame by default. On the Stroke panel, you can choose to align a stroke to the inside, outside, or center of the selected object's frame.

8. Click Object on the Menu bar, then click Corner Options

   The Corner Options dialog box opens. The dialog box consists of four settings, one for each corner of the selected frame. Each setting includes the option to choose a corner style and size.

9. Click the top-left arrow, then click Inverse Rounded, as shown in Figure C-16

   All four boxes change to Inverse Rounded because the Make all settings the same button ▣ is selected. You can apply different styles to each corner by deactivating the Make all settings the same button.

10. Click OK, deselect all, press [W] to view the document in Preview mode, then compare your screen to Figure C-17

11. Save your work

FIGURE C-15: Applying a four-point stroke

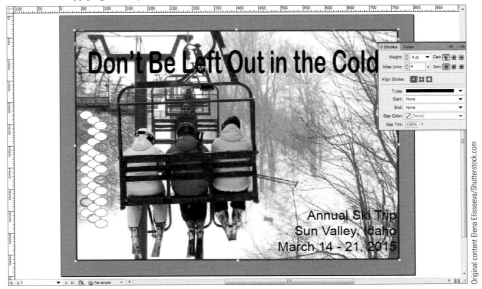

FIGURE C-16: Corner Options dialog box

Top-left arrow

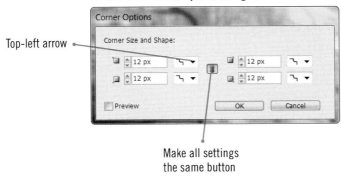

Make all settings
the same button

FIGURE C-17: Modified corners applied to the photo

Inverse
Rounded corner

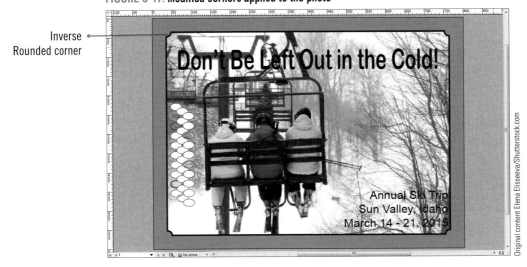

Creating a Multi-State Object

In InDesign, you can create different appearances or **states** for the same object. This makes it possible to demonstrate one layout with two or more options for any of the InDesign objects. For example, you could create a layout with different colored backgrounds or one in which the central photo changes. To create a multi-state object, you first select the object, then click the Convert selection to multi-state object button on the Object States panel. Two copies of the same object appear as thumbnails on the panel. Select one of the object states on the panel and then make changes to it in the Document window. ▨▨▨▨ Jennifer would like to see what the final layout would look like with a red background. You convert the blue background to a multi-state object and change the fill color of one of the object states to RGB Red, and then view each state on the Object States panel.

STEPS

1. **Press [W] to switch back to Normal mode**

2. **Click Window on the Menu bar, point to Interactive, then click Object States**
   The Object States panel opens.

3. **Click the blue rectangle frame, then click the Convert selection to multi-state object button ▨ on the Object States panel**
   Two object states of the blue rectangle appear on the Object States panel, as shown in Figure C-18. By default, they are named State 1 and State 2. You can add descriptive names to object states to help identify them. A dashed line appears around the blue rectangle frame in the Document window.

4. **Verify that State 2 is still selected on the Object States panel, open the Swatches panel, click the Fill button ▨ on the Swatches panel, then click RGB Red on the Swatches panel**
   The frame is filled with 50% red because the original object had a 50% tint applied.

5. **On the Swatches panel, drag the Tint slider to 100%, then compare your screen to Figure C-19**

6. **Close the Swatches panel, then click State 1 and State 2 to compare options for the layout**

7. **Save your work, click File on the Menu bar, then click Exit to exit InDesign**

FIGURE C-18: **Creating a multi-state object**

- Object States panel
- Object states
- Convert selection to multi-state object button

FIGURE C-19: **Viewing the red rectangle frame**

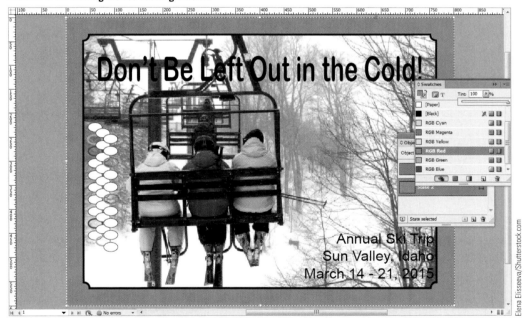

Practice

Concepts Review

Label the elements of the InDesign screen shown in Figure C-20.

FIGURE C-20

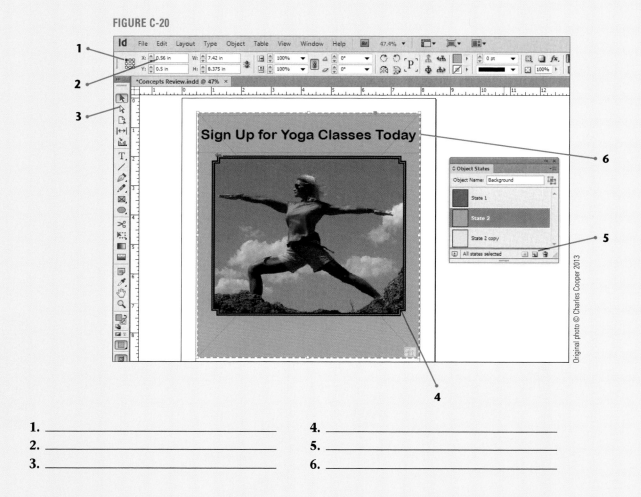

Original photo © Charles Cooper 2013

1. _____
2. _____
3. _____
4. _____
5. _____
6. _____

Match each term with the statement that best describes it.

7. **Live Distribute**
8. **Align**
9. **Group**
10. **Multi-state object**

a. To position one or more objects in relation to other objects or page elements, such as margin guides

b. A good choice when you wish to manually distribute objects

c. An InDesign object that has two or more appearances

d. To combine two or more objects as one object

Select the best answer from the list of choices.

11. Which of the following is a Transform command?
- **a.** Type
- **b.** Rotate
- **c.** Effects
- **d.** Transparency

12. Which InDesign element can you align an object to?
- **a.** Ruler
- **b.** Page
- **c.** Column
- **d.** Gutter

13. Which dialog box allows you to move and copy multiple objects?
- **a.** Move
- **b.** Move and Copy
- **c.** Transform
- **d.** Step and Repeat

14. Which of the following is not an alignment choice for a stroke?
- **a.** Inside
- **b.** Center
- **c.** Middle
- **d.** Outside

Skills Review

1. Create an object.
- **a.** Start InDesign, navigate to the drive and folder where you store your Data Files, then open ID C-2.indd.
- **b.** Save the document as **hang gliding_ID-C**, then reset the Essentials workspace.
- **c.** Click the Rectangle tool on the Tools panel.
- **d.** Position the Rectangle tool pointer on the left side of the page anywhere next to the left side of the photo and inside the left margin guide.
- **e.** Drag to create a small rectangle, then release the mouse button.
- **f.** Verify that the rectangle is still selected, then click the Swatches panel icon on the right to open the Swatches panel.
- **g.** Click the Fill button on the Tools panel, if necessary, then click RGB Yellow on the Swatches panel.
- **h.** Drag the Tint slider on the Swatches panel to 70.
- **i.** Click the Stroke button on the Tools panel, then click [None] on the Swatches panel.
- **j.** Save your work.

2. Transform an object.
- **a.** Make sure the yellow rectangle is selected.
- **b.** Click the upper-left reference point on the Control panel, double-click the X Location value if necessary, type **0**, then press [Tab].
- **c.** Type **0** in the Y Location box, then press [Enter] (Win) or [return] (Mac).
- **d.** Double-click the value in the W (Width) text box in the Control panel, type **800**, then press [Tab].
- **e.** Type **600** in the H (Height) text box, then press [Enter] (Win) or [return] (Mac).
- **f.** Save your work.

3. Arrange and lock an object.
- **a.** Click the Selection tool, then verify that the yellow rectangle is still selected.
- **b.** Click Object on the Menu bar, point to Arrange, then click Send Backward.
- **c.** Click Object on the Menu bar, point to Arrange, then click Send Backward.
- **d.** Verify that the yellow rectangle is still selected, click Object on the Menu bar, then click Lock.
- **e.** Click the photo, then lock it.
- **f.** Deselect all, press [W] to view your work in Preview mode, then save your work.
- **g.** Press [W] to return to Normal view.

Skills Review (continued)

4. **Step and repeat an object.**

   a. Click and hold the Rectangle tool on the Tools panel, click the Ellipse tool, then click in the yellow rectangle above the upper-left corner of the photo.

   b. Type **15** in the Width text box, press [Tab], type **15** in the Height text box, then click OK.

   c. Change the fill color of the circle to RGB Red, then change the stroke color to Black.

   d. Verify that the circle is still selected, click Edit on the Menu bar, then click Step and Repeat.

   e. Click the Preview check box in the Step and Repeat dialog box, if necessary.

   f. Type **32** in the Count text box, press [Tab] until the Vertical Offset text box is highlighted, type **0**, press [Tab], then type **22** in the Horizontal Offset text box. (*Hint*: If you get a warning, change the Horizontal and/or Vertical text box values to 0, then enter the Count value again.)

   g. Click OK to close the Step and Repeat dialog box.

   h. Click the Selection tool, press and hold [Shift], then select the original circle so that all of the circles are selected.

   i. Click Object on the Menu bar, then click Group.

   j. Verify that the group is still selected, then open the Step and Repeat dialog box.

   k. Type **2** in the Count text box, press [Tab] until the Vertical Offset text box is highlighted, type **–8**, press [Tab], type **0** in the Horizontal text box, then click OK.

   l. Save your work.

5. **Use Live Distribute.**

   a. Click the Selection tool on the Tools panel, if necessary.

   b. Click the first group of circles, press and hold [Shift], then click the second and third groups of circles so that all three groups are selected, if necessary.

   c. Position the mouse pointer over the bottom-right selection handle of the bounding box.

   d. Click the selection handle, press [Spacebar], drag the pointer slowly up, down, left and/or right until the three groups of circles overlap to create an interesting pattern.

   e. Verify that the three groups are still selected, click Object on the Menu bar, then click Group.

   f. Save your work.

6. **Use the Direct Selection tool.**

   a. Click the Selection tool on the Tools panel, then click in the pasteboard to deselect all.

   b. Click the Direct Selection tool on the Tools panel, then click any one of the circles.

   c. Show the Swatches panel, if necessary, click the Fill button on the Tools panel, then click [None].

   d. Click the Stroke panel tab to open the Stroke panel, click the Weight list arrow, click 3 pt, then deselect.

   e. Repeat Steps b–d to change the fill to [None] and the stroke weight to 3 pt for any six of the remaining circles.

   f. Save your work.

7. **Modify corners and strokes.**

   a. Click Window on the Menu bar, point to Workspace, then click Reset Essentials.

   b. Click Object on the Menu bar, then click Unlock All on Spread.

   c. Deselect all, click the Selection tool on the Tools panel, then click the photo.

   d. Show the Swatches panel, click the Stroke icon on the Tools panel, then click RGB Blue on the Swatches panel.

   e. Show the Stroke panel, click the Weight list arrow, then click 6 pt.

   f. Click Object on the Menu bar, then click Corner Options.

   g. Click the top-left down arrow, click Bevel, then click OK.

   h. Save your work.

Skills Review (continued)

8. Create a multi-state object.

FIGURE C-21

Original content Danshutter/Shutterstock.com

a. Click Window on the Menu bar, point to Interactive, then click Object States.

b. Click the grouped circle pattern, then click the Convert selection to multi-state object button on the Object States panel.

c. Verify that State 2 is still selected on the Object States panel, open the Swatches panel, click the Fill button on the Tools panel, then click Black on the Swatches panel.

d. Drag the Tint slider to 100% on the Swatches panel.

e. Click the Stroke button on the Tools panel, then click [Paper] on the Swatches panel.

f. Click the Weight list arrow, then click 1 pt on the Stroke panel.

g. Deselect all, press [W] to view your image in Preview mode, then compare your screen to Figure C-21. (*Hint*: Your pattern will differ from the figure.)

h. Save your work, then exit InDesign.

Independent Challenge 1

You are applying for a job as a fabric designer for a teen furniture store. As part of the interview process, you've been asked to pick six colors for furniture and accessories that would appeal to teenagers, and provide a printout of them to the human resources manager. You've decided to use InDesign to create the color set.

FIGURE C-22

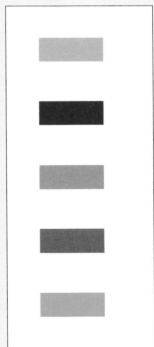

a. Open ID C-3.indd, then save it as **color samples_ID-C**.

b. Select the rectangle, then open the Step and Repeat dialog box.

c. Step and repeat four copies of the rectangle that have a 2" vertical offset and a 0" horizontal offset.

d. Fill the five rectangles with colors and tints of colors from the Swatches panel. Use the Color panel to create new swatches and add them to the Swatches panel. (*Hint*: When you create a color, right-click the Swatch button on the Color panel and then click Add to Swatches.)

e. Do not apply a stroke to the rectangles.

f. Group the five rectangles.

g. Deselect all objects, press [W] to switch to Preview mode, then compare your screen to Figure C-22. (*Hint*: The colors of the rectangles on your screen will be different.)

h. Save the document, then exit InDesign.

Independent Challenge 2

You left your wallet at the movie theatre. A few days later, you receive it in the mail with a note from someone who found it. Everything you had in it is still there. You are so relieved and grateful that you compose a thank you note right away.

a. Start InDesign.

b. Open ID C-4.indd, then save it as **thank you_ID-C**.

c. Create a rectangle that snaps to all four margin guides.

d. Fill the rectangle with a color of your choice.

Independent Challenge 2 (continued)

e. Send the rectangle behind the flower graphic and text box.

f. Format the text using the text formatting features in InDesign, then position the text frame where you want it.

g. Place a 5-point stroke around the photo using the stroke color of your choice.

h. Use the Corner Options dialog box to change the style of the four corners.

FIGURE C-23

Original content Hadrian/Shutterstock.com

Advanced Challenge Exercise

- Click Window on the Menu bar, point to Object & Layout, then click Align.
- Click the background frame, press and hold [Shift], then click the photo.
- On the Align panel, click the Align horizontal centers button, then click the Align vertical centers button.
- If necessary, adjust the location of the text frame.
- Click the page to deselect.

i. Switch to Preview mode, then compare your document to Figure C-23.

j. Save the document, then exit InDesign.

Independent Challenge 3

Your design class is having a contest to design a logo that provides services for the homeless. You use your knowledge of working with InDesign objects to create a winning logo. You then make three versions of the logo using the Object States panel.

a. Start InDesign, create a new document, then save it as **services_ID-C**.

b. Use the shape tools, fill colors, stroke colors and stroke weights to design an interesting logo.

c. Use the Step and Repeat feature, the Align panel, and/or the Live Distribute feature to position the logo elements.

d. Group all of the pieces of the logo so that it is one selectable object.

e. Convert the logo into a multi-state object.

f. Create a third state for the logo.

g. Click State 2 on the Object States panel.

h. Deselect all, use the Direct Selection tool to select individual logo elements and then modify them in some way.

i. Select State 2 copy on the Object States panel, deselect all, then modify individual logo elements.

j. Click each state on the Object States panel to view the different versions of the logo.

Independent Challenge 3 (continued)

FIGURE C-24

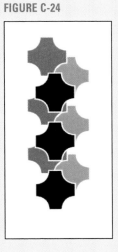

Advanced Challenge Exercise

- Select State 1 on the Object States panel, then change the name to **Logo 1**. (*Hint*: Select the state, then click the state name once. Wait for the text to become highlighted, then type a new name.)
- Change the names of State 2 and State 2 copy to **Logo 2** and **Logo 3**.
- Highlight Multi-state 1 in the Object Name text box on the Object States panel, then type **Logo Design**.

k. Deselect all, press [W] to view the logo in Preview mode, then save your work. Figure C-24 shows a sample logo.

l. Exit InDesign.

Real Life Independent Challenge

InDesign is a great program for creating your own professional-looking printed materials. Design a simple business card with your name and a service that you provide (for example, dog walking or house sitting). Include your telephone number and an email address. Use the shape tools and the Step and Repeat command to create a simple but interesting pattern for your card.

a. Start InDesign, then create a new document that is 3" wide by 2.5" tall, without facing pages and with 0" margins. (*Hint*: Change your Horizontal and Vertical Ruler Units to Inches in the Units & Increments Preferences dialog box, if necessary.)

b. Save the document as **business card_ID-C**.

c. Create a rectangle that is the same size as the document and that snaps to all four edges of the document.

d. Create a text box, then type your name, a fictitious profession and/or company name, phone number, and email address.

e. Format the text to your liking.

f. Create your pattern using one or more of the shape tools, the Swatches panel, and the Step and Repeat command.

FIGURE C-25

UNDER CONTROL
Ann Fisher
Professional Organizer
555-555-1222
yourname@organize.net

g. Use any of the Transform, Arrange, and Align commands to further design your pattern. Be creative.

h. Group and lock objects as you deem necessary.

i. Switch to Preview mode. A sample business card is shown in Figure C-25.

j. Save the document, then exit InDesign.

Visual Workshop

Create a new 8.5" × 11" document that has .5" margins and does not have facing pages. (*Hint*: Change the Horizontal and Vertical Ruler Units to Inches in the Units & Increments Preferences dialog box, if necessary.) Save it as **bars_ID-C**. Using Figure C-26 as a guide, recreate the image. Start by creating a rectangle that is 7.5" wide and 1" tall, and then fill it with red. Snap it to the top and left margin guides. Step and repeat the rectangle. The black rectangle should snap to the top margin guide and should be .5" wide and 8.875" tall. Once the bars are layered correctly, group and lock all of the bars. Switch to Preview mode, save the document, then exit InDesign.

FIGURE C-26

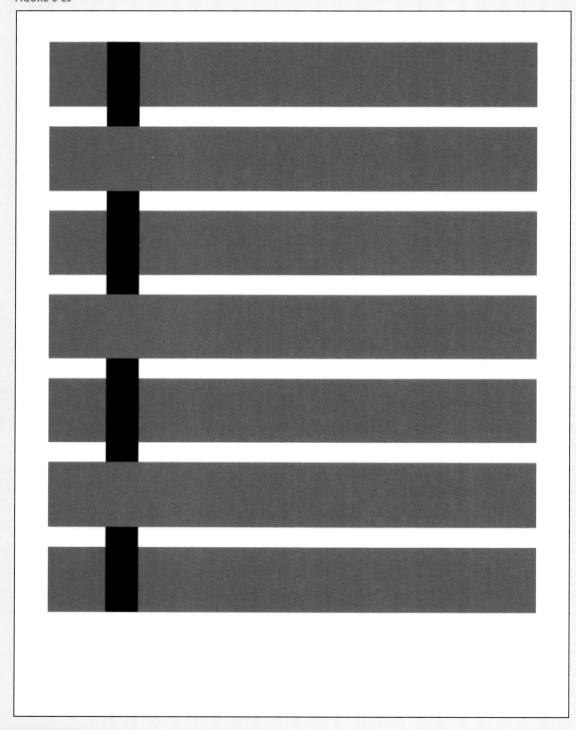

Working with Graphics

In addition to creating your own graphics in InDesign, you can also place graphics from other programs, such as Adobe Illustrator and Photoshop, in InDesign documents. InDesign places graphics into frames; there are many ways that you can manipulate the graphic and the frame to fit your layout needs. Placed graphics are known as **links** because the placed graphic that appears in the document is actually a link to the original graphic file stored on your computer. Information about placed graphics appears on the Links panel. You can use the Links panel to replace one placed object with another, find a placed object in a document, and even edit a placed object by launching the software program that created it. 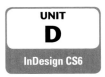 Your client, The Happy Apple, creates an online and print advertisement each week promoting its weekly specials. You work with your contact, Ted, to place the images that are needed into the InDesign document.

OBJECTIVES

Understand bitmap and vector graphics

Place a graphic into a frame

Work with the content indicator

Transform frame contents

Use the Links panel

Replace a linked image and embed a file

Add graphics to a library

Understanding Bitmap and Vector Graphics

Graphic files come in many formats. Two formats that are commonly placed into InDesign documents are bitmap and vector. A **bitmap graphic** is a graphic that is made up of **pixels**: tiny color squares arranged in a grid that are used to display graphics shown on a monitor or television screen. Scanned photographs and photographs taken from a digital camera are bitmap graphics. Files created in an image-editing software program, such as Adobe Photoshop, are another example of bitmap graphics. If you zoom in on a bitmap graphic or greatly increase its size, you can see its pixels. A **vector graphic** is a graphic that is made up of **vectors**, which are straight or curved line segments connected by **anchor points** (small dots), much like a completed connect-the-dots drawing. Vector graphics are created in drawing programs such as Adobe Illustrator. They are an ideal format for illustrations and logos because they can be resized in page layouts without losing image quality. Vector graphics can be manipulated in InDesign using the Pen tool and the Direct Selection tool. You can add, move, and delete anchor points and line segments to change the shape of the vector. ▰▱▰ Before working with the images you'll use in the advertisement, you review the properties of bitmap and vector graphics.

STEPS

1. **Start InDesign, open ID D-1.indd from the drive and folder where you store your Data Files, then save it as** graphics_ID-D

   The file includes one bitmap image of papayas and one vector image of an apple.

2. **Click the** workspace switcher **on the Menu bar, then click** Essentials

3. **Click the** Zoom tool 🔍 **on the Tools panel**

   You use the Zoom tool to enlarge your view of the bitmap image to view the pixels.

4. **Drag a small rectangle with the** Zoom tool pointer ⊕ **over the papayas image in the approximate location shown in Figure D-1, then release the mouse button**

   The dotted rectangle that appears as you drag the Zoom tool pointer is called a **marquee**. Everything inside the marquee will be enlarged on the screen when you release the mouse pointer. At a high zoom percentage, you can easily see the pixels that make up the image.

5. **Click** View **on the Menu bar, then click** Fit Page in Window

6. **Click the** Direct Selection tool � **on the Tools panel, then position the** Direct Selection tool pointer ▸ **near the upper-right edge of the apple until it appears with a small line segment next to it** ▸╱

   When the Direct Selection tool pointer is positioned over the edge of an unselected vector graphic, the anchor points and line segments become visible. As shown in Figure D-2, the pointer is over a line segment, indicated by the tiny line segment icon next to the arrow pointer.

QUICK TIP
In order to manipulate a vector graphic's anchor points and line segments in InDesign, you must copy and paste it from Illustrator to InDesign. If you use the Place command, the vector graphic will not be editable.

7. **Click any one of the** anchor points **on either side of the line segment, then drag slowly in any direction to change the location of the anchor point and the shape of the apple, as shown in Figure D-3**

   Most vector graphics are created in Adobe Illustrator, but they can be manipulated in Adobe InDesign using the similar tools.

8. **Save your work, then close graphics_ID-D.indd**

FIGURE D-1: Viewing pixels

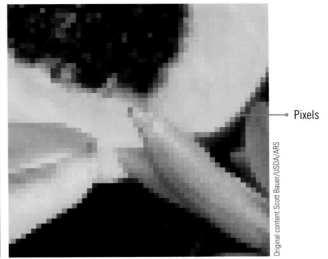

Marquee

Pixels

Original content Scott Bauer/USDA/ARS

Bitmap graphic

FIGURE D-2: Viewing the parts of a vector

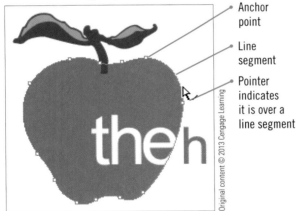

Anchor point

Line segment

Pointer indicates it is over a line segment

Original content © 2013 Cengage Learning

FIGURE D-3: Moving an anchor point

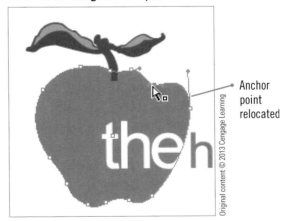

Anchor point relocated

Original content © 2013 Cengage Learning

Understanding resolution issues

Resolution, also known as screen resolution, is the number of pixels per inch (ppi) used to display computer graphics on a monitor. There should be at least 72 pixels per inch in order for a graphic to display correctly. The resolution required for printed materials, also known as the number of lines per inch (lpi) or dots per inch (dpi), is much higher. This is because pixels are converted to dots when graphics are printed. The number of dots per inch determines the quality of the print job. For example, printed newspapers have a lower lpi than a glossy magazine. When working in InDesign, it is important that you avoid resizing bitmap graphics. When you resize a graphic to make it larger, the same number of pixels is forced to fill a larger area. The pixels are spread farther away from each other, resulting in poor print quality. This is why bitmap images are known as being "resolution dependent." Vector graphics, on the other hand, are not made of pixels and are "resolution independent," meaning that you can greatly reduce or increase their size and they will print with the same level of quality.

Placing a Graphic into a Frame

You place graphics into frames. Frames are created using any of the frame tools: the Rectangle, Ellipse, and Polygon tools. After you create a frame, you place a graphic into it using the Place command on the File menu. When you place a graphic into a frame, the upper-left corner of the graphic snaps to the upper-left corner of the frame and then fills the remainder of the frame. If the frame is larger than the graphic, not all of the frame will be filled with the graphic. If the graphic is larger than the frame, part of the graphic will not be seen; it will be cropped by the frame. InDesign offers many solutions for fitting frame contents. Ted has sent over photos of this week's specials for the newsletter. You create a frame for the first one and then place a bitmap graphic into it.

STEPS

1. **Open ID D-2.indd from the drive and folder where you store your Data Files, then save it as** specials_ID-D

2. **Make sure that the Essentials workspace is selected and that the guides are visible**

3. **Click the** Rectangle Frame tool ⊠ **on the Tools panel, then click the** page
   The Rectangle dialog box opens.

4. **Type** 4 **in the Width text box, press [Tab], type** 4 **in the Height text box, then click** OK

5. **Click the** Selection tool ▶ **on the Tools panel, then drag the edge of the frame so that it is aligned with the left margin and the bottom guide, as shown in Figure D-4**
   The smart guides appear green when the frame touches both the left margin guide and the horizontal guide.

> **QUICK TIP**
> You can also place a graphic without first creating a frame. A frame is automatically created for the graphic when it is placed on the page. The frame is the same size as the graphic.

6. **Verify that the frame is still selected, click** File **on the Menu bar, then click** Place
   The Place dialog box opens.

7. **In the Place dialog box, shown in Figure D-5, navigate to the drive and folder where you store your Data Files, click** pizza.psd, **then click** Open
   An image of a pizza against a white background fills the frame from the upper-left corner of the frame, as shown in Figure D-6. The bounding box surrounds the frame.

8. **Save your work, then keep the specials_ID-D.indd document open**

Placing multiple images

Some types of documents require many pictures. A clothing catalog is a good example. When you have many pictures that you plan to place in InDesign, you can select them for placement all at once instead of one at a time. You do this by pressing and holding [Ctrl] (Win) or ⌘ (Mac) as you select multiple graphics in the Place dialog box. The pointer becomes a loaded graphics pointer. It displays the thumbnail of the first selected graphic and the number of total graphics to be placed. Each time you click, a graphic is placed in the document in the order that it was selected in the Place dialog box.

Align the rectangle frame here

FIGURE D-5: **Place dialog box**

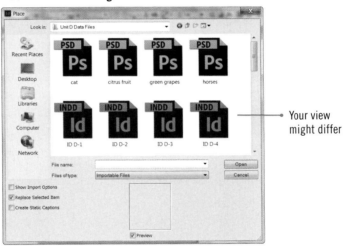

Your view might differ

FIGURE D-6: **pizza.psd graphic placed in the frame**

White background is part of the image

Bounding box

Working with the Content Indicator

When you place a graphic into a frame, you only see the part of the graphic that fits inside the frame. You may want to show a different view of the graphic without changing the frame size. The **content indicator**, a donut-shaped icon, appears over a placed graphic when you move the Selection tool over the graphic. The content indicator allows you to move a graphic in a frame without moving the frame. Once you begin dragging the content indicator, you will see the part of the image that lies outside the frame borders and the part of the image inside the frame borders. You can drag the image until it is cropped to your liking. **Cropping** an image in InDesign means hiding part of it without permanently removing it. 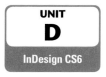 You use the content indicator to move the pizza image so that it is more centered in the frame.

STEPS

1. **Verify that the frame is still selected with the Selection tool** ▶

2. **Position the mouse pointer over the pizza image until the** content indicator ◉ **is visible**

3. **Position the mouse pointer over** ◉ **until you see a** hand pointer ✋, **as shown in Figure D-7**
   You use the hand pointer to drag the graphic.

4. **Click and hold the** image **for a couple seconds, then drag** ◉ **slowly up and to the left until your screen resembles Figure D-8, then release the mouse**
   The area of the graphic outside of the frame appears ghosted. The brown frame represents the borders of the graphic file, not the InDesign frame that the graphic is placed in. When dragging the image you may or may not see transformation values, which are the X and Y coordinates next to the cursor. They show the location of the object's reference point. You can turn transformation values off in the Interface section of the Preferences dialog box. Click the Show Transformation Values check box to remove the check mark.

5. **Double-click the** pizza image
   The image is selected, indicated by the brown outline that surrounds the pizza image.

6. **Double-click the** pizza image **again**
   The frame is selected, indicated by the blue bounding box.

7. **Save your work**

QUICK TIP
Another way to select an image without selecting the frame is to click the image with the Direct Selection tool ▶.

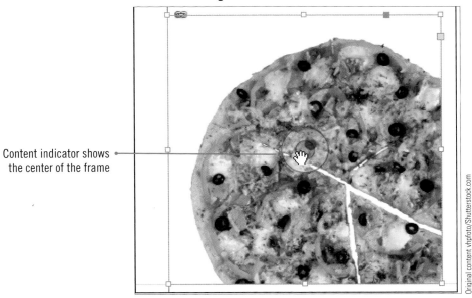

Content indicator shows
the center of the frame

Original content vhpfoto/Shutterstock.com

FIGURE D-8: **Adjusting the view inside the frame**

This Week's Specials

Brown frame represents the
border of the graphic file

Image outside of the
frame is ghosted

Brick Oven Pizza

Blue frame represents
the border of the frame

X: -0.1 in
Y: 1.98 in

Original content vhpfoto/Shutterstock.com

InDesign CS6

Other uses of the Direct Selection tool

The Direct Selection tool has many uses in addition to selecting a placed object separately from its frame. You can use it to select the individual anchor points and line segments of vector graphics, such as rectangles and rectangle frames that you create with InDesign. To select an anchor point or line segment in a graphic, make sure that the graphic is not selected, then click the point or segment you wish to select with the Direct Selection tool. You can then edit the graphic to make a subtle change to the object or to create an entirely new shape. When anchor points are selected and editable, you can drag either the point or one of its adjoining line segments. Dragging an anchor point changes the shape of the object because the line segments attached to either side of it change when the anchor point is moved. Dragging a line segment is one way to resize a shape by moving only one side of it. Press and hold [Shift] while you drag to constrain the shape without changing its horizontal or vertical axis.

Transforming Frame Contents

When the image inside a frame is selected, the Control panel displays options for transforming the frame contents. For example, you can scale an image, rotate it, center it, or flip it. There are also buttons for fitting the image to match the size of the frame and vice versa. Table D-1 describes the fitting options in more detail. ▆▆▆▆ Although you and Ted like how the pizza is framed, you want to scale the pizza image and then center it inside the frame.

STEPS

1. **Verify that the frame is still selected with the Selection tool ▐▶, then click the top-left reference point on the Control panel**

   The image of the pizza is selected. The Control panel displays options for modifying the image, as shown in Figure D-9. Notice the X and Y values change to X+ and Y+. They represent the horizontal and vertical locations of the upper-left corner of the pizza image in relation to the upper-left corner of the frame. They are both negative numbers because they are located above and beyond the upper-left corner of the frame.

2. **Double-click the Scale X Percentage text box ▣ on the Control panel, as shown in Figure D-10, type 86, then press [Enter] (Win) or [return] (Mac)**

   The Scale Y Percentage text box ▣ value changes to 76% automatically because the Constrain proportions for scaling button ▐8▌ is selected. The pizza image is scaled 86%.

3. **Click the Center content button ▣ on the Control panel**

   The pizza image is centered inside the frame, as shown in Figure D-11.

4. **Click the Select container button ▐▲▌ on the Control panel**

   The frame is selected. Clicking the Select container button on the Control panel is equivalent to clicking the image to select the frame.

5. **Save your work**

QUICK TIP

The Control panel has many effects that you can add to frames and images. Select an image or a frame, click the Add an object effect to the selected target button ▐fx▌, then select an effect.

TABLE D-1: Fitting commands

command	button	description	use when
Fit content to frame	▣	Image is resized to fit the exact size of the frame	Frame size must remain the same and it is OK if the image is distorted when stretched or shrunk to fit the frame
Fit frame to content	▣	Frame is resized to the exact size of the image	Picture size must remain at 100% and the frame size does not matter
Center content	▣	Image is centered in the frame without any reduction in image or frame size; if image is larger than the frame, some of the image will be cropped	The image and frame are similar in size and you want to center the content quickly
Fit content proportionally	▣	Image is resized to fit the frame while maintaining its proportion; if the frame and the image are different sizes, some empty space may appear inside the frame	Frame size cannot change and all of the image must be visible; only works well when the frame and image are similar in size
Fill frame proportionally	▣	Entire frame is filled with the image and the image's proportions are preserved; if the image is larger than the frame, some of it will be cropped by the frame border	Frame size cannot change and not all of the image needs to be visible; only works well when the frame and image are similar in size

FIGURE D-9: Viewing the Control panel

Horizontal and vertical locations of the upper-left corner of pizza image in relation to the upper-left corner of the frame

Width and height of pizza image

Upper-left corner of pizza image

Upper-left corner of frame

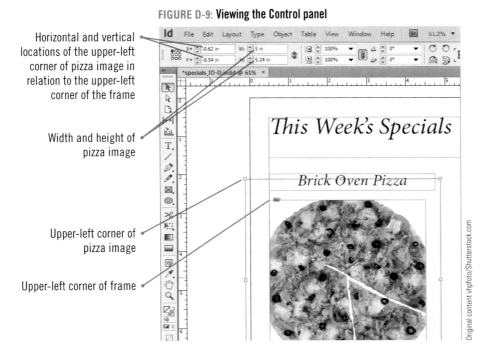

FIGURE D-10: Highlighting the Scale X Percentage value

Scale X Percentage text box

FIGURE D-11: The scaled and centered image

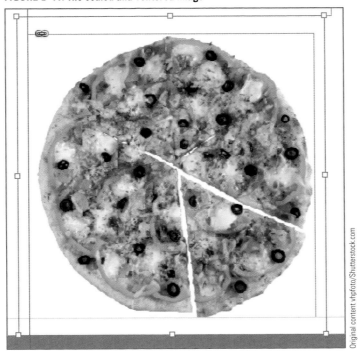

Using the Links Panel

When you place an image in a frame, the frame displays a **preview**, which is a graphical representation of the original image file and not the file itself. A link is automatically established between the preview and the actual image file, which remains in its original location on the local internal hard drive or storage device. Linking images helps to keep an InDesign file size manageable because the size of the placed image files is not added to the InDesign file size. Once images are placed in a document, information about each placed file, such as its name, size, and the page where it appears in the document, is displayed on the Links panel. See Table D-2 on page 88 for more information about each link status. ▓▓▓▓ You place another graphic in the document and then view three links on the Links panel.

STEPS

1. **Click the Rectangle Frame tool ⊠, on the Tools panel, then click an empty part of the page**

2. **Type 5.5 in the Width text box, press [Tab], type 4 in the Height text box, then click OK**

3. **Click the Selection tool ▶ on the Tools panel, then position the new frame in the location shown in Figure D-12**

4. **Verify that the frame is still selected, click File on the Menu bar, click Place, click sushi.psd, then click Open**
   A photo of sushi fills the frame.

5. **Click the Center content button ▣ on the Control panel**
   The image is centered in the frame.

6. **Click the Links panel icon ⬲, if necessary, then compare your screen to Figure D-13**
   The Links panel lists the three images placed in the document: logoWhite.ai, pizza.psd, and sushi.psd. The sushi.psd file is highlighted on the panel because it is still selected on the page. The Links panel includes three information columns—Name, Status ⚠, and Page ▣—and a row of buttons for working with links. The bottom section of the Links panel is called the Link Info section. It displays detailed information about the highlighted link. You can view the next link or the previous link in the list by clicking the Select next link in the list button ▶ or the Select previous link in the list button ◀.

7. **On the Links panel, move the pointer along the blue highlighted area for sushi.psd until you see a ScreenTip stating the path of the file, then continue to move the pointer until you see a ScreenTip that reads OK under the Status column, as shown in Figure D-14**
   There are four possible statuses for each link: OK, Missing, Modified, and Embedded. The OK status indicates that the linked file has not been moved or modified since you placed it in the document.

8. **Click logoWhite.ai on the Links panel, then click the Go to Link button ↗▣ on the Links panel**
   The Happy Apple logo (logoWhite.ai) appears in the document window and is selected. The Go to Link button helps you identify a link when you are not sure what it is or where it is in the document.

Editing a link

You can edit a linked file in InDesign using the Edit Original button on the Links panel or the Edit Original command on the Links panel menu. Click a link on the Links panel that you wish to edit, then click the Edit Original button. The file opens in the software program that it was created in. For example, if you edit a photograph, it will open in the photo-editing program that it originated from. If you edit a file that you did not create, InDesign will open the program on your computer that is associated with the file type. If you want to use a specific program to edit a file, select the file in the Links panel, click the Panel menu button, point to Edit With, then click the name of the program you want to use to edit the file from the list of available programs. When you edit a file, InDesign remains open. When you finish editing the file, close the software program you are using. You'll see the updated file with the edits made to it in InDesign.

FIGURE D-12: Positioning the second frame

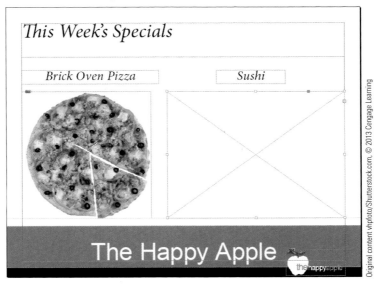

This Week's Specials

Brick Oven Pizza   *Sushi*

The Happy Apple

FIGURE D-13: Links panel

Highlighted link

Show/Hide Link
Information button

Relink button

Go to Link button

Select previous link
in the list button

Page column

Status column

Name column

Select next link in the
list button

Link Info section

FIGURE D-14: Links panel

Name column

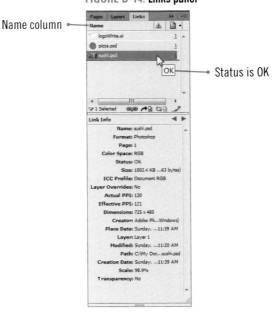

Status is OK

Replacing a Linked Image and Embedding a File

When working with an InDesign publication, it is very likely that you will replace one image with another. To replace a placed image in InDesign, click the image on the Links panel, click the Relink button on the Links panel, then choose a new file in the Relink dialog box. The new image replaces the original image and inherits any fitting commands and transformations that were made to it. For example, if you place an image, rotate it 15°, then replace it with a new image, the new image will be automatically rotated 15°. Small images that do not have a large file size can be embedded in the document. Embedding a file makes it a permanent part of the InDesign file; it is no longer linked. Embedded files remain on the Links panel with an embedded icon. Embedding a file is a great way to protect it from being changed, moved, or deleted. ░░░░ Ted would prefer that you use a different sushi image. You use the Links panel to replace the sushi image with a different image. You also embed the Happy Apple logo.

STEPS

1. **Click** View **on the Menu bar, then click** Fit Page in Window

2. **Click the** Selection tool **on the Tools panel, then click the** sushi image

QUICK TIP

To relink an image without inheriting any previously applied fitting commands and transformations, click Edit (Win) or InDesign (Mac) on the Menu bar, point to Preferences, click File Handling, then remove the check mark in the Preserve Image Dimensions When Relinking check box.

3. **Click the** Relink button **on the Links panel**
   The Relink dialog box opens.

4. **Navigate to the drive and folder where you store your Data Files, click** sushi 2.psd, **as shown in Figure D-15, then click** Open
   The sushi 2.psd file replaces sushi.psd in the document and on the Links panel. The image is automatically resized to fill the frame proportionally because you had previously applied this command to sushi.psd. You want to embed the Happy Apple logo so that it cannot be moved or modified by another person.

5. **Click** logoWhite.ai **on the Links panel**
   To embed the logo, you must first select it.

6. **Click the** Panel menu button **, click** Embed Link, **then save your work**
   The logo is now embedded into the InDesign file. The status changes to Embedded on the Links panel, as shown in Figure D-16. If the Embed Link command is not available you may need to update the link first.

TABLE D-2: Link status

status and icon	indicates	to change status to OK
OK	Linked file has not been changed or moved from its location on the computer since it was placed into InDesign	N/A
Missing ⊘	Linked file has been moved from its location on the computer when it was placed into InDesign	Click the Relink button on the Links panel or double-click the Missing icon; navigate to and select the linked file in the Relink dialog box, then click Open to relink the file and change the status of the missing link back to OK
Modified ⚠	The linked file was modified after it was placed into InDesign	Double-click the Modified icon in the Status column next to the link in question, which updates automatically
Embedded ▣	The file is embedded instead of linked	N/A

FIGURE D-15: Relink dialog box

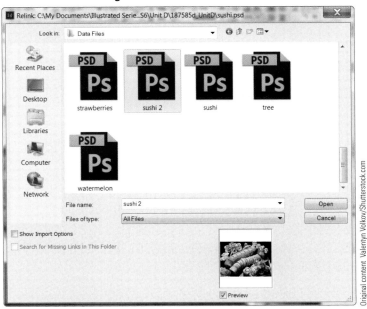

FIGURE D-16: Embedding the logo file

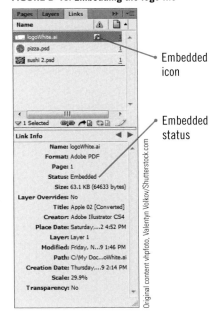

Embedded icon

Embedded status

Changing Links panel options

By default, the Links panel displays three columns of information: Name, Status, and Page. This information is enough for most people to have when creating simple documents. However, depending on how you use InDesign, you may want to display more information about placed files on the Links panel. For example, you may want to view the Dimensions column to view the size of an image. There are over 50 possible columns of information available, including categories such as Shutter, ISO Speed, Author and Location. You can customize the Links panel by adding or removing columns using the Panel Options dialog box. At the top of the Panel Options dialog box, you can choose the row size and whether you want to view image thumbnails in the Name column, the Link Info section, or both.

Adding Graphics to a Library

A **library** is a type of InDesign file that is strictly for storing often-used text, graphics, and even InDesign pages for use in any InDesign document you create. Libraries are very convenient because they store all the formatting that you have applied to objects and text. For example, if you place a graphic that has been resized or centered in its frame in a library, those settings are stored with the graphic. When you use the graphic again in a new document, you won't have to resize or center it. Libraries are easy to work with in InDesign because they are InDesign files (with an .indl extension) that look and work like InDesign panels. 📇📇📇 Ted wants to use the pizza and sushi graphics and the logo again in future InDesign documents, so you create a library file to store them in.

STEPS

1. **Close the Links panel**

2. **Click File on the Menu bar, point to New, then click Library**
   The New Library dialog box opens.

QUICK TIP
To add an entire page of objects to a library as a single item, click the Panel menu button ▾☰, then click Add Items on Page 1. To add all objects on a page as separate library items, click Add Items on Page 1 as Separate Objects.

3. **Navigate to the drive and folder where you store your Data Files, then type specials library_ID-D in the File name text box (Win) or the Save As text box (Mac), as shown in Figure D-17**
   Anyone working on the weekly specials advertisements will be able to access items in the library.

4. **Click Save to close the New Library dialog box**
   The Specials Library appears in the document window. Now you're ready to add items to the library.

5. **Click the Selection tool ▶ on the Tools panel, click the pizza image, then drag it to the library**
   As you drag an item to a library, a plus sign appears next to the pointer indicating that the item is being dragged to the library.

6. **Compare your library to Figure D-18**
   A copy of the pizza image is added to specials library_ID-D.indl. Notice that the original pizza image remains in the document.

QUICK TIP
You can change a library item by selecting it in the library, selecting one or more items in the document, clicking the Panel menu button ▾☰, then clicking Update Library Item.

7. **Add the sushi 2.psd graphic and the Happy Apple logo to the library so that it contains three items**
   The library items are listed alphabetically.

8. **Drag pizza.psd from the library to anywhere on the page**
   Notice that the image is identical to the original pizza image. The image is scaled 76% and centered.

9. **Undo your last step, reset the Essentials workspace, save your work, close specials library_ID-D.indl, press [W] switch to Preview mode, deselect any images if necessary, then compare your screen to Figure D-19**

10. **Close the specials_ID-D.indd file, then exit InDesign**

Viewing and sorting library items

There are three ways to view library items within the library. You can view them as a list, as thumbnails, or as large thumbnails. To change the view of library items, click the Panel menu button, then click List View, Thumbnail View, or Large Thumbnail View. If you have multiple items in a library, it can be helpful to sort them. By default, libraries are sorted alphabetically by name; but you can also sort them by type or sort them so that the newest addition or oldest addition to the library appears first in the library. Sorting library items by type puts items of the same type, like text, together in the library. To sort library items, click the Library menu button, point to Sort Items, then click by Name, by Newest, by Oldest, or by Type.

FIGURE D-17: New Library dialog box

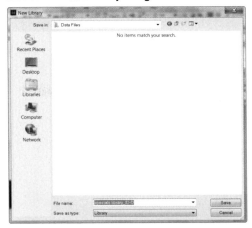

FIGURE D-18: pizza.psd added to specials library_ID-D.indl

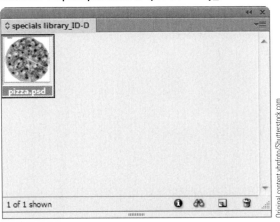

Original content vhpfoto/Shutterstock.com

FIGURE D-19: Finished project

Original content vhpfoto, Valentyn Volkov/Shutterstock.com

Printing an InDesign document with linked files

When you print an InDesign document that contains linked files, the original files that are linked to the document must be present on the same computer in order for the document to print correctly. If you send your InDesign document to a printer or a service bureau for printing, you must send not only the InDesign document, but also all of the linked files in one folder. When an InDesign file and its linked files move from one computer to another, occasionally the InDesign file opens with a warning that the linked images cannot be found. The files are there; the links just need to be re-established to the files in their location on the new computer. A warning dialog box will appear with the name of the first linked file that InDesign cannot find. All you need to do is to re-establish the links by locating the first linked file in the folder that contains it, and the rest of the files in that folder will update automatically.

Practice

Concepts Review

Label the elements of the InDesign screen shown in Figure D-20.

FIGURE D-20

Original content sarsmis/Shutterstock.com

1. _____   4. _____
2. _____   5. _____
3. _____

Match each term with the statement that best describes it.

6. **X+**
7. **Library**
8. **Pixels**
9. **Preview**
10. **Direct Selection tool**

a. Tiny colored squares arranged in a grid that are used to display graphics shown on a monitor or television screen

b. Horizontal location of image inside a frame

c. Used with vector graphics

d. Stores images without removing formatting

e. Appears in a frame

Select the best answer from the list of choices.

11. **Which term refers to hiding part of an image without removing it?**
    a. Resize
    b. Place
    c. Crop
    d. Preview

12. **Which text boxes on the Control panel would you choose to change the size of a photo in a frame?**
    a. X and Y
    b. X+ and Y
    c. Scale X Percentage and Scale Y Percentage
    d. X% and Y%

13. **Which of the following items could you place in an InDesign library?**
    a. Graphic
    b. Dialog box
    c. Content indicator
    d. Panel

14. **What type of graphic file is not linked to an InDesign document?**
    a. Embedded
    b. Linked
    c. Vector
    d. Cropped

Skills Review

1. **Understand bitmap and vector graphics.**
   a. Start InDesign, open ID D-3.indd from the drive and folder where you store your Data Files, then save it as **examples_ID-D**.
   b. Click the workspace switcher on the Menu bar, then click Essentials.
   c. Click the Zoom tool on the Tools panel.
   d. Drag a small rectangle with the Zoom tool pointer over a section of the lollipops image, then release the mouse button.
   e. Click View on the Menu bar, then click Fit Page in Window.
   f. Using the Zoom tool, zoom in on the owl, click the Direct Selection tool on the Tools panel, then position the Direct Selection tool pointer over the top-right ear of the owl.
   g. Click any one of the anchor points on either side of the line segment, then drag slowly in any direction to change the location of the anchor point and the shape of the ear. (*Hint:* You'll want to change the ear and the black shadow behind the ear.)
   h. Save your work, then close examples_ID-D.indd.

2. **Place a graphic into a frame.**
   a. Start InDesign, open ID D-4.indd from the drive and folder where you store your Data Files, then save it as **organic fruit_ID-D**.
   b. Make sure the Essentials workspace is selected.
   c. Click the Rectangle Frame tool on the Tools panel, then click the page.
   d. Type **3.5** in the Width text box, press [Tab], type **4** in the Height text box, then click OK.
   e. Click the Selection tool on the Tools panel, then drag the edge of the frame so that it is left-aligned with the left margin and bottom-aligned with the horizontal guide.
   f. Verify that the frame is still selected, click File on the Menu bar, then click Place.
   g. Navigate to the drive and folder where you store your Data Files, click oranges.psd, then click Open.
   h. Save your work and keep the organic fruit_ID-D.indd document open.

Skills Review (continued)

3. Work with the content indicator.

   a. Verify that the frame is still selected with the Selection tool.

   b. Position the mouse pointer over the image of the oranges so that you see the content indicator.

   c. Position the mouse pointer over the content indicator so that you see a hand pointer.

   d. Click and hold for a moment, drag the content indicator slowly to the left and upward, then release the mouse pointer.

   e. Double-click the image of the oranges to see the brown frame which represents the borders of the oranges image.

   f. Double-click the image of the oranges again to see the bounding box of the frame.

   g. Save your work.

4. Transform frame contents.

   a. Click the Selection tool on the Tools panel, then double-click the image of the oranges.

   b. Double-click the Scale X Percentage text box on the Control panel, type **155**, then press [Enter].

   c. Click the Select container button on the Control panel.

   d. Save your work.

5. Use the Links panel.

   a. Click the Rectangle Frame tool on the Tools panel, then click the page.

   b. Type **5** in the Width text box, press [Tab], type **4** in the Height text box, then click OK.

   c. Click the Selection tool on the Tools panel, then drag the new frame so that its right edge is snapped to the right margin guide and its bottom edge is snapped to the bottom guide.

   d. Verify that the frame is still selected, click File on the Menu bar, click Place, navigate to green grapes.psd, then click Open.

   e. Click the Center content button on the Control panel.

   f. Click the Links panel icon to open the Links panel.

   g. On the Links panel, position the pointer to the right of green grapes.psd under the Status column icon until you see a ScreenTip that reads OK.

   h. Click oranges.psd on the Links panel, then click the Go to Link button.

   i. Save your work.

6. Replace a linked image and embed a file.

   a. Click View on the Menu bar, then click Fit Page in Window.

   b. Click the Selection tool on the Tools panel, then click the green grapes image.

   c. Click the Relink button on the Links panel.

   d. Navigate to the drive and folder where you store your Data Files, click red grapes.psd, then click Open.

   e. Use the content indicator to crop the image so that you see most or all of the grapes in the frame.

   f. Select Organic logo.ai on the Links panel.

   g. Click the Links panel menu button, then click Embed Link.

   h. Save your work.

Skills Review (continued)

7. Add graphics to a library.

   a. Close the Links panel.

   b. Click File on the Menu bar, point to New, then click Library.

   c. If necessary, navigate to the drive and folder where you store your Data Files, then type **fruit library_ID-D** in the File name text box (Win) or the Save As text box (Mac).

   d. Click Save to close the New Library dialog box.

   e. Click the Selection tool on the Tools panel, click the oranges image, then drag it to the library.

   f. Release the mouse button.

   g. Add the red grapes.psd graphic and the Organic Source logo to the library so that your library contains three items.

   h. Drag oranges.psd from the library to anywhere on the page.

   i. Undo your last step, reset the Essentials workspace, then save your work.

   j. Close the library, press [W] to switch to Preview mode, deselect any images if necessary, then compare your screen to Figure D-21.

   k. Close the organic fruit_ID-D.indd file, then exit InDesign.

FIGURE D-21

Independent Challenge 1

You work as a package designer for a pet care product company. You are currently working on a price tag that will be placed on a cat tree. Your last step is to place a picture of a cat and position it well in the space allotted.

a. Start InDesign, open ID D-5.indd, then save it as **cat tree_ID-D**.

b. Create a rectangular frame a little larger than the oval in the middle of the price tag.

c. Place cat.psd into the frame.

d. Fill the frame proportionally.

e. Send the frame to the back.

f. Double-click the cat image with the Selection tool.

g. Make any size or location changes to the image on the Control panel.

h. Use the content indicator to move the image, if necessary.

i. When you are happy with the way that the frame crops the image, lock the image of the cat.

j. Save your work, then compare your screen to Figure D-22.

k. Close the cat tree_ID-D.indd file, then exit InDesign.

Independent Challenge 2

You volunteer two hours a week doing community service work for school credit at your local library. Each week, your supervisor assigns you different tasks. This week, she has asked you to create some fun pages to be distributed at the weekly story hour. The supervisor supplies you with an old version of fun pages and asks you to improve it with better images.

a. Start InDesign, open ID D-6.indd, then save it as **fun pages_ID-D**.

b. Using artwork in your Data Files folder, fill five squares with images of fruit and one square with an image of candy.

c. Use the content indicator and options on the Control panel to crop each picture in an interesting way.

d. Place a 3-point stroke around each frame using a stroke color of your choice.

e. Use the Links panel to swap images, if necessary.

Advanced Challenge Exercise

- Select the set of six frames.
- Click the Add an object effect to the selected target button, then click Drop Shadow.
- Accept the default settings in the Effects dialog box, then click OK.

f. Deselect all, save your work, press [W] to view your work in Preview mode, then compare your screen to Figure D-23.

g. Close the fun pages_ID-D.indd file, then exit InDesign.

Draw an X over the picture that does not belong with the rest of the group.

Independent Challenge 3

You're writing a cookbook and starting to collect images to use in your chapter on smoothies. You decide to place your artwork in an InDesign library because you have spent a lot of time cropping the images carefully. You also add the entire page of images as a new library item and update a library item.

a. Start InDesign, open ID D-7.indd, then save it as **smoothies_ID-D**.

b. Create a new library and name it **cookbook images_ID-D**.

c. Drag each item from the InDesign document to the library.

d. Click the Panel menu button, then click Large Thumbnail View.

e. Click the Panel menu button, then click Add Items on Page 1.

f. Rename the new library item **Smoothie Chapter Opener Art**.

Advanced Challenge Exercise

- In the cookbook images_ID-D library, click Smoothie Chapter Opener Art.
- Click the Library Item Information button (i) on the library.
- In the Description text box, type **This item can also be used for website buttons**, then click OK.

g. Compare your library to Figure D-24, close the smoothies_ID-D.indd file and the cookbook images_ID-D.indl library, then exit InDesign.

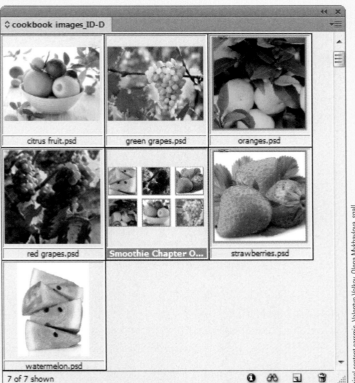

Original content sarsmis, Valentyn Volkov, Olena Mykhaylova, sgall, mikeledray, Africa Studio/Shutterstock.com

Real Life Independent Challenge

Start InDesign and create a new document using the Compact Disc page size option in the New Document dialog box. Name the document **cd cover_ID-D**. Create a CD cover for a band: real or fictitious. Create a frame and then place one of your favorite pictures in the frame. Crop the picture in an interesting way. Add a border to the frame, and then experiment with effects for the frame and the image. Add a title to the CD cover. Save your work, and then close **cd cover_ID-D.indd**.

InDesign CS6

Visual Workshop

Start InDesign, then create a new 8.5" × 11" document with a landscape orientation. Save the document as **horses_ID-D**. Create a rectangular graphics frame that is 7.85 inches wide and 7.50 inches tall. Position the frame as shown in Figure D-25. Place the horses.psd image, then crop the image in the frame exactly how it is cropped in the figure. Show the Links panel and change the Links panel options so that the thumbnail of the horses is displayed in the Link Info section. Save your work, close horses_ID-D.indd, then exit InDesign.

FIGURE D-25

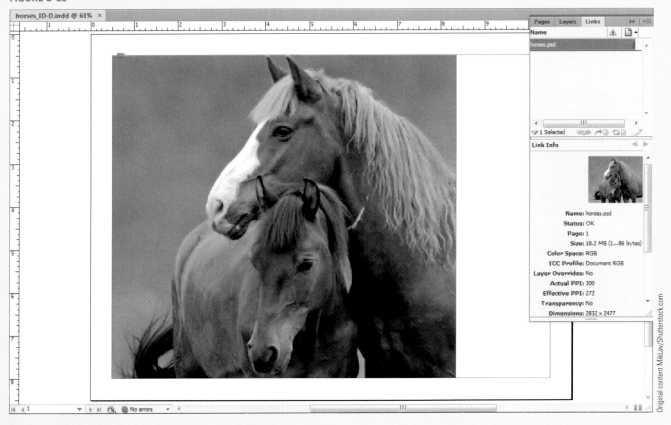

Original content MikLav/Shutterstock.com

Using Master Pages

Files You Will Need:

To view a list of files needed for this unit, see the Data Files Grid in the back of the book.

Most of the pages in multiple-page documents such as magazines and catalogs usually share a similar look. For example, catalog pages are filled with pictures of items for sale and descriptions of those items, and the pictures and descriptions are often in the same location on each page. Imagine if you were creating a 100-page catalog and you had to make sure that all graphics frames and text boxes were in the same locations on all 100 pages. Arranging each page, one at a time, would be time consuming and would likely result in some inconsistencies between pages. The master pages feature in InDesign enables you to apply the same design to multiple pages. Master pages are page designs that are available to be applied to pages in the same way that character styles are available to be applied to text. You create the layout on a master page and then apply it to as many pages as necessary. Think of all the time you can save!  Your next project is to work with the marketing director, Kate, at BreakTime on a booklet announcing its high school summer camp program. The booklet will contain photos and brief descriptions of six new themed camps. You plan to create and use master pages to format the booklet pages consistently.

OBJECTIVES

Create a multipage document

Create master items

Override master items

Modify a master page

Create a new master page

Apply master pages

Work with master pages

Creating a Multipage Document

Most publications that require master pages have left and right pages, such as books, magazines, newspapers, and catalogs. The Pages panel helps you to organize and manage all of the pages in a publication. It displays master page icons and document page icons, which represent the master pages and document pages in your publication, respectively. ▒▒▒▓ Kate would like you to create the camp brochure. You start by creating a new, custom-sized, eight-page document with facing pages and then open the Pages panel to view the master pages and pages.

STEPS

1. **Start InDesign, click** Edit **(Win) or** InDesign **(Mac) on the Menu bar, point to** Preferences, **then click** Units & Increments

2. **Click the** Horizontal list arrow **under Ruler Units, click** Inches **if necessary, click the** Vertical list arrow, **click** Inches **if necessary, then click** OK **to close the dialog box**

> **QUICK TIP**
> Click the Facing Pages check box to remove the check mark if you want to create a multipage document that does not require facing pages, such as flash cards.

3. **Click** File **on the Menu bar, point to** New, **click** Document, **type** 8 **in the Number of Pages text box, then verify that the Facing Pages check box is checked**
   You are creating an eight-page document with left and right pages.

4. **Double-click the** Width value, **type** 6, **press** [Tab], **type** 4 **as the Height value, press** [Tab], **verify that the** Landscape button 📄 **to the right of Orientation is selected, then compare your New Document dialog box to Figure E-1**
   The width of the booklet is greater than the height, so the Landscape button is automatically selected after you enter the Width and Height values.

5. **Click** OK **to close the New Document dialog box, click the** workspace switcher **on the Menu bar, then click** Reset Essentials
   The workspace returns to the Essentials workspace.

> **TROUBLE**
> If you do not see all eight pages in the Pages panel, drag the lower-right corner of the panel down until all eight pages are visible.

6. **Click the** Pages panel button 📑 **on the right side of the workspace to open the Pages panel**
   The Pages panel opens, as shown in Figure E-2. The Pages panel is divided into two sections. The top section displays the available master pages, and the lower section displays the document pages. The default A-Master appears in each new document. It is blank. All new pages in a document have the A-Master applied to them by default. Page 1 is highlighted in blue on the Pages panel because it is the active page in the document window.

7. **Double-click** A-Master **on the Pages panel**
   As shown in Figure E-3, the left and right pages of the A-Master fill the screen. Notice that "A-Master" appears on the left side of the status bar, indicating that the A-Master master page is open in the Document window.

> **QUICK TIP**
> You can also click the arrow next to A-Master in the status bar, and then click the number 1 on the menu to show Page 1 in the Document window.

8. **Double-click the** page 1 icon **on the Pages panel**
   Page 1 appears in the Document window. Notice "1" replaces "A-Master" in the page menu on the status bar.

9. **Double-click** A-Master **on the Pages panel again, then save the document as** camp booklet_ID-E

Inserting pages

To add new pages to a document after it has been created, click the Pages Panel menu button, click Insert Pages to open the Insert Pages dialog box, and then choose how many pages you would like to insert and their locations. For example, you can choose to insert pages at the beginning or end of the document, or before or after a specific page number. To choose which master page should be applied to the newly inserted pages, click the Master list arrow and then choose the name of a master page before closing the Insert Pages dialog box.

FIGURE E-1: New Document dialog box

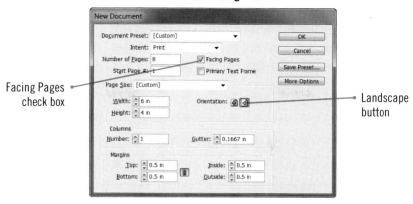

Facing Pages check box

Landscape button

FIGURE E-2: Pages panel

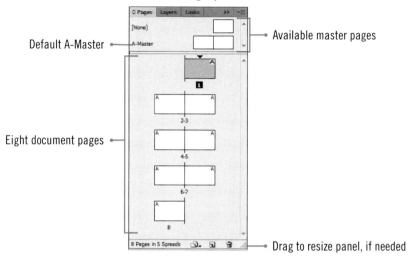

Default A-Master

Available master pages

Eight document pages

Drag to resize panel, if needed

FIGURE E-3: A-Master in the Document window

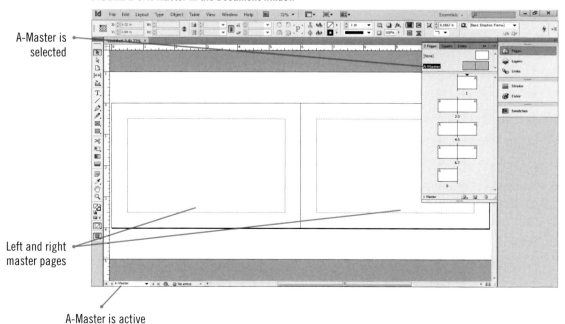

A-Master is selected

Left and right master pages

A-Master is active

Creating Master Items

The objects that you place on master pages are called **master items**. Master items appear on every document page to which the master page is applied. Company logos, page numbers, and empty frames reserved for text and pictures are good examples of master items. If you remove or change a master item on a master page, that item is removed from or changed on the corresponding document pages, as well. ▰▰▰ Kate would like each page in the booklet to include one of the six camp themes and a corresponding photo. You add a page number place holder and a graphics frame as master items to the left page of the A-Master and then copy them to the right page of the master.

STEPS

1. Click the Type tool T on the Tools panel, create a text box on the left page that is .5 inches wide and .3125 inches in height, click the Selection tool ▸, then drag the text box to the location shown in Figure E-4

2. Click T, click inside the text box, click Type on the Menu bar, point to Insert Special Character, point to Markers, then click Current Page Number

   As shown in Figure E-5, the letter "A" appears in the text box as a placeholder for the page number that will appear on all left document pages. The letter "A" is in the default font and point size, Minion Pro, 12 pt. When the current page number marker is placed on a master, InDesign places consecutive page numbers on each document page to which the master is applied. The dotted line surrounding the text box indicates that it is a master item. Next you will format and align the marker.

3. Double-click the A on the left master page to select it, then click the Align center button ≡ on the Control panel

4. Click Object on the Menu bar, then click Text Frame Options

   The Text Frame Options dialog box opens.

5. Click the Align list arrow, click Center, then click OK

   The text is vertically centered within the text box.

TROUBLE

Drag the Pages panel out of the way if necessary.

6. Click the Rectangle Frame tool ⊠ on the Tools panel, then create a frame that snaps to the inside of the four margin guides on the left master page (W: 5, H: 3)

   This frame is also a master item. It will be used for the photos that will be placed on each individual page in the booklet.

QUICK TIP

As you drag, the double-arrow pointer icon indicates that you are making a copy of the selection.

7. Click ▸ on the Tools panel, click the page number text box, press and hold [Shift][Alt] (Win) or [Shift][option] (Mac) click the rectangle frame, then drag the two items to the right master page, snapping the frame to the four margin guides

   A copy of the page number text box and the rectangle frame are placed on the right page. Pressing [Alt] (Win) or [option] (Mac) as you drag makes a copy of the selection, and pressing [Shift] as you drag constrains the selection along its horizontal or vertical axis.

8. Deselect the objects, click the page number text box on the right master page, then position it as shown in Figure E-6

   The master items created on the A-Master are automatically placed on all document pages. Notice the dotted outlines on the page icons on the Pages panel. They represent the page number and rectangle frame on each page.

9. Save your work

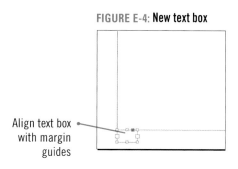

FIGURE E-4: **New text box**

Align text box
with margin
guides

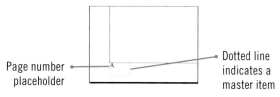

FIGURE E-5: **Viewing the page number placeholder**

Page number
placeholder

Dotted line
indicates a
master item

FIGURE E-6: **A-Master spread**

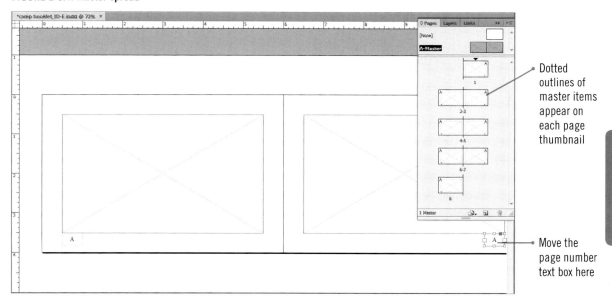

Dotted
outlines of
master items
appear on
each page
thumbnail

Move the
page number
text box here

Numbering options

You can change the InDesign page numbering style using the Numbering & Section Options dialog box. To open the dialog box, click the Pages Panel menu button, then click Numbering & Section Options. Click the Style list arrow, then click a new style, such as a, b, c, d, or 01, 02, 03, and so on. You can also enter a prefix for each page number in the Section Prefix text box, such as "page" or "Page."

You can have more than one page numbering system in a document. For example, some books begin with a preface section using lowercase Roman numerals (i, ii, iii, and so on),

followed by Chapter 1, which starts on page 1 and uses the numbers 1, 2, 3, and so on. To define a new page numbering section, first activate the document page where the new section should start, click the Pages Panel menu button, then click Numbering & Section Options. In the New Section dialog box, click the Start Section check box if necessary, click the Start Page Numbering at option button, and then type a page number. For example, if you choose page 5 in the Pages panel to start a new section, type 1 in the Start Page Numbering at text box to force page 5 to be numbered as page 1.

InDesign CS6

Using Master Pages

InDesign 103

Overriding Master Items

Some master items do not need to be modified on the document pages on which they're placed. A company logo placed in the corner of a master page is a good example; it would look the same on each page. However, empty text boxes and graphics frames placed on master pages need to be modified on document pages when you type text or place items in them. To modify master items on document pages, you must override them. Overriding a master item is how you unlock the master item on the current page so that you can work with it. ⬛⬛⬛ You are ready to place pictures of camp activities that Kate has provided for you on the first seven pages of the booklet. The eighth page will serve as the back cover of the booklet and will not include a photo.

STEPS

1. **Double-click 2-3 below the pages 2 and 3 icons on the Pages panel**

   Note that 2-3 is a spread number. Double-clicking a spread number displays the left and right page of a spread in the Document window.

2. **Press and hold [Shift][Ctrl] (Win) or [Shift]⌘ (Mac), then click the left frame**

   The frame is selected and ready for editing. Pressing and holding [Shift][Ctrl] (Win) or [Shift]⌘ (Mac) when clicking a master item overrides it.

3. **Click File on the Menu bar, click Place, navigate to the drive and folder where you store your Data Files, click sports.psd, then click Open**

4. **Click the Fill frame proportionally button ⬚ on the Control panel, click the image, then drag the content indicator ◉ to move the image in the frame until your screen resembles Figure E-7**

5. **Double-click the Page 3 icon on the Pages panel, click the Pages Panel menu button ▤, then click Override All Master Page Items**

   The master items on the current document page are overridden. The dotted lines around the text box and the rectangle frame on page 3 disappear. Using the Override All Master Page Items command is equivalent to pressing and holding [Shift][Ctrl] (Win) or [Shift]⌘ (Mac) to override a master item.

6. **Place the file sewing.psd in the frame on page 3, then fit and crop the image inside the frame to your liking**

QUICK TIP
The keyboard short-cut for Override All Master Page Items is [Alt][Shift][Ctrl][L] (Win) or [option] [Shift]⌘[L] (Mac).

7. **Using the Override All Master Page Items command, place the following images in the frames on each page, then fit and crop the images as necessary for pages 4–7**

page number	name of picture
4	computer.psd
5	dance.psd
6	canoe.psd
7	adventure.psd

8. **Compare your pages 4–5 to Figure E-8, then save your work**

FIGURE E-8: **Pages 4 and 5 of camp booklet_ID-E.indd**

Removing local overrides

Adding a non-master item to a document page that has a master applied, and overriding a master item on a document page, are known as local changes or local overrides. No matter which local overrides you've made on a document page, you can always return to the look of the original master page by removing the local changes. To do so, select the page on the

Pages panel from which you want to remove local overrides, click the Pages Panel menu button, point to Master Pages then click Remove All Local Overrides. All local items disappear and any modifications you made to master items are undone. For example, if you had placed an image in a graphics frame master item, InDesign removes it from the frame.

Modifying a Master Page

One of the benefits of using master pages is that it is easy to change them at any time in the production process. For example, you can change the size of a frame or remove a text box. The changes you make on the master pages are reflected on the document pages. You can also add new master items to existing master pages. The new items will appear on each document page with that master assigned to it. ▨▨▨▨ Kate would like the photos to have a caption. You add a guide and a text box to the left and right master pages on the A-Master, format the text, and then add titles to each document page.

STEPS

1. **Double-click A-Master on the Pages panel**
   The left and right master pages appear in the workspace.

2. **Place the mouse pointer ⇖ over the horizontal ruler, press and hold [Ctrl] (Win) or ⌘ (Mac), then click and drag a horizontal guide to the 0.125 in mark on the vertical ruler**
   You'll use the guide to position text boxes on each page. Pressing [Ctrl] (Win) or ⌘ (Mac) creates a spread guide, covering both left and right pages.

3. **Click the Type tool T. on the Tools panel, create a text box that is 3.5 inches wide and 0.35 inches tall, click the Selection tool ▸ on the Tools panel, then drag the text box to the left page so that its top snaps to the guide and its left side is aligned with the left side of the graphics frame, as shown in Figure E-9**

4. **Click T., click inside the text box, click the Font style list arrow on the Control panel, click Bold Italic, click the Font size list arrow, click 24 pt, then type Camp Theme**
   Your Control panel should match Figure E-10.

5. **Click ▸, press and hold [Alt] (Win) or [option] (Mac), then drag a copy of the text box to the right page so that its left side aligns with the left side of the graphics frame**
   The two text boxes will be used on each document page to display the camp theme. Each description will be in the same location and have the same formatting applied.

6. **Double-click 2-3 on the Pages panel**
   Pages 2 and 3 of the document open in the workspace. Each page has the Camp Theme text box applied to it.

7. **Click the Pages Panel menu button ▤, click Override All Master Page Items, triple-click inside the Camp Theme text box on the left to switch to the Type tool, then type Sports**

8. **Repeat Step 7 to add the following titles to pages 3–7:**

page number	text
3	Sewing
4	Computer Animation
5	Dance
6	Canoeing
7	Adventure

9. **Compare pages 6 and 7 to Figure E-11, then save your work**

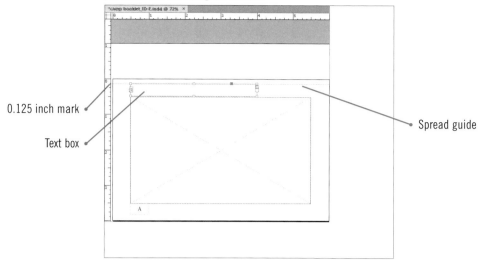

0.125 inch mark

Text box

Spread guide

FIGURE E-10: **Formatting the text**

Text formatting options

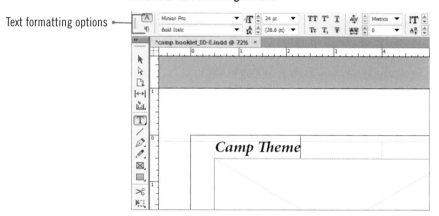

Camp Theme

FIGURE E-11: **Pages 6 and 7 of the camp booklet_ID-E.indd document**

Canoeing

Adventure

6

7

Original content AVAVA, Morgan Lane Photographers/
Shutterstock.com

Moving document pages

Often, you will need to change the order of pages in a document. Moving a page in a document shuffles the pages between the moved page's previous and new locations. For example, if you move page 2 into the page 4 position, page 2 becomes page 4, and pages 3 and 4 are shuffled to become pages 2 and 3. You can move pages in a document by dragging page icons on the Pages panel to new locations on the panel. This works well for short documents, but when you have hundreds of pages in a document, you won't want to scroll through them all to move one or two pages. Instead, you can use the Move Pages command on the Pages Panel menu. The Move Pages dialog box lets you indicate which pages to move and where to move them.

Creating a New Master Page

InDesign documents can have many master pages for many styles of pages. Sometimes, a new master page is only slightly different from one that already exists. For example, in a magazine you have pages with text and photos, and pages with only text. When you create a new master page, you can base it on one that already exists in the document. When you base a new master on an existing master, you start off with an exact copy of the existing master with all of its master items. This allows you to keep the master items (such as page numbers) that you want, delete any master items that you do not want, and modify the master items as necessary. 🔳🔳🔳 You create a new master page based on the A-Master, then modify the new master that Kate can use for the front cover of the booklet.

STEPS

1. **Click the Pages Panel menu button 🔳, then click New Master**

   The New Master dialog box opens. The default prefix assigned to the master is B and the default name for the new master is Master.

2. **Double-click Master in the Name text box, then type Front Cover**

3. **Click the Based on Master list arrow, then click A-Master**

QUICK TIP

To view all of the master pages, drag the double-line between the master pages and the document pages on the Pages panel to resize the top section.

4. **Press [Tab], type 1 in the Number of Pages text box, compare your New Master dialog box to Figure E-12, then click OK**

   Entering 1 in the Number of Pages text box creates a single-page master. The new B-Front Cover master page appears in the top section of the Pages panel, as shown in Figure E-13. The "A" on the B-Front Cover master page icon indicates that it is based on the A-Master. The B-Front Cover master page becomes the active page in the document window. You're ready to customize the B-Front Cover master.

5. **Click the Pages Panel menu button 🔳, then click Override All Master Page Items**

   Like master items on document pages, master items on master pages that are based on another master page are locked and must be overridden to be deleted or modified.

QUICK TIP

The page number text box has the letter "B" in it as a page number placeholder.

6. **Click the Selection tool 🔳 on the Tools panel, click the page number text box, then press [Delete]**

   The Front Cover master page no longer has a page number placeholder.

7. **Drag the Camp Theme text box so that it sits inside and snaps to the left and bottom margin guides, resize it so that it is as wide as the graphics frame, select the text, type BreakTime – Summer 2015 in the text box, then click the Align center button 🔳 on the Control panel**

8. **Click 🔳, click the graphics frame, drag the bottom-middle selection handle up until the height of the graphics frame is 2.5 inches, then compare your screen to Figure E-14**

9. **Save your work**

Primary text frames

If you are planning to create a document with text on every page, you want to create the document with a text frame on every page. A **primary text frame** is a text box master item added to the A-Master when a new document is created. The size of the primary text frame is determined by the page size and margins defined in the New Document dialog box. The text box fills the entire page, snapping to the four margin guides.

For example, if you create an 8.5" × 11" document with 1-inch page margins, the master text frame will be 6.5" × 9". To create a master text frame, click the Primary Text Frame check box in the New Document dialog box when creating a new document. When the new document opens, the A-Master contains a primary text frame and is applied to every page in the document.

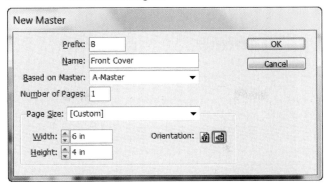

New single master page

Drag to resize sections

"A" indicates that the B-Front Cover master page is based on the A-Master

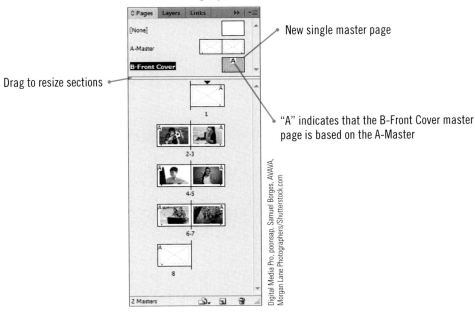

Digital Media Pro, poonsap, Samuel Borges, AVAVA, Morgan Lane Photographers/Shutterstock.com

Height of frame

Drag handle to resize frame

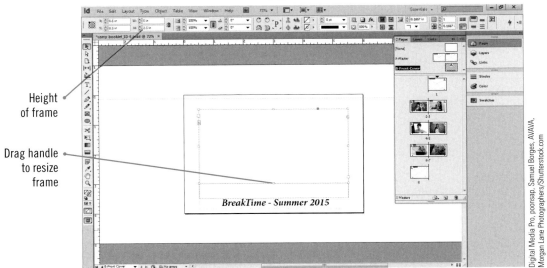

BreakTime - Summer 2015

Digital Media Pro, poonsap, Samuel Borges, AVAVA, Morgan Lane Photographers/Shutterstock.com

InDesign CS6

Applying Master Pages

All new pages in a document have the A-Master applied to them by default, but it is simple to apply a master page other than the A-Master to a document page. To do this, drag the master page icon on the Pages panel to the document page icon on the Pages panel. You can also apply master pages to document pages using the Apply Master to Pages command on the Pages Panel menu. To finish formatting the pages in the camp booklet, you apply the B-Front Cover master page to page 1 of the booklet and then apply a blank master (None) to the last page of the booklet.

1. **Double-click the page 1 icon on the Pages panel**
   Page 1 has the right page of the A-Master applied to it by default.

The page icon named [None] in the top section of the Pages panel is used for inserting blank pages into a document.

2. **Drag the B-Front Cover master page icon from the top section of the Pages panel over the page 1 icon in the lower section of the Pages panel until the page 1 icon is outlined in black, as shown in Figure E-16, then release the mouse button**
   Page 1 has the B-Front Cover master page applied to it, as indicated by the "B" on its page icon, and the B-Front Cover text.

3. **Click the Selection tool ▶ on the Tools panel, press and hold [Shift][Ctrl] (Win) or [Shift]⌘ (Mac), then click the frame to select it**

4. **Click File on the Menu bar, click Place, click camp.psd, then click Open**

5. **Fit and center the image in the frame so that it resembles the placement shown in Figure E-17**

6. **Drag the [None] page icon from the top section of the Pages panel over the page 8 icon in the lower section of the Pages panel, then release the mouse button**
   The last page of the booklet becomes a blank page.

7. **Save your work**

Using options on the Pages Panel menu

To customize the Pages panel, click the Pages Panel menu button, then click Panel Options to open the Panel Options dialog box, as shown in Figure E-15. In the Pages and Masters sections of the dialog box, choose a size for page and master icons by clicking the Size list arrow, then clicking a size. The Show Vertically and Show Thumbnails check boxes in the Pages and Masters sections control how the icons in the panel are displayed. If you remove the Show Vertically check mark, the page icons in the Pages panel will be displayed horizontally; you will only be able to resize the width of the Pages panel, not the height. If you remove the Show Thumbnails check mark, the page icons will be blank in the Pages panel. The Icons section of the dialog box defines which additional icons appear next to the page icons. For example, if the Transparency check box is checked, a small checkerboard icon appears next to the page icon where transparency has been applied to master items. Finally, in the Panel Layout section, you can choose whether you want masters or document pages on top of the panel.

FIGURE E-15: Panel Options dialog box

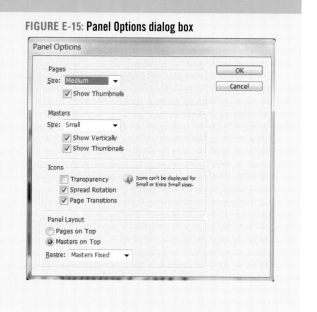

FIGURE E-16: Applying the B-Front Cover master to page 1

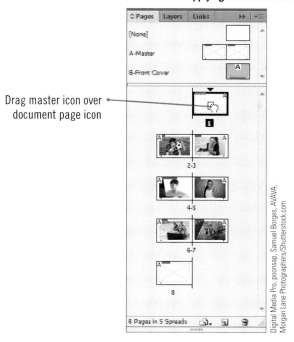

Drag master icon over
document page icon

FIGURE E-17: Front cover of camp booklet_ID-E.indd

BreakTime - Summer 2015

Detaching master items

When you make a change to a master item on a master page, the change is reflected on all document pages. For example, if you change a square graphics frame to a circular graphics frame on the master page, all of the square frames on the document pages will change to circles. However, you can **detach** a master item on a document page so that any changes made to the master item on the master page will not affect the detached master item on the document page. To detach a master item on a document page, select it, click the Pages Panel menu button, point to Master Pages, then click Detach Selection from Master. Detaching a master item is not the same as overriding a master item. Unlike master items that are overridden, detached master items are no longer affected by any changes made to the master page.

Working with Master Pages

The Pages Panel menu is loaded with commands for working with master pages. You can insert and delete master pages and document pages, move document pages, apply color labels to document pages, load master pages from other InDesign documents, find unused master pages, and even save document pages as master pages. ▆▆▆ You apply color labels to pages on the Pages panel to indicate to Kate which artwork is final and which artwork may change, and then save pages 2 and 3 as a new master page to use in future documents.

STEPS

1. **Click the page 1 icon on the Pages panel, press and hold [Ctrl] (Win) or ⌘ (Mac), click the page 5 icon, and then click the page 6 icon**

   The three page icons are selected on the Pages panel. The artwork on these three document pages may change and Kate would like you to apply a gold label to them as a reminder.

2. **Click the Pages Panel menu button ▦, point to Page Attributes, point to Color Label, then click Gold**

   A gold label appears beneath page icons 1, 5, and 6, as shown in Figure E-18.

3. **Click the page 2 icon, press and hold [Ctrl] (Win) or ⌘ (Mac), then click pages 3, 4, and 7**

   Kate would like you to apply a blue label to these icons to indicate that these pages are final.

4. **Click ▦, point to Page Attributes, point to Color Label, then click Blue**

   The icons have a blue label applied to them.

5. **Double-click 2-3 on the Pages panel to open pages 2 and 3 in the Document window**

   You are going to save pages 2 and 3 as a new master page that can be used in the future for similar documents.

6. **Click ▦, point to Master Pages, then click Save as Master**

   A new master named C-Master appears in the list of masters on the Pages panel, as shown in Figure E-19. To use the C-Master in the future, you would load the master page into a new InDesign document using the Load Master command on the Pages Panel menu.

7. **Double-click 6-7 on the Pages panel, deselect all, then close the Pages panel**

8. **Press [W] to view the pages in Preview mode, then compare your pages to Figure E-20**

9. **Save your work, then exit InDesign**

Loading master pages

To load a master page from one document to another, create a new InDesign document with the same size dimensions as that of the master page you plan to load. In the new document, click the Pages Panel menu button, point to Master Pages, then click Load Master Pages. The Open a File dialog box opens for you to navigate to and select the InDesign document that has the master page you wish to load. If the document has more than one master page, all of the master pages are loaded. After the master pages are loaded, you can delete those that you do not need by dragging them from the Pages panel to the Delete selected pages button on the panel. If any of the master pages in the new document and the document being opened share the same name, you will be prompted to replace the existing master page(s) in the new document with the masters that are being loaded or rename the existing master pages.

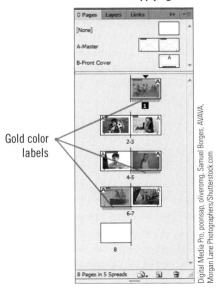

Gold color labels

Digital Media Pro, poonsap, oliveromg, Samuel Borges, AVAVA, Morgan Lane Photographers/Shutterstock.com

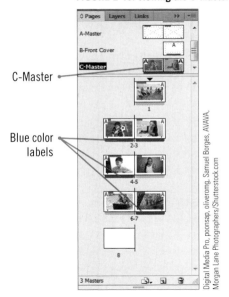

C-Master

Blue color labels

Digital Media Pro, poonsap, oliveromg, Samuel Borges, AVAVA, Morgan Lane Photographers/Shutterstock.com

FIGURE E-20: **Pages 6 and 7 of the Camp booklet**

AVAVA, Morgan Lane Photographers/Shutterstock.com

InDesign CS6

Preventing shuffling

Some multipage documents have spreads that must not be shuffled when other pages are moved. To keep the pages in a spread from being shuffled, select the spread on the Pages panel, click the Pages Panel menu button, then click Allow Selected Spread to Shuffle to remove the check mark. A set of brackets surrounds the page numbers of the spread, indicating that the spread will not be shuffled when pages are moved. If a page is moved before or after one of the pages in a spread, it will be added to the spread. These types of spreads are known as **island spreads**. Island spreads can include as many as 10 document pages.

Practice

Concepts Review

Label the elements of the InDesign screen shown in Figure E-21.

Digital Media Pro, poonsap, oliveromg, Samuel Borges, AVAVA, Morgan Lane Photographers/Shutterstock.com

1. _____   4. _____
2. _____   5. _____
3. _____

Match each term with the statement that best describes it.

6. **Shuffle**
7. **Current page number**
8. **Override**
9. **Load**
10. **Spread number**

   a. Unlock
   b. 4-5
   c. Get a master page from another document
   d. A special character known as a marker
   e. Change the order of pages

Select the best answer from the list of choices.

11. **What type of document would not require facing pages?**
    a. Magazine
    b. Business card
    c. Catalog
    d. Book

12. **Which keys do you use to override an individual master item?**
    a. [Alt][Ctrl] (Win) or [option]⌘ (Mac)
    b. [Shift][Ctrl] (Win) or [Shift]⌘ (Mac)
    c. [Ctrl] (Win) or ⌘ (Mac)
    d. [Alt] (Win) or [option] (Mac)

13. **Which punctuation marks appear around a spread that is not allowed to shuffle?**
    a. Quotation marks
    b. Parentheses
    c. Asterisks
    d. Brackets

Skills Review

1. **Create a multipage document.**
   a. Start InDesign, click File on the Menu bar, point to New, then click Document.
   b. Type **6** in the Number of Pages text box, then verify that the Facing Pages check box is checked.
   c. Double-click the Width value, type **6**, press [Tab], type **8** as the Height value, press [Tab], verify that the Portrait button is selected, then click OK to close the New Document dialog box.
   d. Click the workspace switcher on the Menu bar, then click Reset Essentials.
   e. Click the Pages panel button on the right side of the workspace to open the Pages panel.
   f. Double-click A-Master on the Pages panel.
   g. Double-click the page 1 icon on the Pages panel.
   h. Double-click A-Master on the Pages panel again, then save the document as **desserts_ID-E**.

2. **Create master items.**
   a. Click the Type tool on the Tools panel, create a text box on the left page that is 0.5 inches wide and 0.5 inches in height, click the Selection tool, then drag the text box so that its top snaps to the bottom margin guide. (*Hint*: Try to align the left side of the text box with the left margin guide.)
   b. Click the Type tool, click inside the text box, click Type on the Menu bar, point to Insert Special Character, point to Markers, then click Current Page Number.
   c. Double-click the A on the left master page to select it, then click the Align center button on the Control panel.
   d. Click Object on the Menu bar, then click Text Frame Options.
   e. Click the Align list arrow, click Center, then click OK.
   f. Click the Rectangle Frame tool on the Tools panel, then create a frame that snaps to the inside of the four margin guides on the left master page (W: 5, H: 7). Click the Selection tool on the Tools panel, click the page number text box, press and hold [Shift][Alt] (Win) or [Shift][option] (Mac), click the rectangle frame, then drag the two items to the right master page, snapping the frame to the four margin guides.
   g. Deselect the objects, click the page number text box on the right master page, then position it on the right side of the page so that its right edge aligns with the right margin guide.
   h. Save your work.

3. **Override master items.**
   a. Double-click 2-3 below the page 2 and 3 icons on the Pages panel.
   b. Press and hold [Shift][Ctrl] (Win) or [Shift]⌘ (Mac), then click the left frame.
   c. Click File on the Menu bar, click Place, navigate to the drive and folder where you store your Data Files, click apple pie.psd, then click Open.
   d. Click the Fill frame proportionally button on the Control panel, click the image, then drag the content indicator to move the image in the frame until it is cropped to your liking.
   e. Double-click the page 3 icon on the Pages panel, click the Pages Panel menu button, then click Override All Master Page Items.
   f. Place the file cupcakes.psd in the frame on page 3, then fit and crop the image inside the frame to your liking.

Skills Review (continued)

  g. Using the Override All Master Page Items command, place the following images in the frames on each page, then fit and crop the images as necessary for pages 4–5:

page number	name of picture
4	**chocolate cake.psd**
5	**strawberry shortcake.psd**

  h. Save your work.

4. Modify a master page.

  a. Double-click A-Master on the Pages panel.

  b. Click the Type tool on the Tools panel, then create a text box that is 3.25 inches wide and 0.35 inches tall.

  c. Click the Selection tool on the Tools panel, then drag the text box so that it sits on the top margin guide and is located on the left page. (*Hint*: Try to align the left side of the text box with the left margin guide.)

  d. Click the Type tool, click inside the text box, then type **Name of Dessert**.

  e. Select all of the text, click the Font style list arrow, click Medium, click the Font size list arrow, then click 24 pt.

  f. Click the Selection tool on the Tools panel, press and hold [Alt] (Win) or [option] (Mac), then drag a copy of the text box so that it snaps to the top-left corner of the right page.

  g. Double-click 2-3 on the Pages panel.

  h. Click the Pages Panel menu button, then click Override All Master Page Items.

  i. Double-click inside the Name of Dessert text box on page 2 to switch to the Type tool, triple-click the text to select all of the text, then type **Apple Pie**.

  j. Use Steps g-i as a guide to add the following titles to pages 3–5:

page number	text
3	**Cupcakes**
4	**Chocolate Cake**
5	**Strawberry Shortcake**

  k. Save your work.

5. Create a new master page.

  a. Click the Pages Panel menu button, then click New Master.

  b. Double-click Master in the Name text box, then type **Front Cover**.

  c. Click the Based on Master list arrow, then click A-Master.

  d. Press [Tab], type **1** in the Number of Pages text box, then click OK.

  e. Click the Pages Panel menu button, then click Override All Master Page Items.

  f. Click the Selection tool on the Tools panel, click the page number text box with the letter "B," then press [Delete].

  g. Drag the Name of Dessert text box so that its bottom-left corner snaps to the left and bottom margin guides, resize it so that it is as wide as the graphics frame, then type **Dessert Menu** in the text box.

  h. Click the Selection tool on the Tools panel, click the graphics frame, drag the bottom-middle selection handle up until the height of the graphics frame is 6.25 inches, then save your work.

6. Apply master pages.

  a. Double-click the page 1 icon on the Pages panel.

  b. Drag the B-Front Cover master page icon from the top section of the Pages panel over the page 1 icon in the lower section of the Pages panel until the page 1 icon is outlined in black, then release the mouse button.

  c. Click the Pages Panel menu button, then click Override All Master Page Items.

  d. Click the Selection tool on the Tools panel, then click the frame to select it.

  e. Click File on the Menu bar, click Place, click parfait.psd, then click Open.

  f. Fit and center the image in the frame to your liking.

  g. Drag the [None] page icon from the top section of the Pages panel over the page 6 icon in the lower section of the Pages panel, then release the mouse button.

  h. Save your work.

7. Work with master pages.

  a. Click the page 1 icon on the Pages panel, press and hold [Ctrl] (Win) or ⌘ (Mac), then click the page 4 icon.

  b. Click the Pages Panel menu button, point to Page Attributes point to Color Label, then click Yellow.

  c. Click the page 2 icon, press and hold [Ctrl] (Win) or ⌘ (Mac), then click pages 3 and 5.

  d. Click the Pages Panel menu button, point to Page Attributes point to Color Label, then click Red.

  e. Double-click 2-3 on the Pages panel to open pages 2 and 3 in the Document window.

  f. Click the Pages Panel menu button, point to Master Pages then click Save as Master.

  g. Double-click 4-5 on the Pages panel, deselect all, then press [W] to view the pages in Preview mode.

  h. Close the Pages panel, then compare your pages to Figure E-22.

  i. Save your work, then exit InDesign.

FIGURE E-22

Chocolate Cake   Strawberry Shortcake

YaiSirichai, Hannamariah/Shutterstock.com

Independent Challenge 1

You are spending your senior year in Italy teaching English to young children. You want to create a set of flash cards with the alphabet on one side for your students to use. You use InDesign to create the flash cards.

  a. Start InDesign and open the New Document dialog box.

  b. In the New Document dialog box, deselect the Facing Pages check box, change the Number of Pages to **26**, change the Width to **4** inches and the Height to **6** inches, then click OK.

  c. Save the document as **flash cards_ID-E**.

  d. Open the A-Master master page in the Document window.

  e. Create a text box on the A-Master master page that snaps to all four margin guides. (*Hint*: The width of the text box should be 3 inches and the height of the text box should be 5 inches.)

  f. Insert the Current Page Number placeholder into the text box on the master page.

  g. Format the letter "A" on the master page using any font and large font size that you think would be appropriate for a flash card. (*Hint*: The font size in Figure E-23 is 108 points.)

  h. Center the "A" horizontally in the text box, then center the "A" vertically in the text box using the Text Frame Options dialog box.

  i. Activate page 1 in the Document window.

  j. Click the Pages Panel menu button, then click Numbering & Section Options.

  k. In the Page Numbering area of the Numbering & Section Options dialog box, click the Style list arrow, then click A, B, C, D....

  l. Click OK to close the Numbering & Section Options dialog box.

  m. Double-click the page B icon, then compare your screen to Figure E-23.

  n. Save your work, then exit InDesign.

FIGURE E-23

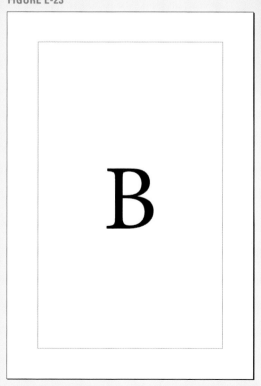

Independent Challenge 2

You work for a graphic design company and are preparing an annual report for a new client. The client would like to see samples of text styles using different fonts and leading amounts. You create three sample pages in InDesign, then save them as three master pages.

a. Start InDesign, then create a new 8.5" × 11", three-page document without facing pages.

b. Save the document as **text samples_ID-E**.

c. Activate the A-Master in the Document window.

d. Create a text box on the A-Master that snaps to all four margin guides.

e. Click the Type tool, click inside the text box, then change the font size to 11 pt.

f. Click Type on the Menu bar, then click Fill with Placeholder Text.

g. Activate page 1 in the Document window.

h. Override the text box master item to select it, select all of the text in the text box on page 1, then change the font and the leading value. (*Hint*: Use the Character panel to change the leading value. Do not resize the text box if the overset text icon appears.)

i. Repeat Step h for page 2 and page 3 using different fonts and leading values.

j. Save each page as a master page and name each new master using the font name chosen for that page.

k. Apply the B-Master to page 1, the C-Master to page 2, and the D-Master to page 3.

l. Delete the A-Master by dragging it to the Delete selected pages button on the Pages panel.

m. Compare one of your pages and your Pages panel to Figure E-24.

FIGURE E-24

 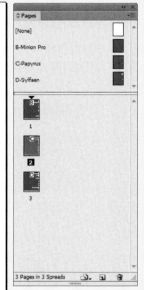

Advanced Challenge Exercise

- Click the Pages Panel menu button, then click Insert Pages.
- In the Insert Pages dialog box, insert two pages after page 3 and apply the C-Master to the two new pages.
- Click OK to close the Insert Pages dialog box.

n. Save your work, then exit InDesign.

Independent Challenge 3

You work for a gift shop and would like to sell your own product: a flip book of daily quotes and inspirations taken from movies. You use InDesign to create the prototype.

a. Start InDesign and create a new 4" × 3", 366-page document with facing pages and a landscape orientation. (*Hint*: One page will be used for the front cover.)

b. Save the document as **quotes_ID-E**.

c. Activate the A-Master in the Document window.

Independent Challenge 3 (continued)

d. Create two text boxes on the left page (one for the page number and one for the quote) and place them where you want.

e. Insert an automatic page number placeholder in the text box designated for the page number and then format the page number.

f. Create a title placeholder, such as "quote," in the quote text box, then format the text using the font, size, and style of your choice.

g. Copy the two text boxes to the right page.

h. Rename the A-Master as **Quote Master**.

i. Create a new master based on the Quote Master, name it **Cover**, and change it to a one-page master.

j. Remove the page number text box on the Cover master, then type **Famous Movie Quotes** in the text box.

k. Format the text to your liking, then apply the Cover master to page 1.

l. Add any design elements that you wish using the basic shape tools.

m. Apply a color label to page 1 to differentiate it from the other pages.

n. Compare your first page to Figure E-25, then save your work.

FIGURE E-25

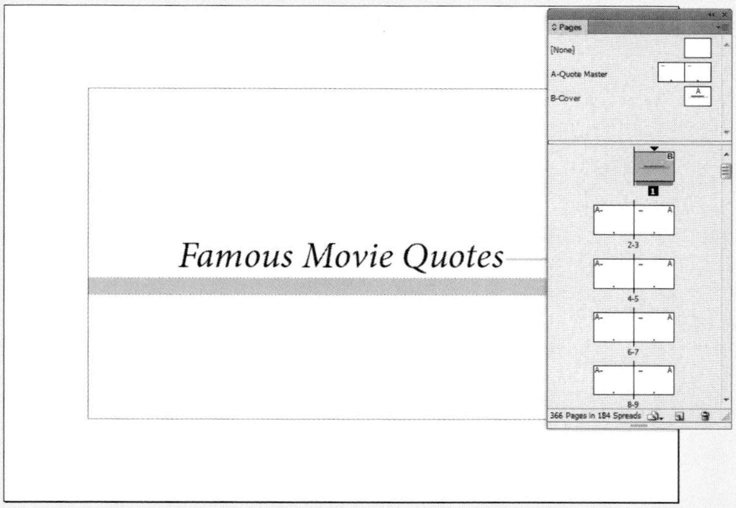

Famous Movie Quotes

Advanced Challenge Exercise

- Display page 1 in the Document window, if necessary.
- Override the text box on page 1.
- Click the Pages Panel menu button, point to Master Pages then click Detach Selection from Master.

o. Close the quotes_ID-E.indd document, then exit InDesign.

Real Life Independent Challenge

You have graduated from college with a degree in photography and have started looking for a job in your field. You decide to create a booklet that contains samples of your photography. You'll use this booklet as your portfolio when applying for jobs.

a. Start InDesign and create a new six-page document with facing pages and any page size that you like.

b. Save the document as **portfolio_ID-E**.

c. Format the left and right master pages with automatic page numbering, one graphics frame (any shape), and one text box that will serve as a title for each piece of artwork.

d. Format the text boxes and the graphics frame any way that you wish.

e. On pages 2 through 6 in the document, override the graphics frame on each page and place a picture in the frame using any of your own photographs. (If you do not have any photos, you can use pictures from the Data Files folders.)

f. On pages 2 through 6, override the text box on each page and type a descriptive title in it for each picture.

g. Create a new master based on the A-Master and name it **Cover**, then change it to a single-page master.

h. Delete the page number from the Cover master page, make any other changes that you want to the master, then apply it to page 1. A graphics frame on the Cover master page is optional.

i. Add any local formatting you wish, such as strokes around the frames, to the document pages.

j. View the Document window in Preview mode, save your work, then exit InDesign.

Visual Workshop

Create a new 8.5" × 11", three-page document with facing pages and 1-inch margins, then save it as **master pages_ID-E**. Activate the A-Master in the Document window and create the master items shown in Figure E-26 on the left and right pages of the master. The text box is 0.5 inches in height, and the font and font size used in the text box are Minion Pro, 30 pt. The frame on each page is 6.5" × 8". Rename the A-Master **Photo Pages**, compare your screen to Figure E-26, save your work, then exit InDesign.

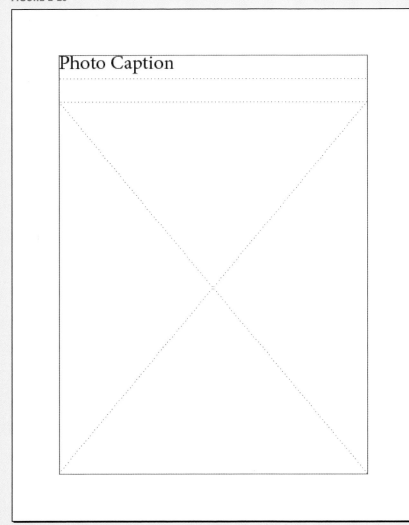

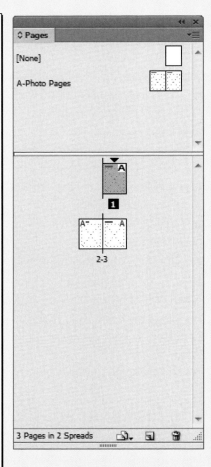

UNIT F
InDesign CS6

Working with Layers

Files You Will Need:

To view a list of files needed for this unit, see the Data Files Grid in the back of the book.

Layers are the levels within an InDesign document on which objects appear. You can organize InDesign objects of the same type onto separate layers. For example, you can place all text boxes on a layer named Text and all graphics on a different layer named Graphics. There are many benefits to using layers. You can hide and show layers, lock and unlock layers, and even suppress the printing of specific layers. To work with layers, you use the Layers panel. Ted, your client at the Happy Apple, needs a slide presentation for an upcoming sales meeting that displays store locations across the United States. You create artwork for one slide in InDesign and use the Layers panel to organize the artwork.

OBJECTIVES

Place an object on a layer

Change layer options

Create a new layer

Duplicate a layer

Lock and hide a layer

Move an object to another layer

Change layer order

Placing an Object on a Layer

Each new InDesign document starts out with an empty layer, named Layer 1, on the Layers panel. When you add an item to the document, whether by placing it or by creating it in InDesign, it is automatically placed as a **page item** on Layer 1 on the Layers panel. Each additional item you place or create in InDesign is also placed on Layer 1 but on one level higher than the last page item. You can view all of the objects and the order that they are stacked on a layer by expanding the layer. You create a new InDesign document, place a map graphic and some text in the document, then view the two page items on Layer 1 on the Layers panel.

STEPS

1. **Start InDesign, create a new 8.5" × 11" document without facing pages, with a landscape orientation, then save it as** store locations_ID-F

2. **Click the** workspace switcher, **click** Reset Essentials, **then click the** Layers panel icon **to open the Layers panel**

   The Layers panel opens with the default layer, Layer 1, highlighted. The pen icon next to Layer 1 on the Layers panel is called the Indicates current drawing layer icon, and it indicates the active layer. Anything added to the InDesign document is added to whichever layer is active on the Layers panel.

3. **Click the** Rectangle Frame tool **on the Tools panel, then create a rectangle frame that snaps to all four margin guides**

   Your rectangle frame should be 10 inches wide and 7.5 inches tall.

4. **On the Layers panel, click the** expand layer arrow **pointing to Layer 1 to expand Layer 1**

   As shown in Figure F-1, the rectangle is the first item on Layer 1. The name <rectangle> is assigned to the object.

5. **Click the** Selection tool **on the Tools panel, verify that the rectangle is still selected, click** File **on the Menu bar, click** Place, **navigate to the drive and folder where you store your Data Files, click** USAmap.ai, **then click** Open

   A map of the United States appears in the frame. If the map image appeared in the loaded cursor icon instead, the rectangle was not selected. Click the rectangle to place the map. You are going to resize the map so that it fits the frame proportionally and then improve its display performance.

6. **Click the** Fit content proportionally button **on the Control panel, click** Object **on the Menu bar, point to** Display Performance, **then click** High Quality Display

   The map fits the frame proportionally and is displayed at a higher quality. The name <USAmap.ai> replaces the name <rectangle> on the Layers panel because the map now fills the frame. The map and the frame are considered one item.

7. **Deselect the map frame, click** File **on the Menu bar, click** Place, **click** Legend.doc, **then click** Open

   The loaded cursor appears showing a thumbnail view of the text that will be placed.

8. **Click in the approximate location shown in Figure F-2 to place the map legend text in the** lower-left corner **of the Document window**

   The legend text is added to the top of Layer 1. The name assigned to the Legend.doc page item is "Legend," followed by the first few words in the document. It is one level higher than the USAmap.ai page item on Layer 1 because it was placed after the map artwork was placed. In the Document window, the legend text box is above the bottom of the rectangle frame.

9. **Save your work**

FIGURE F-1: Viewing the rectangle frame on Layer 1

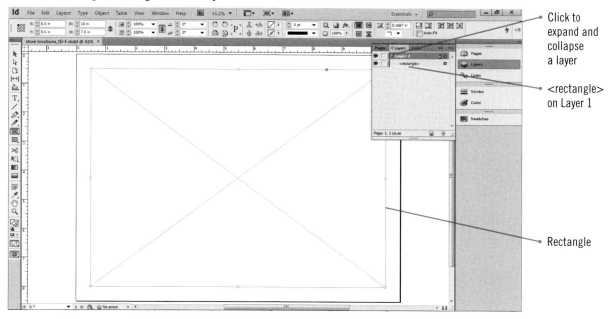

Click to
expand and
collapse
a layer

<rectangle>
on Layer 1

Rectangle

FIGURE F-2: Layers panel

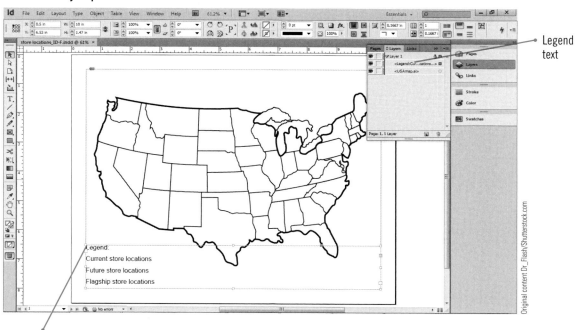

Legend
text

Click here to place
the legend text

Original content Dr_Flash/Shutterstock.com

InDesign CS6

Changing Layer Options

Each layer on the Layers panel has a unique selection color assigned to it. The **selection color** of a layer is the color of the bounding box that appears around selected objects on that layer. For example, the selection color for Layer 1 is Light Blue. When you select items on Layer 1, their selection color is Light Blue. You can change the selection color for a layer if you want to color-code layers in a document. You can also change the name of a layer. Naming layers is helpful to describe a layer's content, especially if you use layers to organize your document elements. For example, when creating a newsletter, you may want to place all text objects on a layer named Text. Ted asks you to name each layer and color-code it so that other employees will be able to easily identify the document items in your absence. You use the Layers panel to rename Layer 1 and change its selection color.

STEPS

1. **Click the Layers Panel menu button ▼≡, then click Layer Options for "Layer 1"**

   The Layer Options dialog box opens. In this dialog box, you can change the name of Layer 1, change its selection color, and adjust other layer options. Layers are automatically named by InDesign using the next consecutive number: Layer 1, Layer 2, Layer 3, and so on.

   QUICK TIP
   You can also open the Layer Options dialog box by double-clicking a layer name on the Layers panel.

2. **Type United States Map in the Name text box**

   This layer will be for the map artwork and the legend. The name of the layer will make the layer easy to locate in the future after more layers are added.

3. **Click the Color list arrow, click Black, then compare your Layer Options dialog box to Figure F-3**

   The bounding box of selected objects on the United States Map layer will be Black instead of the default color, Light Blue. Because the map is black and the legend text is black, it makes sense to change the selection color to Black.

4. **Click OK to close the Layer Options dialog box**

   The changes made to Layer 1 appear on the Layers panel.

5. **Click the Selection tool ▶ on the Tools panel, if necessary, then click the map image**

   As shown in Figure F-4, the bounding box of the map has a black selection color. A small black square called the Indicates selected items icon ▣ appears filled in the layer color next to the Indicates current drawing layer icon ♨ on the United States Map layer and next to <USAmap.ai> to indicate that the map is selected on the artboard.

6. **Click the Hand tool ✋ on the Tools panel, then drag the Document window left so that the right side of the map is not blocked by the Layers panel**

7. **Deselect all, then save your work**

Selecting page items

When working on an InDesign document that you are unfamiliar with, it is likely that you will not know which items on the artboard correspond with a page item on the Layers panel. To find out what a page item is referring to, select the page item on the Layers panel, click the Layers Panel menu button, then click Select Item(s). The object or objects become selected in the Document window. To select items and fit them in the window to see them more clearly, choose Select and Fit Item instead. Selecting a layer is also referred to as **targeting** the layer.

FIGURE F-3: Layer Options dialog box

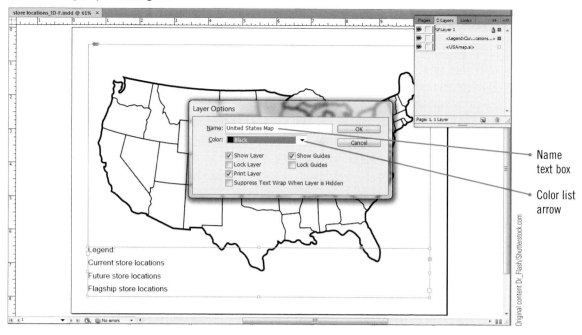

Name text box

Color list arrow

FIGURE F-4: Selecting the map image

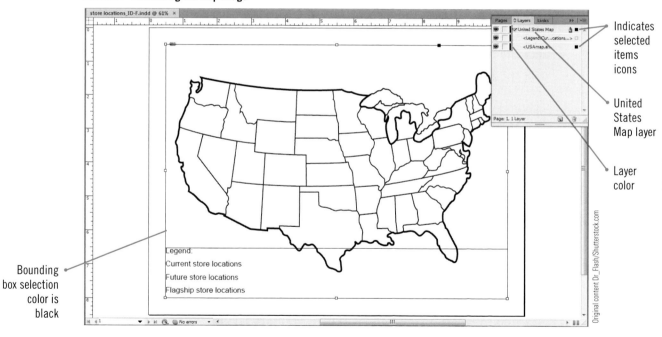

Indicates selected items icons

United States Map layer

Layer color

Bounding box selection color is black

Using the Arrange commands with multiple layers

When you have more than one layer in an InDesign document, the Arrange commands (Send to Back, Bring to Front, Send Backward, and Bring Forward) are applied only to the page items on the currently active layer on the Layers panel. For example, if you have three page items on Layer 3 and you send one of them to the back using the Send to Back command, it will go to the bottom of the stack of the three page items on Layer 3, rather than to the back of all of the objects in the document.

Creating a New Layer

Having more than one layer in a document helps you keep InDesign objects organized. Once items are on individual layers, you can hide and show those layers to view different versions of the same document. Placing items on individual layers also makes it easy to select those items in one step. If you press [Alt] (Win) or [option] (Mac) while clicking a layer on the Layers panel, all items on that layer are selected. There are two ways to create new layers. You can click the Create new layer button on the Layers panel or click the Layers Panel menu button, then click New Layer. The New Layer dialog box is identical to the Layer Options dialog box. 👆 You create a new layer in the Store Locations document on which to put artwork that represents current Happy Apple store locations. By placing the current store artwork on its own layer, you'll be able to work with it as a unit.

STEPS

QUICK TIP

If you click the Create new layer button 🔲 on the Layers panel to create a new layer, the New Layer dialog box does not open; instead, the new layer is automatically assigned a color, named with the next consecutive layer number, and placed at the top of the Layers panel.

1. **Click the Layers Panel menu button ▥, then click New Layer**

   The New Layer dialog box opens, where you can choose a name and selection color for the layer before it appears on the Layers panel.

2. **Type Current Store Locations in the Name text box, click the Color list arrow, click Green, then click OK to close the New Layer dialog box**

   As shown in Figure F-5, the new layer is placed above the United States Map layer. New layers are automatically placed above the currently selected layer on the Layers panel. The order of layers on the Layers panel represents the same order of objects on those layers in the Document window. Objects on the Current Store Locations layer will be on top of or "in front" of the objects on the United States Map layer in the document.

3. **Click and hold the Rectangle tool 🔳 on the Tools panel until you see a menu of tools, then click the Ellipse tool 🔘**

4. **Click the page to open the Ellipse dialog box, type .25 in the Width text box, press [Tab], type .25 in the Height text box, then click OK**

   A small circle appears on the page. The circle will represent current store locations on the map. The circle has a green selection color because it was created when the Current Store Locations layer was the active layer.

5. **Click the Zoom tool 🔍 on the Tools panel, then click the circle to enlarge your view**

6. **Click the Fill button ◩ on the Tools panel, click the Swatches panel button ▦ on the right side of the workspace to open the Swatches panel, then scroll down and click C=75 M=5 Y=100 K=0 (green)**

   The circle's fill color changes to green.

7. **Click the Stroke button ▢ on the Swatches panel, then click [None] on the Swatches panel, if necessary**

QUICK TIP

Press [Alt] (Win) or [option] (Mac), then click a layer on the Layers panel to select all of the objects on that layer.

8. **Click the Selection tool ▶ on the Tools panel, then drag the circle to the approximate location shown in Figure F-6 (Maine)**

9. **Press and hold [Alt] (Win) or [option] (Mac), click and drag the circle in a downward direction to create a copy of it as shown in Figure F-7, create two more copies of the circle, then place them in the approximate locations in New England shown in Figure F-8**

   The four green circles represent the four current store locations in New England.

10. **Save your work**

Current Store
Locations layer

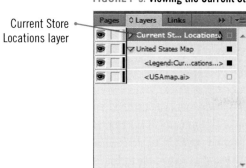

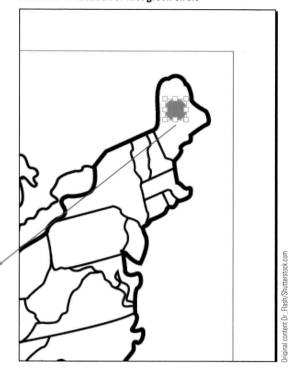

Circle has a green
bounding box

Original content Dr_Flash/Shutterstock.com

FIGURE F-7: **Copying the green circle**

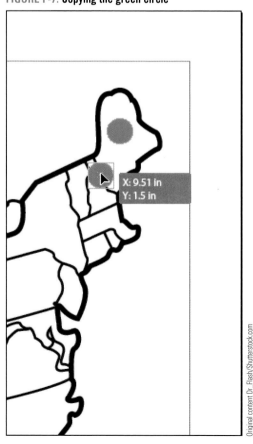

X: 9.51 in
Y: 1.5 in

Original content Dr_Flash/Shutterstock.com

FIGURE F-8: **Four current store locations**

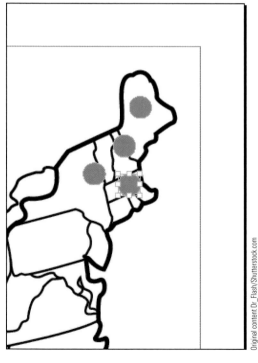

Original content Dr_Flash/Shutterstock.com

InDesign CS6

Duplicating a Layer

Duplicating a layer means choosing a layer on the Layers panel and creating an exact copy of the layer and the objects on it, which is a great way to save yourself time and ensure consistency in your document. Once you duplicate a layer, you can rename it, remove or modify objects on it, and/or add new objects to it. InDesign names duplicated layers with the same name as the layer that was used to create the duplicate, followed by the word "copy." They are also assigned the same selection color. It is a good idea to rename the duplicate layer and assign a new selection color to it for clarification. You duplicate the Current Store Locations layer so that you can use the circles with a new fill color to represent future store locations on a separate layer. You also change the duplicate layer name and selection color to distinguish it from other layers.

STEPS

1. **Close the Swatches panel, open the Layers panel, then verify that the Current Store Locations layer is still active on the Layers panel**

    Clicking a layer on the Layers panel activates that layer.

> **QUICK TIP**
> You can also duplicate a layer by dragging the layer to the Create new layer button ⬛ on the Layers panel, then releasing the mouse button.

2. **Click the Layers Panel menu button ▾, then click Duplicate Layer "Current Store Locations"**

    A new layer "Current Store Locations copy" appears at the top of the Layers panel with green as the selection color. No change takes place in the Document window because the four green circles on the Current Store Locations copy layer are in the identical locations as the four green circles on the Current Store Locations layer.

3. **Double-click the Current Store Locations copy layer on the Layers panel to open the Layer Options dialog box**

4. **Type Future Store Locations in the Name text box, click the Color list arrow, then click Dark Blue**

5. **Click OK, then compare your Layers panel to Figure F-9**

6. **Click the Selection tool ▶ on the Tools panel, if necessary, then click the lowest green circle on the map**

7. **Show the Swatches panel, click the Fill button ⬜ on the Swatches panel, change the fill color of the selected circle to C=100 M=90 Y=10 K=0 (dark blue), drag the circle to the location in northern California shown in Figure F-10, then deselect the circle**

    When you drag the dark blue circle on the Future Store Locations layer away from its original location, the green circle on the Current Store Locations layer is visible. Notice it has the green selection color, and the remaining three circles that have not yet been moved have the dark blue selection color that was assigned to the new layer.

8. **Show the Layers panel, press [Alt] (Win) or [option] (Mac), then click the Future Store Locations layer on the Layers panel to select all of the objects on the Future Store Locations layer, show the Swatches panel, then click C=100 M=90 Y=10 K=0 (dark blue)**

    All of the circles on the Future Store Locations layer are filled with dark blue.

9. **Deselect all, then drag each blue circle to the approximate locations on the West Coast shown in Figure F-11, deselect the circles, then save your work**

FIGURE F-9: **Duplicate layer on Layers panel**

FIGURE F-9: **Duplicate layer on Layers panel**

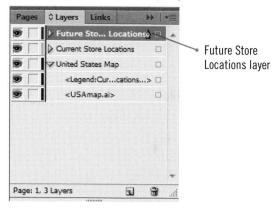

Future Store
Locations layer

FIGURE F-10: **Repositioned circle**

Repositioned
circle on the
Future Store
Locations layer

Circle on the
Current Store
Locations layer
is now visible

Original content Dr_Flash/Shutterstock.com

InDesign CS6

FIGURE F-11: **Positioning the dark blue circles**

Original content Dr_Flash/Shutterstock.com

Locking and Hiding a Layer

You can lock and hide an entire layer or individual page items on a layer. Locking protects the entire layer or the page items on a layer from being moved, selected, or deleted accidently. InDesign documents can become complicated quickly, especially when you are creating a document with lots of detailed objects, such as a street map or a diagram. Objects on locked layers cannot be selected, so they also cannot be moved or deleted. You can also temporarily hide and show layers or page items on layers. Hiding layers can help you focus on one layer without being distracted by the objects on other layers. It also helps you to see what the document would look like without the objects on that layer, without having to delete those objects. 🔲🔲🔲🔲 You check the accuracy of your map by hiding and showing each layer, then you lock the United States Map page item to make sure that it does not get moved or deleted by accident.

STEPS

1. **Show the Layers panel, if necessary, then click the** Toggles visibility icon 🔲 **to the left of the Future Store Locations layer**

   As shown in Figure F-12, the Future Store Locations layer is hidden from view and the dark blue circles on the layer are no longer visible. When you hide the currently active layer, 🔲 disappears and a red slash appears through the Indicates current drawing layer icon 🔲. You cannot place or create content on a hidden layer.

2. **Click** 🔲 **to the left of the Current Store Locations layer on the Layers panel**

   The green circles on the Current Store Locations layer are hidden from view in the document. Hiding multiple layers is a good way to check if InDesign objects are placed on the layers they are supposed to be placed on. For example, if one green circle was still in view after the Current Store Locations layer was hidden, that would indicate that the green circle had been on the United States Map layer by mistake.

3. **Click** 🔲 **to the left of the United States Map layer on the Layers panel**

   All three layers in the document are hidden and the document is blank.

4. **Click the** empty gray square **where** 🔲 **once was next to each of the three layers on the Layers panel**

   The 🔲 icon reappears next to all three layers, and the map, green circles, and dark blue circles reappear.

5. **Click the** empty gray square **between** 🔲 **and the** <USAmap.ai> **object on the United States Map layer on the Layers panel**

   As shown in Figure F-13, the Toggles page item lock icon 🔲 appears next to the layer and a lock icon appears on the image's bounding box, indicating that the layer is locked. If you wanted to lock the legend text, too, you would lock the United States Map layer. When you lock a layer, all page items on that layer are locked.

6. **Click the** Selection tool 🔲**, if necessary, then click the** map image **on the page**

   As long as the United States Map layer is locked, the map image on the layer cannot be selected or changed.

7. **Double-click the** United States Map layer **on the Layers panel to open the Layer Options dialog box**

   As shown in Figure F-14, the check boxes in the Layer Options dialog box show you the status of the layer. This layer is not locked; the USAmap.ai page item on the layer is locked. This layer is not hidden, and it will print. You can change layer settings by adding or removing check marks in the check boxes.

8. **Click** OK**, then save your work**

FIGURE F-12: **Hidden Future Store Locations layer**

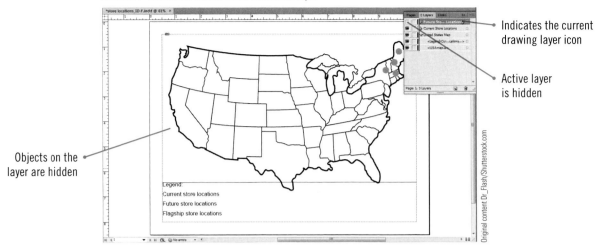

Indicates the current
drawing layer icon

Active layer
is hidden

Objects on the
layer are hidden

FIGURE F-13: **Viewing the locked page item**

Toggles page
item lock icon

Map is locked

FIGURE F-14: **Layer Options dialog box**

Moving an Object to Another Layer

It is not unusual to discover that an object belongs on a different layer after you've created the object. Fortunately, it is possible to move an existing page item from one layer to another layer in a document. To move an InDesign object to a new layer, select the object on the page, then drag the Indicates selected items icon next to the page item being moved on the Layers panel to a new layer. ▰▰▰▰ Ted informs you that two of the future Happy Apple stores in California are going to be flagship stores that include a dining area, gardening center, and natural pharmacy, in addition to the supermarket. To distinguish these two flagship stores from the two other future stores on the West Coast, you create a new layer, move two circles from the Future Store Locations layer to the new layer, and then apply a new fill color to the two circles.

STEPS

1. **Click the Future Store Locations layer at the top of the Layers panel, then click the Create new layer button** ▣ **on the Layers panel**

   Layer 4 appears at the top of the Layers panel. New layers are placed above the selected layer in the panel.

2. **Double-click Layer 4 to open the Layer Options dialog box**

3. **Change the name of the layer to Flagship Store Locations and the selection color to Red, then click OK**

4. **Click the lowest dark blue circle on the state of California to select it, as shown in Figure F-15**

   The Future Store Locations layer becomes the active layer on the Layers panel, and the Indicates selected items icon ▣ appears next to the Future Store Locations layer on the Layers panel. When you click an object in a document, the layer that the page item is on becomes the active layer.

5. **Click the expand layer arrow** ▷ **next to the Future Store Locations layer to expand the layer**

   You verify that the circle is selected because ▣ appears next to the selected <circle> object. You will move this item to the Flagship Store Locations layer.

6. **Drag** ▣ **on the <circle> page item to the Flagship Store Locations layer on the Layers panel, as shown in Figure F-16, then release the mouse button**

   As you drag ▣, the pointer becomes a pointing finger icon ⌐ᐟᔦ The blue circle is now on the Flagship Store Locations layer and its selection color changed to red.

7. **Click the other dark blue circle on the state of California, then drag** ▣ **from the Future Store Locations layer to the Flagship Store Locations layer on the Layers panel**

8. **Expand the Flagship Store Locations layer, then compare your Layers panel to Figure F-17**

   Both circles are on the new layer.

9. **Select both circles in the document, show the Swatches panel, then change the fill color of the two circles on the Flagship Store Locations layer to C=15 M=100 Y=100 K=0 (red), deselect all, then save your work**

Merging layers

When creating an InDesign document, you may end up with more layers than you really need, or you may wish to consolidate, or **merge**, multiple layers into one general layer. When you merge layers together, the objects on each of the layers that are merged become objects on the single layer that results. To merge multiple layers into a single layer, press and hold [Ctrl] (Win) or [⌘] (Mac), then click all of the layers on the Layers panel that you wish to merge. Click the Layers Panel menu button, then click Merge Layers. The name of first layer that was selected is retained as the name of the single merged layer. You may want to rename the merged layer so that it better describes its new contents.

FIGURE F-15: Selected circle

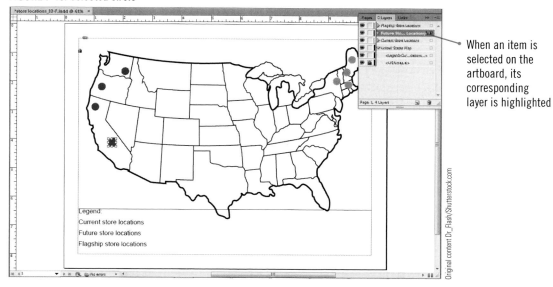

When an item is selected on the artboard, its corresponding layer is highlighted

Original content Dr_Flash/Shutterstock.com

FIGURE F-16: Moving the <circle> page item to the Flagship Store Locations layer

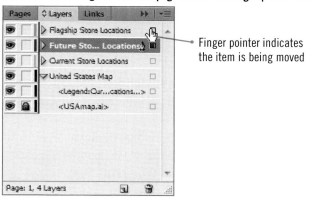

Finger pointer indicates the item is being moved

FIGURE F-17: Viewing the Flagship Store Locations layer

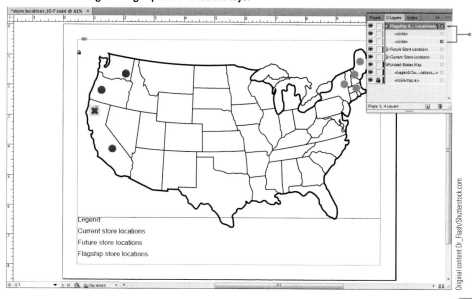

Two <circle> page items on the Flagship Store Locations layer; your selected circle might differ

Original content Dr_Flash/Shutterstock.com

InDesign CS6

Changing Layer Order

The order of layers on the Layers panel is identical to the vertical stacking order of InDesign objects on the page. The top layer in the panel represents the top object(s) on the page and the bottom layer represents the bottom object(s) on the page. To change the order of layers on the Layers panel, you drag the layer to a new location in the panel, then release the mouse button when a black line appears above the layer you are dragging to. ▂▂▂▂ Ted asks you to add a grand opening graphic to the map to announce the opening date of the two flagship stores. You place the grand opening graphic on a new layer and then move the new layer beneath the Flagship Store Locations layer so that the graphic appears beneath the two red circles in the document.

STEPS

1. **Verify that the** Flagship Store Locations layer **is targeted on the Layers panel, then click the** Create new layer button ▣ **on the Layers panel**

   Layer 5 appears at the top of the Layers panel.

2. **Double-click** Layer 5 **to open the Layer Options dialog box, rename the layer** Opening, **click** OK **to accept the default selection color, then close the dialog box**

3. **Click** File **on the Menu bar, click** Place, **then double-click** grand opening.ai

   The mouse pointer is loaded with grand opening.ai, a vector image.

4. **Click anywhere on the state of California, then compare your screen to Figure F-18**

   The grand opening graphic is placed on the currently active Opening layer, which is above the Flagship Store Locations layer on the Layers panel. The graphic blocks or partially blocks the two red circles on the Flagship Store Locations layer.

5. **Using Figure F-19 as a guide, drag the** Opening layer **below the Flagship Store Locations layer until you see a black line below the Flagship Store Locations layer, then release the mouse button**

   The Opening layer is now below the Flagship Store Locations layer on the Layers panel and in the document. In the document, the red circles appear on top of the grand opening graphic and are no longer blocked by it.

6. **Click the** Selection tool ▶ **on the Tools panel, if necessary, verify that the grand opening graphic is still selected, type** 50 **in the Scale X Percentage text box** ▣ **on the Control panel, then press** [Tab]

7. **Drag the** grand opening graphic **so that its location is approximately the same as that shown in Figure F-20**

   Next you will remove the white area behind the grand opening graphic so that it will not block the state lines. You do this in InDesign using the Clipping Path feature.

8. **Verify that the** grand opening graphic **is still selected, click** Object **on the Menu bar, point to** Clipping Path, **then click** Options **to open the Clipping Path dialog box**

9. **Click the** Type list arrow, **click** Detect Edges, **then click** OK

10. **To finish the map, click the** United States Map layer **on the Layers panel, place the file named** Legend dots.ai **next to the legend text**

11. **Deselect all, press** [W] **to view the document in Preview mode, compare your finished map and Layers panel to Figure F-21, save, then exit InDesign**

Pasting layers into a document

You can paste objects and their corresponding layers from one InDesign document into another using the Paste Remembers Layers command on the Layers panel menu. Click the Layers Panel menu button, then click Paste Remembers Layers to add a check mark before the command. Next, copy or cut the InDesign objects and paste them into the new document.

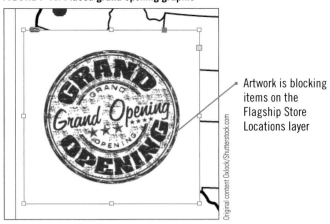

Artwork is blocking items on the Flagship Store Locations layer

Original content Oxlock/Shutterstock.com

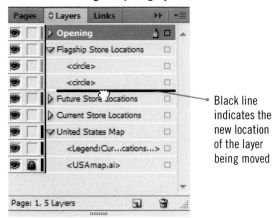

Black line indicates the new location of the layer being moved

FIGURE F-20: **Resized and repositioned graphic**

Original content Dr_Flash, Oxlock/Shutterstock.com

FIGURE F-21: **The finished map**

Original content Dr_Flash, Oxlock/Shutterstock.com

Practice

Concepts Review

Label the elements of the InDesign screen shown in Figure F-22.

FIGURE F-22

Original content Ann Fisher

1. _____   4. _____
2. _____   5. _____
3. _____

Match each term with the statement that best describes it.

6. **Locked layer**   a. Used to move an object to a new layer
7. **Page item**   b. Objects on it cannot be selected
8. **Newly created layer**   c. Indicates the active layer
9. **Indicates selected items icon** ▣   d. Name given to an object on a layer
10. **Indicates current drawing layer icon** ◭   e. Appears above the selected layer on the Layers panel

Select the best answer from the list of choices.

11. On the Layers panel, what do you click to unlock a layer?

    a.   **c.** ▣

    b. 👁   **d.** 🖊

12. Which of the following moves a layer to a new location on the Layers panel?

    a. Use the Move Layer command.

    b. Drag the layer in the panel.

    c. Press and hold [Alt] (Win) or [option] (Mac), then drag the layer in the panel.

    d. Drag the Indicates selected items icon ▣ on the layer you want to move.

13. When does the word "copy" appear after a layer name on the Layers panel?

    a. When the layer has been duplicated   **c.** When an object has been moved to the layer

    b. When an object on the layer has been copied   **d.** When the layer has been moved

Skills Review

1. Place an object on a layer.

    a. Start InDesign, create a new 8.5" × 11" document without facing pages and with a portrait orientation, then save it as **new york coffee_ID-F**.

    b. Click the workspace switcher, click Reset Essentials, then click the Layers panel icon to open the Layers panel.

    c. Click the Rectangle tool on the Tools panel, then create a rectangle frame that snaps to all four margin guides.

    d. On the Layers panel, click the expand layer arrow to expand Layer 1.

    e. Click the Selection tool on the Tools panel, click File on the Menu bar, click Place, navigate to where you store your Data Files, click New York.tif, then click Open.

    f. Click the Fit content proportionally button on the Control panel, then click the Center content button on the Control panel.

    g. Click Object on the Menu bar, point to Display Performance, then click High Quality Display.

    h. Deselect the map frame, click File on the Menu bar, click Place, click New York Legend.doc, then click Open.

    i. Align the loaded cursor with approximately the 9-inch mark on the vertical ruler, then click to place the New York legend text in the lower-left corner of the document window. (*Hint*: Be sure all four lines of the legend are visible.)

    j. Save your work.

2. Change layer options.

    a. Click the Layers Panel menu button, then click Layer Options for "Layer 1".

    b. Type **New York Map** in the Name text box.

    c. Click the Color list arrow, then click Light Blue.

    d. Click OK to close the Layer Options dialog box.

    e. Click the Selection tool on the Tools panel, if necessary, then click the map image to view the Light Blue selection color.

    f. Deselect all, then save your work.

3. Create a new layer.

    a. Click the Layers Panel menu button, then click New Layer.

    b. Type **Current Locations** in the Name text box, click the Color list arrow, click Yellow, then click OK to close the New Layer dialog box.

    c. Click the Rectangle tool on the Tools panel. (*Hint*: The Rectangle tool may be hidden beneath the Ellipse tool.)

    d. Click the page to open the Rectangle dialog box, type **.25** in the Width text box, press [Tab], type **.25** in the Height text box, then click OK.

    e. Click the Zoom tool on the Tools panel, then click the square to enlarge your view as necessary.

Skills Review (continued)

f. Click the Fill button on the Tools panel, open the Swatches panel, then scroll down and click C=0 M=0 Y=100 K=0 (yellow).

g. Click the Stroke button on the Tools panel, then click [None] on the Swatches panel, if necessary.

h. Click the Selection tool on the Tools panel, then drag the square to just inside the upper-right corner of the map of New York.

i. Press and hold [Alt] (Win) or [option] (Mac), click and drag the square in a downward direction to create a copy of it as shown in Figure F-23, then create two more copies of the square, and place them in the approximate locations shown in the figure.

j. Save your work.

4. Duplicate a layer.

a. Show the Layers panel, then verify that the Current Locations layer is still active on the Layers panel.

b. Click the Layers Panel menu button, then click Duplicate Layer "Current Locations".

c. Double-click the Current Locations copy layer on the Layers panel to open the Layer Options dialog box.

d. Type **Future Locations** in the Name text box, click the Color list arrow, click Dark Blue, then click OK.

e. Click the Selection tool on the Tools panel, if necessary, then click the yellow square nearest to the bottom of the map.

f. Change the fill color of the selected square to C=100 M=90 Y=10 K=0 (dark blue), drag the square approximately 1 inch to the left, then deselect.

g. Press [Alt] (Win) or [option] (Mac), click the Future Locations layer on the Layers panel to select all of the objects on the layer, then click C=100 M=90 Y=10 K=0 (dark blue) on the Swatches panel.

h. Drag the blue squares to the approximate locations shown in Figure F-24, deselect, then save your work.

5. Lock and hide a layer.

a. Open the Layers panel, if necessary, then click the Toggles visibility button to the left of the Future Locations layer on the Layers panel.

b. Click the Toggles visibility button to the left of the Current Locations layer on the Layers panel.

c. Click the Toggles visibility button to the left of the New York Map layer on the Layers panel.

d. Click the empty gray square where the Toggles visibility icon once was next to each of the three layers on the Layers panel.

e. Click the empty gray square between the Toggles visibility icon and the <New York.tif> object on the Layers panel.

f. Double-click the New York Map layer on the Layers panel to open the Layer Options dialog box, then view the settings for the New York Map layer.

g. Click OK, then save your work.

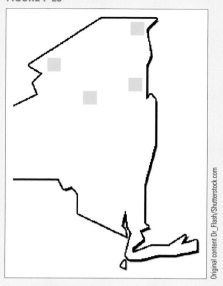

Original content Dr_Flash/Shutterstock.com

FIGURE F-24

Original content Dr_Flash/Shutterstock.com

Skills Review (continued)

6. Move an object to another layer.

a. Click the Future Locations layer at the top of the Layers panel, then click the Create new layer button on the Layers panel.

b. Double-click Layer 4 to open the Layer Options dialog box.

c. Change the name of the layer to **Cafe/Bookstore Locations** and the selection color to Grass Green, then click OK.

d. Click the blue square on the far left to select it.

e. Click the triangle next to the Future Locations layer to expand the layer.

f. Drag the Indicates selected items icon on the <rectangle> page item to the Cafe/Bookstore Locations layer on the Layers panel, then release the mouse button.

g. Click the next, left-most blue square on the state of New York, then drag the Indicates selected items icon from the Future Locations layer to the Cafe/Bookstore Locations layer on the Layers panel.

h. Expand the Cafe/Bookstore Locations layer to view both squares on the Cafe/Bookstores layer.

i. Change the fill color of the two squares on the Cafe/Bookstore Locations layer to C=75 M=5 Y=100 K=0 (green).

j. Deselect all, then save your work.

7. Change layer order.

a. Verify that the Cafe/Bookstore Locations layer is targeted on the Layers panel, then click the Create new layer button on the Layers panel.

b. Double-click Layer 5 to open the Layer Options dialog box, rename the layer **New Store**, then click OK to accept the chosen selection color and close the dialog box.

c. Click File on the Menu bar, click Place, then double-click Opening Soon.ai.

d. Click the loaded cursor anywhere on the far-left green square on the map to place the Opening Soon graphic.

e. Drag the New Store layer below the Cafe/Bookstore Locations layer until you see a black line below the Cafe/Bookstore Locations layer, then release the mouse button.

f. Click the Selection tool on the Tools panel, if necessary, then drag the Opening Soon graphic so that the word "Soon" is slightly above the green square.

g. To finish the map, click the New York Map layer on the Layers panel, place the file named Legend squares.ai, then move the legend squares into position next to the legend text.

h. Deselect all, press [W] to view your work in Preview mode, then compare your finished map and Layers panel to Figure F-25.

i. Save your work, then exit InDesign.

FIGURE F-25

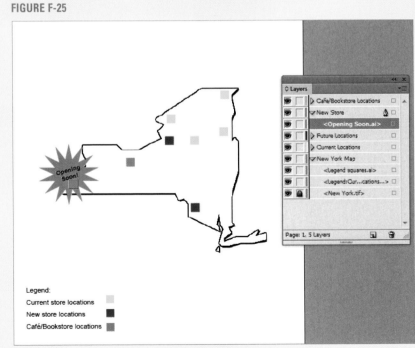

InDesign CS6

Independent Challenge 1

You were recently hired as a designer for a snowboarding magazine. Each month you update the magazine cover for the new issue. During your first week, you realize that the previous designer did not use layers when assembling the magazine cover template. You decide to add layers to it in order to keep the page elements organized.

a. Start InDesign, open ID F-1.indd, then save it as **snowboard magazine_ID-F**.

b. Open the Layers panel.

c. Create five layers named **Date**, **Title**, **Subtitle**, **Picture**, and **In this Issue**.

d. Expand Layer 1, then drag each page item to its corresponding layer. (*Hint*: The orange rectangle and the title "<Snowboard>," are one item. "The Top 10 Mountains" is the subtitle.)

e. Delete Layer 1 by clicking the Layers Panel menu button, then click Delete Layer "Layer 1".

f. Rearrange the order of the layers, as necessary, so that you see all five page elements.

g. Hide and show each layer to make sure that each item is placed correctly.

h. Press [W] to view your page in Preview mode, then save your work.

i. Compare your screen and your Layers panel to Figure F-26, then exit InDesign.

FIGURE F-26

Working with Layers

Independent Challenge 2

You volunteer at a local farm stand each summer. Every weekday, the farm offers a different item for $1.00 until it runs out of the item. You are in charge of creating ads for the sale item each morning. You have figured out how to make a different ad each day using the same InDesign document.

a. Start InDesign, open ID F-2.indd, then save it as **quick ad_ID-F**.

b. Duplicate Layer 1, rename the new layer **Monday**, then change the selection color for the Monday layer to the color of your choice.

c. Hide Layer 1, select the Monday layer, then change the "Day of Week" text in the text box on the Monday layer to **Monday**.

d. Duplicate the Monday layer, rename the new layer **Tuesday**, then change the selection color for the Tuesday layer.

e. Hide the Monday layer, target the Tuesday layer, then change the "Monday" text in the text box to **Tuesday**.

f. Repeat Steps d-e to create new layers for Wednesday, Thursday, and Friday. (*Hint*: Remember to duplicate the layers instead of creating new layers.)

g. Check your work by showing each layer with all other layers hidden. (*Hint*: Press and hold [Alt] (Win) or [option] (Mac), then click the Toggles visibility button for a layer to show that layer and hide all others.)

h. Select the Friday layer, then hide all other layers on the Layers panel.

i. Place the file named red grapes.psd in the circle graphics frame, then fill the frame proportionally.

Advanced Challenge Exercise

- Show all of the layers on the Layers panel.
- Click the Layers Panel menu button, then click Paste Remembers Layers to put a check mark next to it, if necessary.
- Click Edit on the Menu bar, then click Select All.
- Click Edit on the Menu bar, then click Copy.
- Create a new InDesign document with the default settings.
- Click Edit on the Menu bar, then click Paste.
- Press and hold [Alt] (Win) or [option] (Mac), then click the Toggles visibility icon on the Monday layer to show that layer and hide all others.

j. Deselect all, press [W] to view the page in Preview mode, then compare your screen to Figure F-27.

k. Save your work, then exit InDesign.

FIGURE F-27

Independent Challenge 3

You volunteer two hours a week doing community service work for school credit at your local library. Each week, you create some fun pages to be distributed at the weekly story hour. Since taking an InDesign class in school, you realize that you could improve the fun page document by organizing the page elements in layers.

a. Start InDesign, open ID F-3.indd, update links if necessary, then save it as **fun page layers_ID-F**.

b. Rename Layer 1 as **Text**.

c. Create five new layers named **Grapes**, **Watermelon**, **Strawberries**, **Citrus Fruit**, and **Candy**.

d. Place each page item on the appropriate layer, then hide and show each layer to check your work.

e. Lock the Text layer.

f. Press and hold [Alt] (Win) or [option] (Mac), click Grapes on the Layers panel to select all of the objects on it, change the stroke color of the red and green grape images to C=100 M=90 Y=10 K=0.

g. Deselect all objects, show all layers, then save your work.

h. Press [W] to view the page in Preview mode, compare your screen and your Layers panel to Figure F-28, then exit InDesign.

FIGURE F-28

Real Life Independent Challenge

Determine two items that you no longer use but you think you could sell online. Before you post information about the items online, place a picture of each item in InDesign and add descriptions.

    a. Start InDesign and create a new single-page 8.5" × 11" document without facing pages and with 1-inch margins.

    b. Save the document as **online sale_ID-F**.

    c. Place at least two images of your own items in the document. (*Hint*: If you do not have your own photos, you may use the two clock images in the Data Files folder.)

    d. Write a description for each item.

    e. Place each item on a new layer and name the layer so that it describes the item on it.

    f. Create a layer named **Text**, then place all of the text descriptions on the text layer.

    g. Arrange the images and descriptions on the page as you like.

    h. Drag the Text layer to the bottom of the Layers panel.

Advanced Challenge Exercise

- Select one layer, press and hold [Shift], then click the remaining layers.
- Click the Layers Panel menu button, then click Merge Layers.
- Change the name of the merged layer to **Sale Items**.

    i. Save your work, then exit InDesign.

Visual Workshop

Start InDesign and create a new 8.5" × 11" document with facing pages. Save the document as **guide layers_ID-F**. Using Figure F-29 as a guide, open the A-Master and create all of the guides shown in the figure on the left and right pages of the A-Master. Place the horizontal guides on a layer named **Horizontal guides** and the vertical guides on a layer named **Vertical guides**. (*Hint*: Thumbnail images of the guides do not appear on the Layers panel.) Compare your screen to Figure F-29, save your work, then exit InDesign.

FIGURE F-29

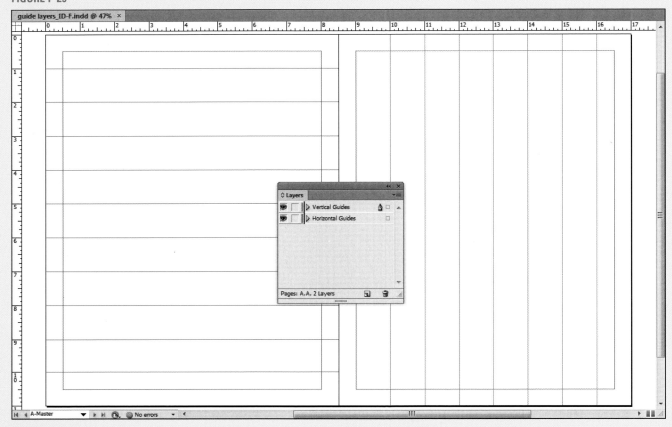

Working with Color and Tables

Files You Will Need:

To view a list of files needed for this unit, see the Data Files Grid in the back of the book.

Color is a dynamic part of any InDesign document and can greatly enhance a document's appearance. InDesign offers an endless supply of colors to use for printed documents and for the web. You can make your own process colors and save them in the Swatches panel or choose from several spot color libraries. You can also use two or more colors to create a fill in which colors blend from one to another, called a **gradient fill**. Using tables in InDesign helps you organize and display text in rows and columns, similar to a spreadsheet. There are many ways to format tables to create a professional presentation of your information, such as by applying colors and styles to table cells and text.  The Happy Apple is raising money for a local animal shelter. At the checkout line, customers will be able to purchase a paper apple for $1.00 to hang in the store window. Ted asks you to create two apple cutouts, each with a different color, for customers to choose from. He also asks you to create a table showing the progress of the six Happy Apple stores that are participating in the fundraiser.

OBJECTIVES

Create a process color

Select a spot color

Create a gradient

Use the Gradient Swatch tool

Create a table

Format table cells

Insert, merge, and split table cells

Set tabs in a table

Creating a Process Color

A **process color** is a color that is made from using the four process inks: cyan, magenta, yellow, and black, also known as **CMYK**. Process inks are inks that are used for color printing; they are made by combining different percentages of one or more of these four colors, similar to combining the ingredients in a recipe. For example, the color red is made from 50% yellow and 50% magenta. Process colors are designated for documents that will be printed on paper. These colors are affected by the type of paper they are printed on and other elements such as light and air, and therefore are not guaranteed to look the same every time when printed. ![icon] You open an InDesign document containing two apple graphics, create a new process color, and then apply it to one of the apple graphics.

STEPS

1. **Start InDesign, open ID G-1.indd, then save it as** apple cutouts_ID-G

   The open document contains two apple vector graphics that were copied and pasted from Adobe Illustrator to InDesign. The images are modifiable because they were pasted rather than placed as preview files into the document.

2. **Click** Window **on the Menu bar, point to** Workspace, **then click** Reset Essentials

3. **Click the** Direct Selection tool ![icon] **on the Tools panel, verify that the Fill button** ![icon] **is active on the Tools panel, then click the** apple on the left

   The apple is grouped to the stem and leaves. The Direct Selection tool selects just the apple.

4. **Click the** Swatches panel button ![icon] **on the right side of the workspace to open the Swatches panel, then drag the lower-right corner of the Swatches panel down so that you can see all of the colors in it, as shown in Figure G-1**

   The top nine colors, starting with Paper, are the default colors on the Swatches panel. The three bottom colors are the three colors applied to the apple and stem in each of the graphics. Notice that all of the colors are named using C, M, Y, and K, followed by a percentage. The gray square icon to the right of each color indicates that each color is a process color. The color c15m100y100k0 is selected on the Swatches panel because it is the color that is applied to the selected object.

5. **Verify that the apple is still selected, click the** Swatches Panel menu button ![icon], **then click** New Color Swatch

   The New Color Swatch dialog box opens, displaying the last swatch that was selected on the Swatches panel.

6. **Click the** Name with Color Value check box **to remove the check mark, then type** Golden Delicious **in the Swatch Name text box**

   By deselecting the Name with Color Value check box, you can add your own descriptive name, rather than using the default CMYK naming convention. Named colors, like Golden Delicious, are useful for making global changes to a document. If you edit a named color, everywhere the named color is applied in the document is automatically updated.

7. **Double-click the** Cyan text box, **type** 10, **press [Tab], type** 12, **press [Tab], type** 90, **press [Tab], type** 0, **then compare your New Color Swatch dialog box to Figure G-2**

   The color created from this combination of CMYK appears in the preview box.

8. **Click** OK **to close the New Color Swatch dialog box**

   The new color, Golden Delicious, is applied to the selected apple and appears at the bottom of the Swatches panel, as shown in Figure G-3. If you wanted to continue to create additional new colors, you could click Add instead of OK in the dialog box. When you click Add, the new color is added to the Swatches panel and the New Color Swatch dialog box remains open.

9. **Click the** Color panel button ![icon] **to open the Color panel, click the** Color Panel menu button ![icon], **then click** CMYK

   The Color panel shows the CMYK combination for the Golden Delicious color swatch.

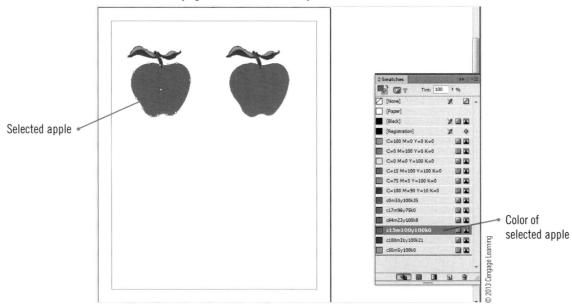

Selected apple

Color of selected apple

FIGURE G-2: **New Color Swatch dialog box**

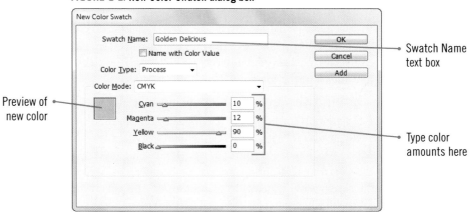

Swatch Name text box

Preview of new color

Type color amounts here

FIGURE G-3: **New process color applied to artwork**

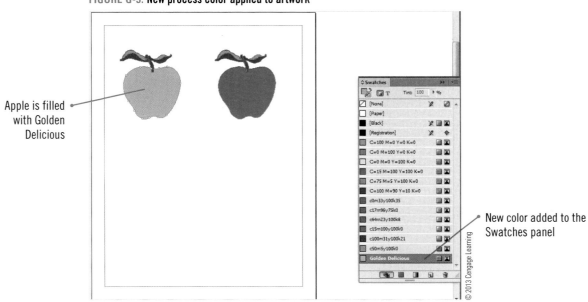

Apple is filled with Golden Delicious

New color added to the Swatches panel

© 2013 Cengage Learning

InDesign CS6

Selecting a Spot Color

Spot colors are another type of color used for documents printed on paper. Unlike process colors that you can create yourself, **spot colors** are manufactured by paint companies. Spot colors are helpful to use when you are unsuccessful at creating a color you need with CMYK. They are more reliable than process colors because they print exactly the same each time they are used. Spot colors can be used for documents printed on your home computer, but they are often used for high-end commercial documents such as magazines and catalogs that will be printed on large printing presses. Spot colors are listed on the Swatches panel. You choose a spot color for the second apple and then apply it to the apple shape.

STEPS

1. **Deselect the Golden Delicious apple, open the Swatches panel, click the** Swatches Panel menu button **, then click** New Color Swatch

   The New Color Swatch dialog box opens.

2. **Click the** Color Type list arrow, **then click** Spot

3. **Click the** Color Mode list arrow, **then click** PANTONE+ Solid Coated

   Pantone is the company name of a large color manufacturer. Solid Coated is a category of paint that Pantone makes.

4. **Click the** PANTONE text box, **then type** 390

   The color PANTONE 390 C, a light green, is selected in the list, as shown in Figure G-4. Some PANTONE colors are based on the CMYK color mode and others are based on the Lab color mode. The Lab color space includes all perceivable colors. Its gamut exceeds both RGB and CMYK color models. You want to apply this to the next apple to make it the color of a Granny Smith apple.

5. **Click** OK **to close the New Color Swatch dialog box**

   PANTONE 390 C appears at the bottom of the Swatches panel, as shown in Figure G-5. To the right of the color, the square icon with the circle at its center indicates that the color is a spot color. Next to the spot color icon is either a CMYK mode or Lab mode icon. If the color mode is CMYK, you can position the mouse pointer over the CMYK mode icon to view the combination of CMYK you would use to create a process color that is the closest possible match to the spot color. This is known as a **process match**. Creating a process match is useful when the color you need does not have to be a perfect match and you don't want to purchase the spot color ink.

6. **Click the** Fill button ▱ **on the Tools panel, if necessary**

7. **Click the** Direct Selection tool ▸, **click the** apple **on the right, then click** PANTONE 390 C **on the Swatches panel**

   The apple is filled with a light green color, PANTONE 390 C.

8. **Deselect all, compare your screen to Figure G-6, then save your work**

Creating a new tint swatch

If you need a lighter version of a color, you can make a tint swatch from it. To create a tint swatch from an existing color, select the color on the Swatches panel, click the Swatches panel menu button, then click New Tint Swatch. Drag the Tint slider to the left in the New Tint Swatch dialog box until the desired percentage appears in the text box to the right, then click OK. The new tint swatch appears on the Swatches panel with the same name and tint percentage next to the name.

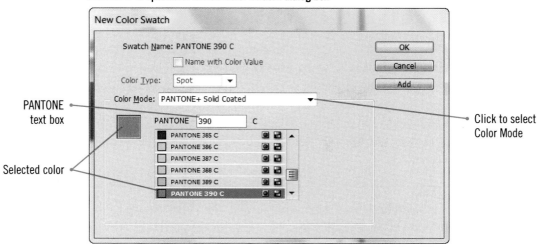

PANTONE text box

Selected color

Click to select Color Mode

FIGURE G-5: **Viewing PANTONE 390 C on the Swatches panel**

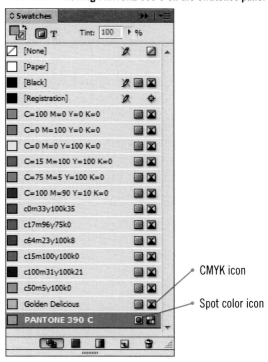

CMYK icon

Spot color icon

FIGURE G-6: **Spot color applied to apple**

Pantone 390 C spot color

© 2013 Cengage Learning

InDesign CS6

Creating a Gradient

A **gradient** is a type of fill for an object that contains at least two colors that gradually blend from one to the other, such as from black to white. **Linear** gradients blend from one point to another horizontally, vertically, or diagonally, depending on the angle of the gradient. **Radial** gradients blend from the center outward to the border(s) of the object. Gradient fills can add texture to an object and also give the illusion of lightness and darkness in an object. In addition to filling objects, you can apply a gradient to strokes and text in InDesign. ░░░░ You create a gradient fill for the apple leaves to give them a more three-dimensional look.

On the Swatches panel, the Show All Swatches button is selected by default, and all color swatches and gradient swatches are displayed in the panel. Click the Show Color Swatches button to show only color swatches in the panel. Click the Show Gradient Swatches button to display only the gradient swatches in the panel.

1. **Click the Swatches Panel menu button ⬛, then click New Gradient Swatch**

   The New Gradient Swatch dialog box opens with the default Linear type and the default gradient colors (white to black) showing in the Gradient Ramp, as shown in Figure G-7. The two icons below the Gradient Ramp are called **color stops**. The first color stop, located at 0% on the Gradient Ramp, represents the starting color of the gradient. The second color stop, located at 100% on the Gradient Ramp, represents the ending color of the gradient. A diamond icon appears above the Gradient Ramp. By default its location is at 50%, which indicates the point in the gradient where there is 50% of each color. You can drag the diamond slider to change its location.

2. **Click the right color stop, click the Stop Color list arrow, then click Swatches**

   The colors on the Swatches panel are available in the dialog box.

3. **Scroll down in the list of swatches, then click c100m31y100k21 (dark green)**

   Green is applied to the 100% color stop and becomes the last color in the new gradient. The gradient blends from white to green, as shown in Figure G-8.

To remove a color from a gradient, drag a color stop off of the Gradient Ramp.

4. **Click just below the Gradient Ramp anywhere between the color stops to add a new color stop, then drag the new color stop until you see approximately 50% in the Location text box**

   The new color will begin halfway between the starting color stop and the ending color stop. Diamond icons now appear halfway between the 0% and 50% color stops, and halfway between the 50% and 100% color stops.

5. **Using Figure G-9 as a guide, drag the sliders for the middle color stop to C=36 M=0 Y=70 K=0**

   The gradient blends from white to a lighter green and then to a darker green.

To rename a gradient swatch, double-click it to open the Gradient Options dialog box, then change its name in the Swatch Name text box.

6. **Click OK to close the dialog box**

   The gradient swatch is added to the bottom of the Swatches panel and is named New Gradient Swatch by default.

7. **Click the Zoom tool 🔍 on the Tools panel, then drag the Zoom tool pointer ⬚ around the left apple to zoom in on it**

8. **Click the Direct Selection tool ⬚, click the dark green part of the left leaf, click New Gradient Swatch on the Swatches panel, then apply the New Gradient Swatch to the dark green part of the right leaf**

   The New Gradient Swatch is applied to the left and right leaves, as shown in Figure G-10.

9. **Apply the New Gradient Swatch to the dark green areas of the left and right leaves on the Granny Smith apple, then save your work**

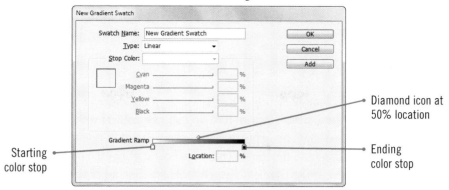

Starting color stop

Diamond icon at 50% location

Ending color stop

FIGURE G-8: **Applying a new color to the last color stop**

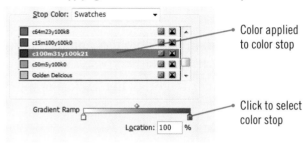

Color applied to color stop

Click to select color stop

FIGURE G-9: **Choosing the color for the middle color stop**

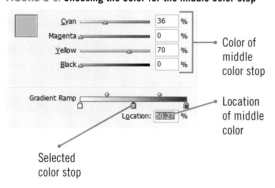

Color of middle color stop

Location of middle color

Selected color stop

FIGURE G-10: **Gradient applied to leaves**

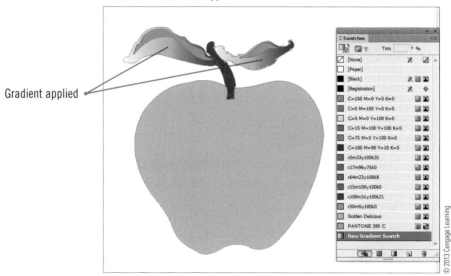

Gradient applied

© 2013 Cengage Learning

Using the Gradient Feather tool

The Gradient Feather tool 🔲 functions similarly to the Gradient Swatch tool. In fact, the only difference is that the Gradient Feather tool applies opacity values to each color stop so that in changing a gradient fill, you can also control the opacity or transparency of each stop in the gradient. Before applying the Gradient Feather tool, double-click it on the Tools panel to open the Effects dialog box. Here you can adjust the default settings for Opacity for each stop along the Gradient Ramp. You can also change the location of color stops and the angle of the gradient fill.

Using the Gradient Swatch Tool

You can use the Gradient Swatch tool to change the start and end points, direction, and/or angle of a gradient fill. To use the Gradient Swatch tool, you select an object with the gradient fill, then drag the tool over the object. As you drag, a temporary line appears. The start point, end point, direction, and angle of the line created by dragging the tool become the new start point, end point, direction, and angle of the gradient fill, respectively. The Gradient Swatch tool only changes the gradient fill of the selected object or objects; it does not affect the gradient swatch on the Swatches panel. You use the Gradient Swatch tool to change the start and end points and the direction of the gradient fill on each set of leaves so that the two apples are not identical.

STEPS

1. Click the Zoom tool 🔍 on the Tools panel, then drag the Zoom tool pointer ⊕ around the Golden Delicious apple to zoom in on it, if necessary

2. Click the Direct Selection tool 🔾 on the Tools panel, then click the left leaf of the Golden Delicious apple that is filled with the gradient

3. Click the Gradient Swatch tool 🔳 on the Tools panel
   The mouse pointer becomes a crosshair icon.

4. Using Figure G-11 as a guide, click slightly above the left leaf, drag in a downward direction to the bottom of the leaf, then release the mouse button
   As shown in Figure G-12, the gradient fills the left leaf from just above the top of it to just below the bottom of it, instead of from left to right, giving the leaf an entirely new look, since the bottom is darker than the top. The angle of the gradient follows the angle of the line created when you dragged. The parts of the leaf not included within the line are filled with the beginning and ending colors used in the gradient.

5. Press and hold the [Spacebar] to switch to the Hand tool 🖑, then drag the page to the left until you see the Granny Smith apple

6. Click 🔾, then click the section of the right leaf filled with the gradient

7. Click 🔳, drag the Gradient Swatch tool pointer -¦- from the bottom of the leaf to the top, then release the mouse button

8. Click the Selection tool 🔾 on the Tools panel, deselect the leaf, then double-click 🖑 on the Tools panel to view the entire page in the Document window

9. Save your work, then compare your screen to Figure G-13

Using the Gradient panel

The Gradient panel includes the same options as the New Gradient Swatch dialog box for creating a new gradient. When you use the Gradient panel to create a new gradient, you will need the Swatches panel and/or the Color panel open at the same time so that you can choose colors for each color stop. When you select a color stop and are ready to choose a swatch on the Swatches panel to apply to that color stop, be sure to press and hold [Alt] (Win) or [option] (Mac) before clicking the swatch. Otherwise, the selected object will be filled with the color swatch chosen on the Swatches panel. Pressing [Alt] (Win) or [option] (Mac) ensures that the color chosen on the Swatches panel is only applied to the color stop of the gradient fill.

FIGURE G-11: Changing the gradient fill of the left leaf

Start dragging here

Stop dragging here

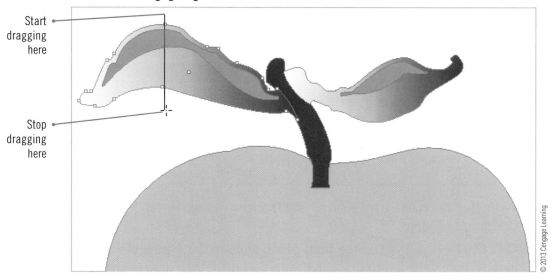

© 2013 Cengage Learning

FIGURE G-12: Viewing the result of the Gradient tool

Gradient is reversed

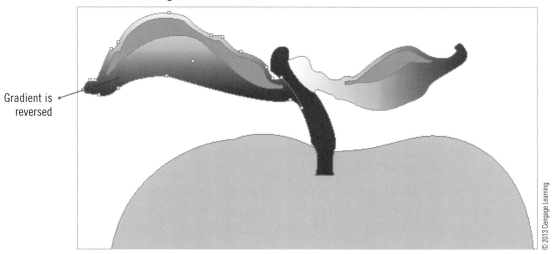

© 2013 Cengage Learning

FIGURE G-13: Viewing the gradient fills

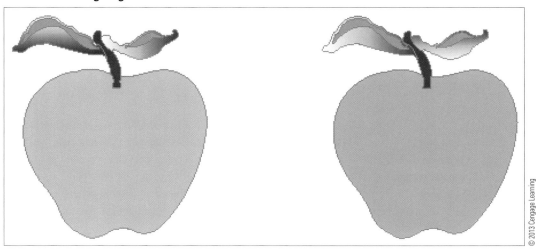

© 2013 Cengage Learning

Creating a Table

There are some types of information, such as weekly schedules, that are best presented in documents as tables. In InDesign, a **table** is a rectangular object that is made up of many smaller rectangles called **cells**. Cells are laid out horizontally in **rows** and vertically in **columns**. Tables are used primarily for text, but it is possible to insert graphics into cells too. To create a table, you must first create a text box to put the table into. To make changes to a table, you can select individual cells, rows, or columns, or you can select the entire table. ▓▓▓ You are ready to create a table that shows how much money has been raised so far. The Happy Apple will match the donation for each dollar donated.

STEPS

1. **Verify that the rulers are displayed and that you can see the entire page in the Document window**

2. **Click the Type tool T on the Tools panel, position the Type tool pointer ⌶ at approximately the 5-inch mark on the vertical ruler, then drag to create a text box that snaps to the left, bottom, and right margin guides, as shown in Figure G-14**

   The text box in the figure is selected so that you can see its four borders.

3. **Click T if necessary, click inside the text box, click Table on the Menu bar, then click Insert Table**

   The Insert Table dialog box opens.

4. **Type 7 in the Body Rows text box, press [Tab], type 3 if necessary in the Columns text box, then click OK**

   A table with seven rows and three columns appears in the text box.

5. **Position the mouse pointer on the top edge of the first column of the table until the pointer becomes a black arrow ↓, as shown in Figure G-15, then click the mouse button**

   The first column of cells is selected. When an element of the table is selected, settings for modifying the table appear on the Control panel.

6. **Click the mouse button outside of the table area to deselect the column, position the mouse pointer on the upper-left corner of the table so that the mouse pointer becomes a diagonal black arrow ↘, then click the mouse button to select the entire table**

   The entire table is selected. Selecting the entire table is useful to make changes to every cell in the table at once.

7. **Click in the top cell of the first table column, type Store Locations, press [Tab], type Number of Apples Sold, press [Tab], type Total Amount Donated, then press [Tab]**

   The insertion point appears in the second cell of the first table column. Pressing [Tab] when in a table cell moves the insertion point to the next cell in the table.

8. **Type the text shown in Figure G-16 in the remaining table cells**

9. **Save your work**

Using the Table panel

The Table panel includes some of the same options for modifying a table that are on the Control panel when a table or table element is selected. Both panels include buttons that allow you to rotate the text inside a cell, change the number of columns and rows, choose an exact width or height for table cells, and change the cell inset value. The **inset** value is the amount of space between the top, bottom, right, and/or left sides of text and its cell borders. The Table panel menu includes the same menu items found on the Table menu on the Menu bar, such as Merge Cells, Table Options, and Cell Options. Choosing whether to use the Table panel, Control panel, or Table menu is merely a matter of preference. To open the Table panel, click Window on the Menu bar, point to Type & Tables, then click Table.

FIGURE G-14: Creating a text box

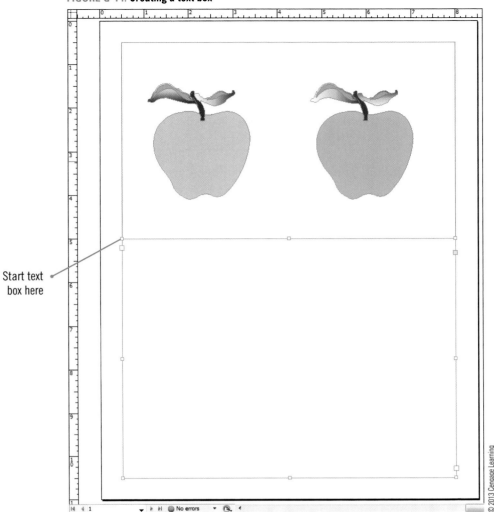

Start text
box here

© 2013 Cengage Learning

FIGURE G-15: Preparing to select a column

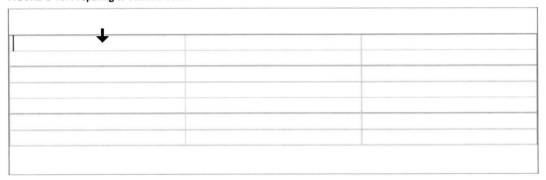

FIGURE G-16: Text entered into table

Store Locations	Number of Apples Sold	Total Amount Donated
Presque Isle, Maine	550	$1,100.00
Bangor, Maine	360	$720.00
Burlington, Vermont	471	$942.00
Concord, New Hampshire	292	$584.00
Hartford, Connecticut	379	$758.00
Cambridge, Massachusetts	650	$1,300.00

Formatting Table Cells

There are many formatting options for table cells. You can format the text inside cells the same way that you format text inside a text box. You can apply borders and shading to table cells, and also change the width and height of table cells in order to fit more information inside them. ▓▓▓ After entering all of the data in the table, you are ready to format the table cells. You increase the height of each table cell, vertically align the text inside the cells, and then change the weight and color of the cell borders.

QUICK TIP

To apply formatting to table rows and columns, click Table on the Menu bar, point to Table Options, then click one of the choices in the menu, such as alternating fills.

1. **Click the Type tool [T] on the Tools panel, if necessary, select the entire table, click Table on the Menu bar, point to Cell Options, then click Rows and Columns**

   The Cell Options dialog box opens with the Rows and Columns tab displayed.

2. **Click the Row Height list arrow, then click Exactly**

   The Exactly setting is used when you want the row height to be an exact number. The At Least setting is used when the height of a row should be at least a specific value that you choose.

3. **Double-click the value in the Row Height text box, type .35, press [Tab], then click the Preview check box to add a check mark**

   The height of each table row changes to 0.35 inches tall. Compare your screen and Cell Options dialog box to Figure G-17.

4. **Click the Text tab in the Cell Options dialog box, click the Align list arrow, then click Align Center**

   The text is vertically centered inside each of the cells.

5. **Click the Strokes and Fills tab**

   Notice that there is already a default 1-pt black stroke applied to table cells.

6. **Click the Weight list arrow, click 2 pt, click the Color list arrow, click C=75 M=5 Y=100 K=0 (green), then click OK**

7. **Click the Selection tool [▸] on the Tools panel, deselect the table, then press [W]**

   A 2-pt green border is added to the table cells, as shown in Figure G-18.

8. **Save your work**

Using colors from Illustrator in InDesign

When you copy an Illustrator object and paste it in InDesign, the colors applied to the object appear automatically in the InDesign Swatches panel whenever the document is open. This is a great way to incorporate a color palette into other InDesign elements, such as text, frame borders, and other InDesign objects. When *placing* an Illustrator object into InDesign, the Illustrator object is placed as a bitmap image. Its colors cannot be modified in InDesign and they are not added to the InDesign Swatches panel.

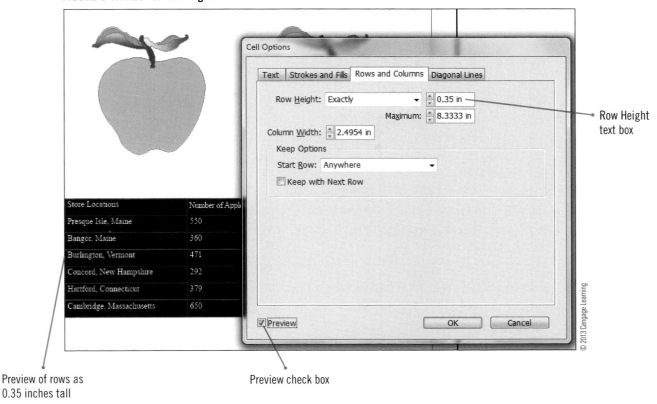

Row Height text box

Preview of rows as 0.35 inches tall

Preview check box

© 2013 Cengage Learning

FIGURE G-18: New formatting applied to table cells

Store Locations	Number of Apples Sold	Total Amount Donated
Presque Isle, Maine	550	$1,100.00
Bangor, Maine	360	$720.00
Burlington, Vermont	471	$942.00
Concord, New Hampshire	292	$584.00
Hartford, Connecticut	379	$758.00
Cambridge, Massachusetts	650	$1,300.00

InDesign CS6

Converting text to tables and tables to text

You can easily convert existing text to a table using the Convert Text to Table command on the Table menu. Select the text that you wish to convert to a table, click Table on the Menu bar, then click Convert Text to Table. The Convert Text to Table dialog box opens. In this dialog box, you need to indicate how you initially separated the text horizontally and vertically. Typically, you would use a tab, a space, or a comma to separate pieces of text horizontally, and a paragraph return to separate pieces of text vertically. Whatever you used will determine how the text will be separated into columns and rows. Click the Column Separator list arrow, then click the item (Tab, Comma, or Paragraph) that you used to separate the pieces of text horizontally. Click the Row Separator list arrow, then click the item (Tab, Comma, or Paragraph) that you used to separate the pieces of text vertically. You can also convert tables into text by selecting a table and then clicking the Convert Table to Text command on the Table menu. In the Convert Table to Text dialog box, you indicate what type of separator you would like to use to separate each piece of text.

Inserting, Merging, and Splitting Table Cells

When working with tables, you may need to add table rows and/or columns because you don't have enough or delete them because you have too many. You can easily add rows and columns in a table using the Insert Row or Insert Column dialog box. You can choose how many rows or columns you want to insert, and if they should be added above or below the selected row or column. To delete a row or column, select the row or column, click Table on the Menu bar, point to Delete, then click Row or Column. You can also combine, or **merge**, table cells into one cell and break up, or **split**, a table cell into smaller cells. ▓▓▓▓▓ You realize you need a heading row and a totals row for the table, so you insert two new rows, merge the cells in the new top row for the heading, and split the last table cell in the new bottom row to add the company goal next to the total dollar amount.

STEPS

1. **Press [W] to switch to Normal mode, click the Type tool ⊤ on the Tools panel, position the mouse pointer on the left edge of the top row of the table until the pointer becomes a black arrow ➔, then click the mouse**

   The top row is selected.

QUICK TIP

You can also press [Ctrl][F9] (Win) or ⌘[F9] (Mac) to insert a row.

2. **Click Table on the Menu bar, point to Insert, then click Row**

   The Insert Row(s) dialog box opens.

3. **Click the Above option button if necessary, then click OK**

   A new row is inserted above the selected row.

4. **Select the new row, then click the Merge cells button ⊠ on the Control panel**

   The three cells in the top row are merged into one cell.

5. **Click the merged cell, type The Happy Apple Fundraiser, change the font size of the text in the merged cell to 18 pt, click the Align center button ≣ on the Control panel, click the Selection tool ▶, deselect all, then compare your table to Figure G-19**

6. **Click ⊤, select the bottom table row, click Table on the Menu bar, point to Insert, click Row, click the Below option button in the Insert Row(s) dialog box, then click OK**

7. **Click the first cell of the bottom row, type Total, press [Tab], type 2,702, then press [Tab]**

8. **Click Table on the Menu bar, point to Select, then click Cell**

   The current cell is selected.

9. **Click Table on the Menu bar, click Split Cell Vertically, then deselect the cell**

   As shown in Figure G-20, the cell is split evenly into two cells.

10. **Click the left side of the split cell, type $5,404.00, press [Tab], type Goal: $3,000.00, then save your work**

Creating a table style

To add visual interest to your table, you may want to fill table cells with color. For example, you can apply alternating fill colors to rows in order to place emphasis on specific rows and make the table easier to read, or just to make the table more attractive. Once you have finished formatting a table, you can save all of the formatting as a table style in the Table Styles panel and then apply the style to new tables in the future. To create a new table style, click the Table Styles Panel menu button, then click New Table Style. The New Table Style dialog box opens with the General category displayed. The Style Settings section lists a summary of the style currently applied to the table. You can further modify the table style using the categories provided on the left of the dialog box. When you close the dialog box, the new style is added to the Table Styles panel.

FIGURE G-19: **Viewing the merged cell**

The Happy Apple Fundraiser		
Store Locations	Number of Apples Sold	Total Amount Donated
Presque Isle, Maine	550	$1,100.00
Bangor, Maine	360	$720.00
Burlington, Vermont	471	$942.00
Concord, New Hampshire	292	$584.00
Hartford, Connecticut	379	$758.00
Cambridge, Massachusetts	650	$1,300.00

Merged cell

FIGURE G-20: **Viewing the split cell**

The Happy Apple Fundraiser			
Store Locations	Number of Apples Sold	Total Amount Donated	
Presque Isle, Maine	550	$1,100.00	
Bangor, Maine	360	$720.00	
Burlington, Vermont	471	$942.00	
Concord, New Hampshire	292	$584.00	
Hartford, Connecticut	379	$758.00	
Cambridge, Massachusetts	650	$1,300.00	
Total	2,702		

Setting Tabs in a Table

Tab stops are ruler settings that work together with the [Tab] key to allow you to position, or **justify**, text at specific horizontal locations within a text box or table cell. Using tab alignments, you can left-, right-, or center-justify text. You can also align numbers by their decimal point using the Align to Decimal button. You use the Align to Decimal button to align the dollar amounts in the third column of the table.

STEPS

1. **Click the Type tool T. on the Tools panel, if necessary, then drag from the second cell of the third column ($1,100.00) through the remaining six cells in the column**
   The text in the second cell and in all cells beneath it in the column is selected.

2. **Click Type on the Menu bar, then click Tabs**
   The Tabs panel appears directly above the selected text, as shown in Figure G-21. The Tabs panel includes a ruler and four alignment buttons in its upper-left corner.

3. **Click the Align to Decimal button ↓ on the Tabs panel, then click directly above the 1-inch mark on the ruler on the Tabs panel**
   As shown in Figure G-22, the Align to Decimal tab stop appears in the ruler. The numbers in the column shift to the right and are aligned by their decimal points at the location of the Align to Decimal tab stop. The text "1 in" in the X text box on the Tabs panel indicates the location of the selected tab stop.

4. **Drag the Align to Decimal tab stop on the ruler to the right to approximately the 1.25-inch mark in order to move the aligned numbers to a new position**
   The numbers in the selected cells move $^1\!/_4"$ to the right. The information in the right half of the split cell also moves $^1\!/_4"$ to the right.

5. **Select just the cell that contains Goal: $3,000.00, drag the Align to Decimal tab stop down and off of the tab ruler to remove the tab setting for this cell, close the Tabs panel, then deselect all**
   Dragging a tab stop out of the ruler removes the tab stop for the selected text only.

6. **Select all of the numbers in the second column, click Type on the Menu bar, click Tabs, then set an Align to Decimal tab stop at the 1-inch mark**

7. **Close the Tabs panel, select the second row, click the Font Style list arrow on the Control panel, then click Bold Italic to format the column headings**

8. **Deselect all, press [W] to switch to Preview mode, then compare your finished table to Figure G-23**

9. **Save your work, then exit InDesign**
   You can also type a number in the X text box to place the selected tab stop type at that spot on the ruler.

FIGURE G-21: **Tabs panel above selected text**

Tab buttons

Ruler

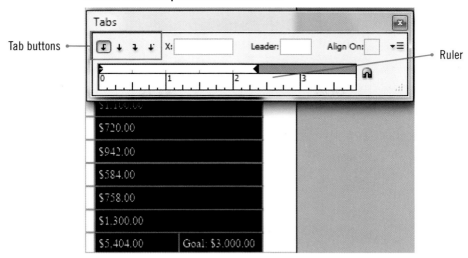

FIGURE G-22: **Align to Decimal tab set**

X text box

Align to
Decimal button

Align to Decimal
tab stop

1-inch mark
on ruler

Numbers are
aligned by
decimal point

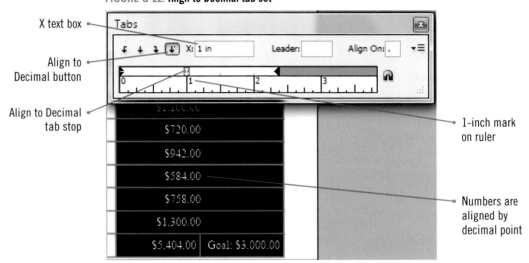

FIGURE G-23: **Finished table**

The Happy Apple Fundraiser			
Store Locations	*Number of Apples Sold*	*Total Amount Donated*	
Presque Isle, Maine	550	$1,100.00	
Bangor, Maine	360	$720.00	
Burlington, Vermont	471	$942.00	
Concord, New Hampshire	292	$584.00	
Hartford, Connecticut	379	$758.00	
Cambridge, Massachusetts	650	$1,300.00	
Total	2,702	$5,404.00	Goal: $3,000.00

Practice

Concepts Review

Label the elements of the InDesign screen shown in Figure G-24.

FIGURE G-24

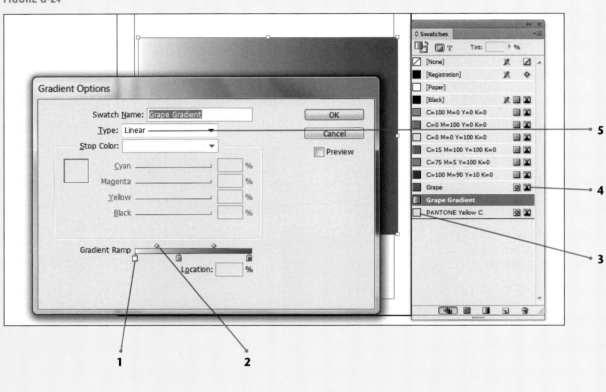

1. _____   4. _____
2. _____   5. _____
3. _____

Match each term with the statement that best describes it.

6. **Merge**
7. **Linear**
8. **Color stop**
9. **Spot color**
10. **Process color**

a. A type of gradient fill
b. Made from cyan, magenta, yellow, and/or black
c. Found on the Gradient Ramp
d. A color made by an ink manufacturer
e. Combining two or more table cells

Select the best answer from the list of choices.

11. **Which of the following are associated with table columns and rows?**
    - **a.** Alternating fills
    - **b.** Exact width or height measurements
    - **c.** Borders
    - **d.** All of the above

12. **What is the Gradient Swatch tool used for?**
    - **a.** Create a gradient
    - **b.** Change a gradient
    - **c.** Apply a gradient
    - **d.** None of the above

13. **What are process inks used for?**
    - **a.** Web graphics
    - **b.** Color printing
    - **c.** Multimedia
    - **d.** Creating spot colors

14. **What is Pantone an example of?**
    - **a.** Process color
    - **b.** Process match
    - **c.** Manufacturer of spot colors
    - **d.** CMYK color

15. **Which of the following steps do you perform to add a new color stop to the Gradient Ramp?**
    - **a.** Click just below the Gradient Ramp
    - **b.** Double-click the far-left color stop
    - **c.** Double-click the first color stop
    - **d.** Click the Gradient Panel menu button, then click New Color Stop

Skills Review

1. **Create a process color.**
   a. Start InDesign, open ID G-2.indd, then save it as **fall schedule_ID-G**.
   b. Click Window on the Menu bar, point to Workspace, then click Essentials or, if Essentials is already selected, click Reset Essentials.
   c. Click the Swatches panel button to open the Swatches panel, then drag the lower-right corner of the Swatches panel down so that you can see all of the colors in it.
   d. Click the Swatches Panel menu button, then click New Color Swatch.
   e. Type **0** in the Cyan text box if necessary, press [Tab], type **45**, press [Tab], type **100**, press [Tab], then type **0**.
   f. Click the Name with Color Value check box to remove the check mark, then type **Pumpkin Orange** in the Swatch Name text box.
   g. Click OK to close the New Color Swatch dialog box, click the far-left leaf, click the Fill tool on the Tools panel if necessary, click Pumpkin Orange on the Swatches panel, then deselect the leaf.
   h. Click Color on the right side of the workspace to open the Color panel, then notice the CMYK combination for the Pumpkin Orange color swatch.
   i. On the Swatches panel, create a new process color: **0%** Cyan, **25%** Magenta, **100%** Yellow, and **0%** Black.
   j. Name the color **Gold**, click OK, apply the Gold fill color to the middle leaf, then select the middle leaf.
   k. Create a third new process color using **25%** Cyan, **100%** Magenta, **100%** Yellow, and **0%** Black.
   l. Name the color **Rust**, click OK, then apply the Rust fill color to the far-right leaf.
   m. Deselect the far-right leaf, then save your work.

2. **Select a spot color.**
   a. Click the Swatches Panel menu button, click New Color Swatch, click the Color Type list arrow, then click Spot.
   b. Click the Color Mode list arrow, then click PANTONE+ Solid Coated.
   c. Click the PANTONE text box, type **1605**, then click OK to close the New Color Swatch dialog box.
   d. Open the Color panel and notice the spot color along with its process match.
   e. Click the stem on the far-left leaf, press and hold [Shift], click the other two leaf stems in the document, then release [Shift].
   f. On the Swatches panel, click PANTONE 1605 C, deselect all, then save your work.

Skills Review (continued)

3. Create a gradient.

  a. Click the Swatches Panel menu button, then click New Gradient Swatch.

  b. Click the first color stop on the Gradient Ramp in the New Gradient Swatch dialog box, click the Stop Color list arrow, click Swatches if necessary, then click Gold in the list of swatches.

  c. Click just below the Gradient Ramp anywhere between the first color stop and the second color stop to add a new color stop, then drag the new color stop until you see approximately 50% in the Location text box.

  d. Click the new color stop, click the Stop Color list arrow, then click Swatches.

  e. Click Pumpkin Orange in the list of swatches, click the third color stop, then click Rust in the list of swatches.

  f. Click OK to close the dialog box.

  g. Click the Selection tool if necessary, click the middle leaf, then click New Gradient Swatch on the Swatches panel.

  h. Click Window on the Menu bar, point to Color, click Gradient to see the selected gradient on the Gradient panel, close the Gradient panel, then save your work.

4. Use the Gradient Swatch tool.

  a. Verify that the middle leaf is still selected, then click the Gradient Swatch tool on the Tools panel.

  b. Position the Gradient Swatch tool approximately at the bottom of the stem, drag straight up to the approximate middle of the leaf, then release the mouse button. (*Hint*: The top points of the leaf are rust-colored.)

  c. Click the Selection tool, deselect all, then save your work.

5. Create a table.

  a. Click the Type tool, then create a text box below the three leaves that is 6 inches wide and 3.5 inches tall and whose bottom edge snaps to the bottom margin guide.

  b. Show the Align panel, align the text box to the horizontal center of the page, then close the Align panel. (*Hint*: Select Align to Page in the Align panel.)

  c. Click the Type tool if necessary, click inside the text box, click Table on the Menu bar, then click Insert Table.

  d. Type **6** in the Body Rows text box, press [Tab], type **3** if necessary, then click OK.

  e. Position the mouse pointer on the top edge of the first column of the table so that the pointer becomes a black arrow, then click to select the column.

  f. Position the mouse pointer on the upper-left corner of the table so that the mouse pointer becomes a diagonal black arrow, then click to select the table.

  g. Click in the top cell of the first table column, type **Weekday**, press [Tab], type **Name of Class**, press [Tab], type **Drop-In Cost**, then press [Tab].

  h. Enter the following text in the remaining table cells, then save your work.

Monday	Pilates	$18.00
Tuesday	Hatha Yoga	$16.00
Wednesday	Ballet Stretch	$12.00
Thursday	Vinyasa Yoga	$16.00
Friday	Zumba	$20.00

6. Format table cells.

  a. Select the entire table, click Table on the Menu bar, point to Cell Options, then click Rows and Columns.

  b. Click the Row Height list arrow, then click Exactly.

  c. Double-click the value in the Row Height text box, type **.375**, press [Tab], then select the Preview check box.

  d. Click the Text tab in the Cell Options dialog box, click the Align list arrow, then click Align Center.

  e. Click the Strokes and Fills tab, click the Weight list arrow, click 1 pt if necessary, click the Color list arrow, click Pumpkin Orange, click OK, deselect the table, press [W] to switch to Preview mode, then save your work.

Skills Review (continued)

7. Insert, merge, and split table cells.

a. Press [W] to switch to Normal mode, click the Type tool if necessary, select the top table row, click Table on the Menu bar, point to Insert, click Row, click the Above option button if necessary, then click OK.

b. Select the new row, then click the Merge cells button on the Control panel.

c. Click the merged cell, type **Fall Class Schedule**, change the font size of the text in the merged cell to 24 pt, click the Align center button on the Control panel, then deselect all.

d. Select the bottom table row, click Table on the Menu bar, point to Insert, click Row, click the Below option button in the Insert Row(s) dialog box, then click OK.

e. Click the first cell of the bottom row, type **Saturday**, press [Tab], type **Nia**, then press [Tab].

f. Click Table on the Menu bar, point to Select, then click Cell.

g. Click Table on the Menu bar, click Split Cell Vertically, then deselect the cell.

h. Click the left side of the split cell, type **$14.00**, press [Tab], type **Two classes**, then save your work.

8. Set tabs in a table.

a. Click the Type tool if necessary, drag from the second cell of the third column ($18.00) through the remaining six cells in the column, then click Type on the Menu bar, then click Tabs.

b. Click the Align to Decimal button on the Tabs panel if necessary, then click directly above the 0.5-inch mark on the ruler on the Tabs panel.

c. Select only the cell that contains "Two classes," then drag the Align to Decimal tab stop down and off of the ruler to remove the tab stop for this cell only, close the Tabs panel, then deselect all.

d. Select the first row of the table, click the Font Style list arrow on the Control panel, click Bold Italic to format the title, deselect all, press [W], then compare your finished table to Figure G-25.

e. Save your work, close fall schedule_ID-G.indd, then exit InDesign.

Fall Class Schedule			
Weekday	Name of Class	Drop-In Cost	
Monday	Pilates	$18.00	
Tuesday	Hatha Yoga	$16.00	
Wednesday	Ballet Stretch	$12.00	
Thursday	Vinyasa Yoga	$16.00	
Friday	Zumba	$20.00	
Saturday	Nia	$14.00	Two classes

© 2013 Cengage Learning

Independent Challenge 1

You are a textbook cover designer, and you have been asked to design the cover for a 10th grade math book. You first want to create a palette of three vibrant colors that work well together and that you will use when you design the cover.

a. Start InDesign, create a new default document, then save it as **textbook colors_ID-G**.

b. Create three rectangles on the page that are 3 inches wide and 2 inches tall.

c. Create three new colors and name them in the Swatches panel. Create colors that you think would appeal to the audience, then apply each new color as a fill color to one of the rectangles.

d. Overlap the rectangles in any arrangement to demonstrate how the colors look together.

e. Save your work, press [W], then compare your screen to Figure G-26.

FIGURE G-26

InDesign CS6

Independent Challenge 1 (continued)

Advanced Challenge Exercise

- Select all three rectangles, then press and hold [Alt] (Win) or [option] (Mac) while you drag them below to create a copy.
- Create a tint swatch for each of the three new colors, using 75% for each tint swatch.
- Apply the three tint swatches to the copied rectangles, then save your work.

f. Close textbook colors_ID-G.indd, then exit InDesign.

Independent Challenge 2

You're creating an ad for a local car dealer. You create colorful gradient fill for the balloon graphic.

a. Start InDesign, open ID G-3.indd, then save it as **car ad_ID-G**.

b. Create two new process colors and name them on the Swatches panel.

c. Select two PANTONE solid coated spot colors and save them on the Swatches panel.

d. Apply the four new colors to four of the balloons.

e. Using the four new colors, create a new four-color, radial gradient swatch and name it **Balloon Gradient**.

f. Apply the Balloon Gradient as the fill color to the last unfilled balloon in the document.

g. Use the Gradient Swatch tool to change the highlight point by clicking the balloon anywhere but center.

h. Save your work, press [W], then compare your screen to Figure G-27. (*Hint*: Your balloons will differ.)

FIGURE G-27

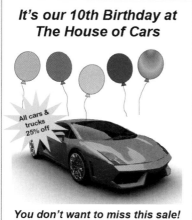

Advanced Challenge Exercise

- Click the Type tool, then select all of the text in the text box at the top of the document.
- Click the Balloon Gradient on the Swatches panel.
- Select all of the text in the text box at the bottom of the document, then apply the Balloon Gradient swatch to the text.
- Click the Selection tool, select the balloon with the gradient fill, then double-click the Gradient Feather tool.
- Change the Opacity of the first color stop to 50%, change the Opacity of the second color stop to 75%, click OK, deselect all, then save your work.

i. Close car ad_ID-G.indd, then exit InDesign.

Independent Challenge 3

The local high school lacrosse team needs new equipment and uniforms. As the volunteer manager of the team, you plan to present a document outlining the needs of the team to the school budget committee. You plan to incorporate the team colors, aqua and gray, into the document. You use a table in InDesign to present the information.

a. Start InDesign, create a new 8.5" × 11" document with 1-inch margins, without facing pages, and with Portrait orientation, then save the document with the name **lacrosse_ID-G**.

b. Create a text box that snaps to all four margin guides.

c. Insert a table in the text box with seven rows and three columns.

Independent Challenge 3 (continued)

d. Enter the following text in the first seven rows. (*Hint*: Include the header row.)

Quantity	Equipment	Price (each)
12	Lacrosse sticks	$87.00
12	Lacrosse helmets	$109.00
12	Team jerseys	$26.00
12	Arm pads	$35.00
12	Lacrosse shorts	$24.99

e. Merge the first two cells in the bottom row, type **Total** in the merged cell, press [Tab], then type **$3,383.88**.

f. Select the table, then change the cell height to exactly 1 inch.

g. Change the text alignment to Center, change the font size of all text in the table to 18 pt, then center-align the cells in the Quantity and Equipment columns.

h. Insert a new row above the top row, merge the new row, type **Fairbanks High School Lacrosse Team**, center the new heading, then change the font size to 24 pt.

i. Create two new process colors named **Aqua** and **Light Gray**. (*Hint*: Apply your own CMYK percentages.)

j. Click Table on the Menu bar, point to Table Options, then click Alternating Fills.

k. Apply alternating fills using 100% Light Gray and 10% Aqua for all rows.

l. Apply the Aqua color to the heading text, then add Aqua, 2-pt borders around each cell in the table.

m. Use an Align to Decimal tab stop to align all of the amounts in the third column and then center-align the "Price (each)" text above the amounts.

n. Save your work, then press [W].

o. Compare your screen to Figure G-28, close lacrosse_ID-G.indd, then exit InDesign.

FIGURE G-28

Fairbanks High School Lacrosse Team		
Quantity	Equipment	Price (each)
12	Lacrosse sticks	$87.00
12	Lacrosse helmets	$109.00
12	Team jerseys	$26.00
12	Arm pads	$35.00
12	Lacrosse shorts	$24.99
Total		$3,383.88

Real Life Independent Challenge

Tables are a great tool to help you organize information. Use InDesign to create a table of your weekly schedule. You can include school, work, and/or all extracurricular activities, such as exercise classes, meetings, and tasks.

a. Start InDesign, create a new document with 1-inch margins, without facing pages, and with Landscape orientation, then name it **weekly schedule_ID-G**.

b. Create an 9" × 5" text box that snaps to the left and right margin guides.

c. Insert a table in the text box that has five rows and five columns.

d. Type the days of the week from Monday through Friday in the five cells in the first row, then fill the cells below the column headings with your activities for each day, such as **School 7-2**. (*Hint*: You do not have to add times to each item or use all of the rows. If you run out of rows, you can add more by clicking in the last cell of the last column, then pressing [Tab].)

e. Insert a new row above row 1, merge the cells in row 1, then type **My Schedule** in the merged cell.

f. Delete any extra rows, if necessary, then format the text as you like.

g. Format the cells using the Cell Options dialog box (use color), save your work, then exit InDesign.

Visual Workshop

Start InDesign and create a new 8.5" × 11" document without facing pages. Save the document as **rainbow gradient_ID-G**. Using Figure G-29 as a guide, create a rectangle and place it just above the approximate center of the page. Create a color swatch named **Orange** from 0% Cyan, 50% Magenta, 100% Yellow, and 0% Black. Create a linear gradient named **Rainbow** using the Orange swatch and the default red, yellow, green, and blue colors on the Swatches panel. (*Hint*: Orange should appear in the gradient between red and yellow.) Space each color stop 25% to the right of the previous color stop on the Gradient Ramp. Select the blue color stop on the Gradient Ramp, compare your screen to Figure G-29, save your work, then exit InDesign.

FIGURE G-29

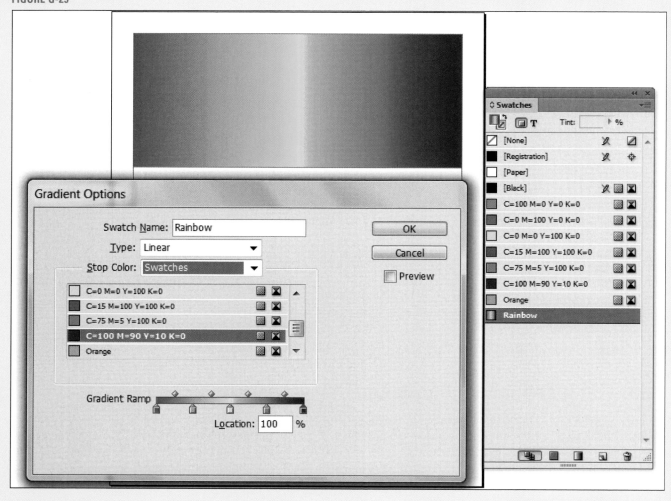

Working with Color and Tables

Integration

InDesign CS6

Adding Interactivity

Files You Will Need:

To view a list of files needed for this unit, see the Data Files Grid in the back of the book.

Interactive documents include buttons and links that you click to visit specific sections in a document, website, or digital publication. Imagine viewing a college catalog online; you could click a link for only those schools that are in a specific part of the country or only those schools that offer a culinary program. In InDesign, you can build interactivity into a document by adding buttons, hyperlinks, and animation. You can also program buttons to play sounds and video. When you export the document as a PDF or a Flash Player file, the interactive elements become active. You can open PDF files in Adobe Reader and view Flash Player files in a web browser. The Happy Apple website is created in InDesign. It has been recently updated with new content and events including a fundraiser to benefit an animal shelter. Ted asks you to incorporate the necessary interactive elements to complete the job. You create a variety of buttons and hyperlinks using the interactive features in InDesign.

OBJECTIVES

Creating a hyperlink

Testing a hyperlink

Creating a button

Creating a rollover and a click appearance

Creating an animation

Assigning a Go To State action to a button

Exporting a document as a Flash Player file

Creating a Hyperlink

A **hyperlink** is an interactive element that takes you from one place in a document or on a web page to another place. That place may be a new document, a website, a different web page, or an email window. You use the Hyperlinks panel to create a hyperlink. A hyperlink can appear as rectangle or it can be invisible. A hyperlink requires a source and a destination. The **source**—the actual link that a user will click—can be a text selection, a text frame, or a graphics frame. The **destination** is the place the source jumps to. Hyperlinks are only active in InDesign documents that have been exported as Adobe PDF or SWF files, although you can test them on the Hyperlinks panel. Your first job is to add a hyperlink to the name of the animal shelter. The hyperlink will take viewers to the animal shelter's website.

STEPS

1. **Start InDesign, open the file ID H-1.indd, then save it as happy apple website_ID-H**
   The layout for The Happy Apple website opens with text and pictures.

2. **Click the workspace switcher on the Menu bar, then click Digital Publishing**
   The Digital Publishing workspace offers useful panels for creating websites and other digital publications.

3. **Click the Zoom tool 🔍 on the Tools panel, then zoom in on the picture of the dog and text, as shown in Figure H-1**

4. **Click the Type tool T on the Tools panel, then highlight the text Buddy Dog Humane Society**

5. **Click the Hyperlinks panel icon to open the Hyperlinks panel**
   The Hyperlinks panel opens in the workspace.

6. **Click the Hyperlinks Panel menu button, then click New Hyperlink**
   The New Hyperlink dialog box opens, as shown in Figure H-2. In the dialog box, you can choose the type of link, such as a URL, the name of the destination, and the appearance of the hyperlink. Notice that the Appearance section describes the physical characteristics that will be used for the hyperlink. You can choose whether you want the hyperlink to be visible or not. By default, hyperlinks are invisible rectangles.

7. **Click the Link To list arrow, click URL, if necessary, then click the Shared Hyperlink Destination check box to remove the check mark**
   A **Uniform Resource Locator (URL)** is the address of a website on the Internet.

8. **Click after the // in the Destination URL text box, then type www.buddydoghs.com**
   The URL, www.buddydoghs.com, the Buddy Dog Humane Society website, is the destination for the hyperlink. The hyperlink will appear on top of the selected text as an invisible rectangle.

9. **Click the Style list arrow, then click Blue Underline**
   Blue Underline is a character style that was created in this document. All character styles in an InDesign document are available in the New Hyperlink dialog box.

10. **Click OK to close the New Hyperlink dialog box, then save your work**
    The New Hyperlink dialog box closes. The hyperlink has been added to the document on top of the high-lighted text, but it is invisible because its appearance is set to Invisible Rectangle. The Blue Underline style is applied to the text. You will test the hyperlink in the next lesson.

FIGURE H-1: Zooming in on photo of dog and text

Help Support a Pup
For the entire month of May, The Happy Apple is collecting donations for the Buddy Dog Humane Society. Make your donations at the store or online. Click here to see our progress.

Original content Ann Fisher

FIGURE H-2: New Hyperlink dialog box

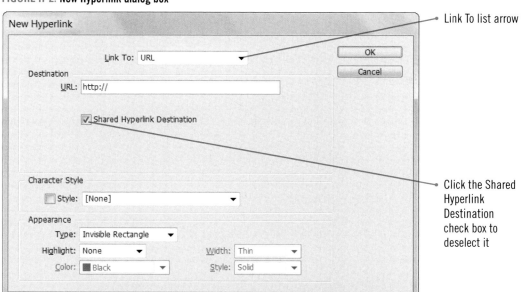

Link To list arrow

Click the Shared Hyperlink Destination check box to deselect it

Using the Web swatch library

If you use InDesign to create pages or graphics for the web, you should apply color from the Web swatch library to the objects in your documents in order for them to display correctly on the web. Colors in the Web swatch library are displayed the same on both Windows and Macintosh computers, and are all made from a combination of RGB instead of CMYK. To access the Web swatch library, click the Swatches Panel menu button, click New Color Swatch, click the Color Type list arrow, click Spot, click the Color Mode list arrow, then click Web.

Testing a Hyperlink

Hyperlinks only work in an exported document, whether it is an interactive PDF or a Shockwave Flash file. However, you can test a link in InDesign using the Hyperlinks panel. To test a hyperlink, you first select the name of the hyperlink on the Hyperlinks panel, then click the right arrow button, called the *Go to destination of the selected hyperlink or cross-reference button*. The destination will open in a new window. The left arrow button called the *Go to source of the selected hyperlink or cross-reference button*, highlights the source of the active hyperlink on the Hyperlinks panel. This is useful if you have multiple hyperlinks and cannot figure out their sources. You are now ready to test the hyperlink using the Hyperlinks panel.

STEPS

1. **Click the Selection tool ▶ on the Tools panel, then click the page to deselect the highlighted text**

   The text is formatted with the Blue Underline style. The hyperlink is above the text and is invisible.

2. **Click Buddy Dog Humane Society on the Hyperlinks panel to highlight it**

   The URL for the hyperlink appears in the URL text box in the panel, as shown in Figure H-3.

3. **Click the Go to destination of the selected hyperlink or cross-reference button ⇨ on the Hyperlinks panel**

   The Buddy Dog Humane Society website opens in the browser, as shown in Figure H-4. Your window may slightly differ from the figure.

4. **Close the browser, then close the Hyperlinks panel**

5. **Save your work**

Working with effects

You can apply 10 effects to InDesign objects from the Object Effects menu. The Effects dialog box opens with the effect that you chose both highlighted and checked on the left side of the dialog box. The main panel of the dialog box displays all of the possible settings for that effect. The settings that you first see are the default settings. For example, the Drop Shadow settings use a 75% opaque black color for the shadow. Each effect has dials, check boxes, menus, and text boxes for you to use to enter new setting values. You can preview the changes by clicking the Preview check box in the lower-left corner of the dialog box. If you want to apply an effect just to an object's stroke, fill, or text, click the Settings for list arrow above the list of effects on the left side of the dialog box, then click Fill, Stroke, or Text.

You can apply more than one effect to an object at a time. Click the effect check box or highlight the effect name to choose that effect. If you click the effect check box, the main panel continues to display the settings for the highlighted effect, even if it's not the one whose check box you just selected. In this case, the new effect is added to the object using InDesign's default settings. However, if you click the name of the effect, the effect is highlighted and its corresponding check box is automatically checked. The main panel displays the settings for the highlighted effect, allowing you to modify the new effect's settings while adding it to the object. To remove an effect, remove the check mark next to the effect name. The Transparency effect does not have a check box. Simply click Transparency to apply it, and deselect it to remove it. Effects are listed on the Effects panel after they are applied to an object.

FIGURE H-3: Hyperlink to Buddy Dog Humane Society

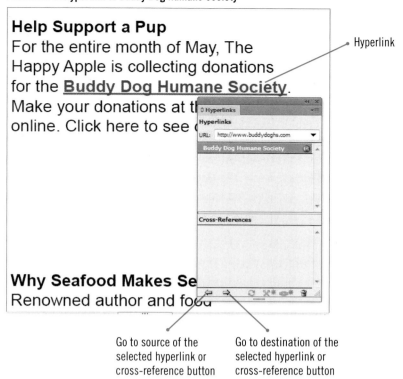

Hyperlink

Go to source of the selected hyperlink or cross-reference button

Go to destination of the selected hyperlink or cross-reference button

FIGURE H-4: Buddy Dog Humane Society website

Website Buddy Dog Humane Society (www.buddydoghs.com)

Creating a Button

In InDesign, a **button** refers to an interactive, clickable item that becomes active when the document is exported as an interactive Portable Document Format (PDF) or SWF file. You can create a button using just about any object in InDesign. You can use a shape, a placed image, or even a text box as a button. To create a new button, select the object that you would like to use as a button, then click the Convert to Button command on the Object menu. The Buttons and Forms panel opens, prompting you to choose an action and an event for the new button. The **event** refers to the required treatment of the button, such as a rollover or a click, and the **action** refers to what will happen as a result of the action, such as opening a web page. ▰▰▰▰ Each week, The Happy Apple website features one of the dogs or cats available for adoption from the pet shelter. You create a button that will show the pet of the week.

STEPS

1. **Click** File **on the Menu bar, click** Place, **navigate to the drive and folder where your Data Files are stored, click** Puppy Button.ai, **click** Open, **then click the** page **to place the button**
   A button appears next to dog photo.

2. **Click the** Selection tool ▶ **on the Tools panel, drag the** puppy button **to the location shown in Figure H-5, then deselect the button**
   The button may appear blurry because the zoom level is high. Change the display performance to High Quality, if necessary.

3. **Click the** puppy button **to select it**
   Next, you will convert the button artwork to an interactive button.

QUICK TIP
You can also convert an object to a button by clicking the Convert Button button 🔲 on the Buttons and Forms panel. You can convert a button back into an object by clicking the Convert Object button 🔲 on the Buttons and Forms panel.

4. **Click** Object **on the Menu bar, point to** Interactive, **then click** Convert to Button
   The Buttons and Forms panel opens, displaying the button with the name Button followed by a number in its Normal appearance; the way it will look on the website or in a PDF document before it is clicked. The Buttons and Forms panel allows you to create a button name, and choose an action and an event for the button. As shown in Figure H-6, a dashed border appears around the button artwork, indicating that the graphic is now a button.

5. **Highlight the text in the Name text box, then type** For Adoption button

6. **Click the** Event list arrow, **then click** On Click
   The On Click event is assigned to the button, indicating that users must click the button to trigger an action. You assign an event that will jump to a new web page and show a picture of a dog that is available for adoption.

QUICK TIP
You can remove an action by clicking the Delete selected action button ➖ on the Buttons and Forms panel.

7. **Click the** Add new action for selected event button 🔳 **on the Buttons and Forms panel, then click** Go To Next Page
   When the button is clicked in the exported document, page 2 of the InDesign document will open. Page 2 represents another web page in The Happy Apple website. In a later lesson, you will export the file as a **Shockwave Flash (SWF)** file and test the button.

8. **Save your work**

Adding sample buttons

In a multipage document that users will view in Adobe Reader or Adobe Acrobat or on the web, you may need to create buttons for the viewer to use to navigate through the document or to view additional information. InDesign comes with preset buttons stored in the Sample Buttons panel that can help you easily add this interactivity. Each button is programmed with a prewritten script, called an action, that runs when the user clicks the button or moves the mouse pointer over it. To access the Sample Buttons panel, click the Buttons and Forms panel menu button, then click Sample Buttons and Forms.

FIGURE H-5: **Placing the button artwork**

Puppy Button.ai
placed in InDesign

FIGURE H-6: **Converting the button artwork to an InDesign button**

Dashed border   Normal appearance   Your button name
indicates button   may differ

Creating a Rollover and a Click Appearance

When you create a button, you can choose to change its appearance, or **state**, when an event takes place. For example, it's common to change the button's appearance when a user rolls the mouse over the button or when the user clicks the button. To define the new appearance, you first select the button, then click either [Rollover] or [Click] on the Buttons and Forms panel. Make the changes you would like to make to the button and you're done. The button's new appearance appears on the Buttons and Forms panel. The white apple logo in the top-left corner of the Document window is a button that will be used to swap the image of the citrus fruit to another image. You create a rollover effect for the apple button so that when a user rolls the mouse over the button, it changes from white to green. Then you change the click appearance so that when clicked, a drop shadow appears behind the apple button.

STEPS

1. **Double-click the Hand tool** 🖐 **on the Tools panel to zoom out to see the entire page**

2. **Click the Selection tool** ▶ **on the Tools panel, then click the white apple**

   The white apple has already been converted to a button in InDesign. Notice that it is listed on the Buttons and Forms panel as Apple, as shown in Figure H-7.

3. **On the Buttons and Forms panel, click [Rollover] in the Appearance section, as shown in Figure H-8, then double-click the white apple so that just the white part of the apple is selected**

   The [Rollover] appearance becomes active on the Buttons and Forms panel. You want to modify the button's appearance in its rollover state by changing its fill color to green.

4. **Click the Swatches panel icon** 🎨 **to open the Swatches panel**

5. **Scroll down, then click c50m5y100k0**

   The apple fill color changes to green. In the exported SWF file, the apple will change from white to green when the mouse pointer rolls over it.

6. **Verify that the apple button is selected, then click the [Click] appearance on the Buttons and Forms panel**

7. **Click Object on the Menu bar, point to Effects, then click Drop Shadow**

   The Effects dialog box opens with the Drop Shadow effect selected, as shown in Figure H-9. A **drop shadow** is an effect that adds the illusion of depth to an object by placing a shadow behind it. The Drop Shadow effect has many settings that you can adjust in the Effects dialog box, but the default settings are acceptable for the rollover.

8. **Click OK to accept the default settings in the Effects dialog box**

   A drop shadow appears behind the apple graphic and the preview of the apple in the [Click] section of the Buttons and Forms panel updates to show the drop shadow, as shown in Figure H-10.

9. **Save your work**

   In a later lesson, you will export the InDesign document as an SWF file and test the Rollover and Click actions.

FIGURE H-7: Viewing the Apple button on the Buttons and Forms panel

Apple button

Name of button

FIGURE H-8: Viewing the [Rollover] appearance for the Apple button

FIGURE H-9: Effects dialog box

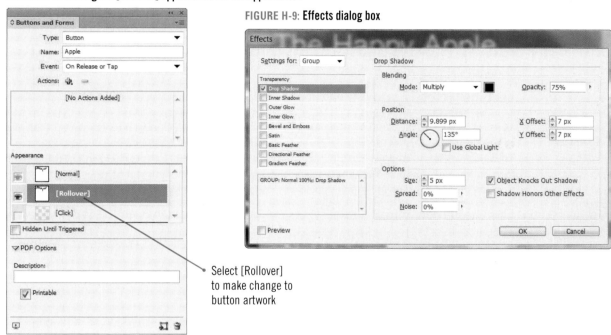

Select [Rollover] to make change to button artwork

FIGURE H-10: Viewing the Rollover and Click appearances on the Buttons and Forms panel

Drop shadow effect

Rollover appearance

Click appearance

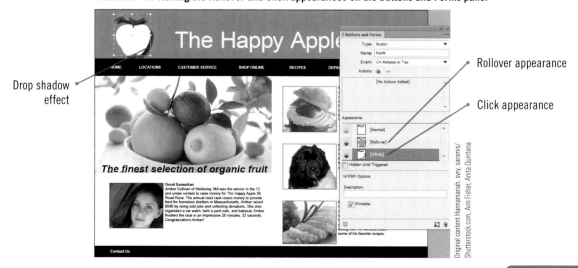

Adding Interactivity

Creating an Animation

Animation is an effect that you can apply to an InDesign object to cause it to move in a specific way, such spin or bounce. Animating objects can add a lot of fun and visual interest to an InDesign document. Using the Animation panel is easy; you select the object that you wish to animate, then choose a type of animation from the Preset menu on the Animation panel. You can choose how many seconds the animation should last, how many times it should occur, and the event that will cause it to occur. The Animation panel uses a pink butterfly to represent the selected InDesign object that is being animated. The motion of the butterfly mimics how the InDesign object will animate when exported. Before exporting the InDesign document, you can preview how animated objects will behave using the SWF Preview panel. You animate the apple to zoom in when the web page loads in the browser. You then preview the animation on the SWF Preview panel.

STEPS

1. **Select the apple on the artboard**

2. **Click the Animation panel icon to open the Animation panel**
   The Animation panel opens in the workspace.

3. **Notice that name "Apple" appears in the Name text box on the Animation panel, as shown in Figure H-11**

4. **Click the Preset list arrow, then click Zoom In (2D)**
   The butterfly shows a preview of how the apple will look when animated.

5. **Click the Event(s) list arrow, then click On Page Load, if necessary**
   The apple will zoom in once when the web page is loaded. An animation icon appears next to the button icon on the apple graphic. You can choose how many times an animation will occur by changing the value in the Play text box. You are ready to preview the animation in the SWF Preview panel

> **QUICK TIP**
> You can also **loop** an animation, which means to have it continually play without stopping, by clicking the Loop check box.

6. **Click the Preview Spread button on the Animation panel to open the SWF Preview panel**

7. **Click the Play preview button on the SWF Preview panel to preview the animation of the apple, as shown in Figure H-12**
   The apple zooms in one time when the page is loaded in the panel.

8. **Close the SWF Preview panel, then save your work**

Using the Preflight panel

When you complete a document, it is very important to find and correct any errors in the document to ensure that it prints correctly. The Preflight feature is an InDesign utility that you can use to check an open document for errors such as missing fonts, missing or modified links, and overset text. Any errors that are found are listed in the Preflight panel; you can use this list to fix any problems by substituting fonts, fixing overset text issues, and/or updating missing and modified files.

A green circle on the left side of the status bar indicates that there are no preflight errors in a document; when the circle is red, there are errors. You can create customized preflight profiles in which you indicate what you would like the Preflight panel to flag as errors to be fixed. For example, you may want InDesign to flag font sizes smaller than 12 points as an error because your document cannot contain any font sizes smaller than 12 points.

FIGURE H-11: Viewing the Animation panel

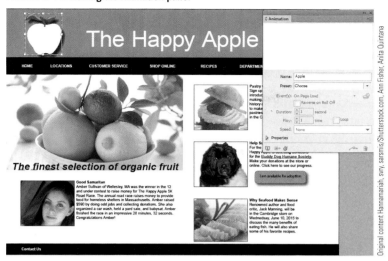

FIGURE H-12: Viewing the animation on the SWF Preview panel

SWF Preview panel

Click to preview
animation

Click to open SWF
Preview panel

Assigning a Go To State Action to a Button

Earlier in this book, you learned about object states. The ability to create multiple appearances for one object, play a big role in interactive websites and other digital publications. Each time you shop online and click buttons to view different colored versions of the same item, you are experiencing the power of object states. The Buttons and Forms panel includes an action called Go To State. All object states created in the Object States panel are listed on the Buttons and Forms panel. After choosing the Go to State action, you then choose the name of the state that should be in view when a button is clicked. ▨▨▨▨▨ You assign the Go To State action to the apple button. When clicked, the view of the citrus fruit will change to a picture of strawberries.

STEPS

1. **Click Window on the Menu bar, point to Interactive, then click Object States**
2. **Click the Selection tool ⬉ on the Tools panel, then click the large image of citrus fruit**
   As shown in Figure H-13, the citrus fruit image is a multi-state object named Fruit. It has two states associated with it, Citrus Fruit, and Strawberries.
3. **Close the Object States panel**
4. **Click the apple button, then open the Buttons and Forms panel**
5. **On the Buttons and Forms panel, select the Click appearance, click the Event list arrow, then click On Click, if necessary**
   The action will be executed once the button is clicked.
6. **Click the Add new action for selected event button ⊕, then click Go To State**
7. **Click the Object list arrow, then click Fruit, if necessary**
8. **Click the State list arrow, then click Strawberries**
   When the apple button is clicked, the Strawberries state of the Fruit object will appear in the Document window. Compare your Buttons and Forms panel to Figure H-14.
9. **Save your work**

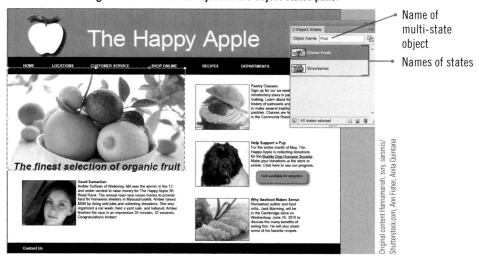

Name of
multi-state
object

Names of states

FIGURE H-14: Choosing the object and state for the Go To State action

Add new action for
selected event
button

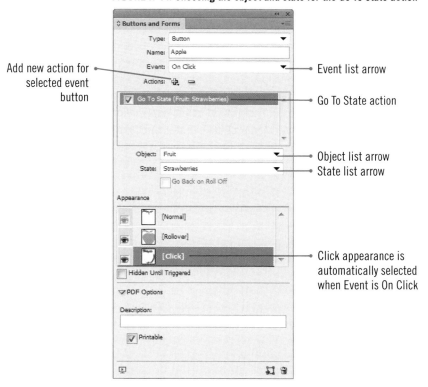

Event list arrow

Go To State action

Object list arrow

State list arrow

Click appearance is
automatically selected
when Event is On Click

Integration

Exporting a Document as a Flash Player File

Shockwave Flash (or SWF) is a very popular format for online animations and games. SWF files are scalable and compact, which makes them perfect for the web. SWF files can be viewed by anyone with Flash Player installed on his or her computer. To export an InDesign document as an SWF file, choose Flash Player (SWF) in the Save as type list (Win) or Format list (Mac) in the Export dialog box. If you wish to quickly preview an SWF file in a browser window after exporting, be sure to click the Generate HTML File check box and the View SWF After Exporting check box in the Export SWF dialog box that opens before the file export is complete. All hyperlinks and buttons are active in the exported SWF file. ░░░ You export the happy apple website_ID-H. indd document as an SWF and then view the animation and test the buttons in a browser window.

STEPS

1. **Click File on the Menu bar, then click Export**
   The Export dialog box opens.

2. **Navigate, if necessary, to the drive and folder where you store your Data Files, click the Save as type list arrow (Win) or the Format list arrow (Mac) at the bottom of the Export dialog box, then click Flash Player (SWF), if necessary**
   The .swf filename extension is added to happy apple website_ID-H in the File name (Win) or Save As text box (Mac).

3. **Click Save**
   The Export SWF dialog box opens, as shown in Figure H-15, showing the default General settings for exporting a document as an SWF file. You can change the settings depending on your needs. The Export section allows you to choose a selection, a range of pages, or all pages to export. You can also choose to view the SWF file after the export is complete. The Size section lets you control the output size of the exported file. You can choose a transparent background or the paper color of the document. Finally, you can choose to include the interactivity and media applied, or not, and any page transitions that may have been applied.

> **QUICK TIP**
> You can apply page transitions to multipage documents in the Pages panel.

4. **In the Export SWF dialog box, verify that the All Pages option button is selected and that the Paper Color option button is selected as the Background, then click OK to accept the default settings in the Export SWF dialog box**
   The SWF file opens in your default browser, as shown in Figure H-16. Notice the apple zooms in once the page is loaded.

5. **Rollover the white apple and notice that it turns green**

6. **Click the green apple and notice the drop shadow effect and the citrus fruit image change to the strawberries image**

7. **Click the Buddy Dog Humane Society hyperlink to open the Buddy Dog Humane Society website**

8. **Close the Buddy Dog Humane Society website to return to the happy apple website, then click the I am available for adoption button to view the pet of the week**

9. **Close the browser window, then exit InDesign**

Understanding Global Security

If you receive a warning in the browser, click Settings in the dialog box. In the Global security settings for content creators box, click Edit locations, click Add location, click Browse for files, navigate to where you store the file, then click Confirm. Close the browser window, then go back to InDesign and re-export the file.

FIGURE H-15: Export SWF dialog box

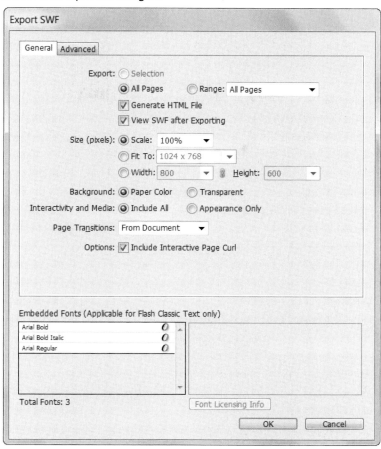

FIGURE H-16: The Happy Apple website

Practice

Concepts Review

Label the elements of the InDesign screen shown in Figure H-17.

FIGURE H-17

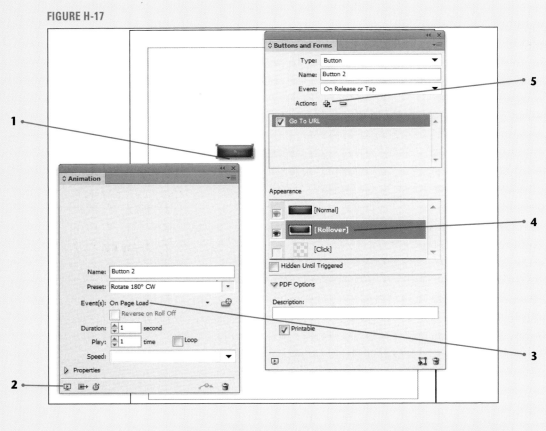

1. _____   4. _____
2. _____   5. _____
3. _____

Match each term with the statement that best describes it.

6. **Button**   a. Where the source jumps to
7. **Preset**   b. Can be visible or invisible
8. **Destination**   c. Allows you to jump to another location
9. **Action**   d. Applied to a button
10. **Hyperlink**   e. An animation style

Select the best answer from the list of choices.

11. **Which of the following is an event?**
    - **a.** On Click
    - **b.** Fly in from Right
    - **c.** Go to Next Page
    - **d.** Go To State

12. **Which of the following refers to a prewritten script?**
    - **a.** Template
    - **b.** Event
    - **c.** Destination
    - **d.** Action

13. **A hyperlink has both a destination and a _____.**
    - **a.** package
    - **b.** source
    - **c.** template
    - **d.** folder

Skills Review

1. **Create a hyperlink.**
   - **a.** Start InDesign, open the file ID H-2.indd from the drive and folder where you store your Data Files, then save it as **happy camper website_ID-H**.
   - **b.** Click the workspace switcher on the Menu bar, then click Digital Publishing.
   - **c.** Click the Zoom tool on the Tools panel, then zoom in on the picture of the boy holding the stick and the text next to it.
   - **d.** Click the Type tool, then highlight the text "ceramics studio."
   - **e.** Click the Hyperlinks panel icon to open the Hyperlinks panel.
   - **f.** Click the Hyperlinks Panel menu button, then click New Hyperlink.
   - **g.** Click the Link To list arrow, click URL, if necessary, then click the Shared Hyperlink Destination check box to remove the check mark.
   - **h.** Click after the // in the Destination text box, then type **www.clayroom.com**.
   - **i.** Click the Style list arrow, then click Blue Underline.
   - **j.** Click OK to close the New Hyperlink dialog box.

2. **Test a hyperlink**
   - **a.** Click the Selection tool on the Tools panel, then click the page to deselect the highlighted text.
   - **b.** Click ceramics studio on the Hyperlinks panel to highlight it.
   - **c.** Click the Go to destination of the selected hyperlink or cross-reference button on the Hyperlinks panel to test the hyperlink.
   - **d.** Close the browser window, then close the Hyperlinks panel.
   - **e.** Save your work.

3. **Create a button.**
   - **a.** Double-click the Hand tool to zoom out.
   - **b.** Click the Selection tool on the Tools panel, then click the Today's Yoga Pose button.
   - **c.** Click Object on the Menu bar, point to Interactive, then click Convert to Button.
   - **d.** On the Buttons and Forms panel, highlight the text in the Name text box, then type **Yoga button**
   - **e.** Click the Event list arrow, then click On Click.
   - **f.** Click the Add new action for selected event button on the Buttons panel, then click Go to Next Page.
   - **g.** Save your work.

Skills Review (continued)

4. Create a rollover and a click appearance.

   a. Double-click the Hand tool on the Tools panel to zoom out to see the entire page.

   b. Click the Selection tool on the Tools panel, then click the black and white illustration of canoes. (*Hint*: This image is a button named Canoes.)

   c. On the Buttons and Forms panel, click [Rollover] in the Appearance section.

   d. Click the Swatches panel icon to open the Swatches panel, then click the Stroke button on the Swatches panel.

   e. Scroll down in the Swatches panel, then click RGB Red.

   f. Verify that the Canoes button is selected, then click the [Click] appearance on the Buttons and Forms panel. (*Hint*: When the canoes image is rolled over in the exported .swf file, a red border will appear around the image.)

   g. Click Object on the Menu bar, point to Effects, then click Drop Shadow.

   h. Click OK to accept the default settings in the Effects dialog box.

   i. Save your work.

5. Create an animation

   a. Select the Canoes button on the artboard.

   b. Click the Animation panel icon to open the Animation panel.

   c. Notice that Canoes appears in the Name text box of the Animation panel.

   d. Click the Preset list arrow, then click Fly in from Right.

   e. Click the Event(s) list arrow, then click On Page Load, if necessary.

   f. Click the Preview Spread button on the Animation panel to open the SWF Preview panel.

   g. Click the Play preview button on the SWF Preview panel to preview the animation.

   h. Save your work, then close the SWF Preview panel.

6. Assign a Go To State action to a button.

   a. Click Window on the Menu bar, point to Interactive, then click Object States.

   b. Click the Selection tool on the Tools panel, then click the large image of the campers playing tug of war. (*Hint*: The image of tug of war is a multi-state object named Campers. It has two states associated with it, Tug of War and Hikers.)

   c. Close the Object States panel.

   d. Click the Canoes button, then open the Buttons and Forms panel.

   e. On the Buttons and Forms panel, select the Click appearance, click the Event(s) list arrow, then click On Click.

   f. Click the Add new action for selected event button, then click Go To State.

   g. Click the Object list arrow, then click Campers, if necessary.

   h. Click the State list arrow, then click Hikers.

   i. Save your work.

7. Export a document as a Flash Player File

   a. Click File on the Menu bar, then click Export.

   b. Navigate, if necessary, to the drive and folder where you store your Data Files, click the Save as type list arrow (Win) or the Format list arrow (Mac) at the bottom of the Export dialog box, then click Flash Player (SWF), if necessary.

   c. Click Save.

Skills Review (continued)

d. In the Export SWF dialog box, verify that the All Pages option button is selected and that the Paper Color option button is selected as the Background, then click OK to accept the default settings in the Export SWF dialog box.

e. Compare your website to Figure H-18.

f. Notice the Canoes button flies in from the right once the page is loaded.

g. Rollover the Canoes button and notice that it turns red.

h. Click the Canoes button and notice the drop shadow effect and the tug of war image change to the hikers image.

i. Click the ceramics studio hyperlink to open the Clayroom website.

j. Close the Clayroom website to return to the happy camper website, then click the Today's Yoga Pose button to view the daily yoga pose.

k. Close the browser window, save the document, then exit InDesign.

FIGURE H-18

Original content oliveomg, ACACA, poonsap, Digital Media Pro, Jeremy/ Shutterstock.com, Ann Fisher;

Integration

Independent Challenge 1

You've created a logo for a client, and now she would like you to make another version of it that can be used on her website as a button. She also would like you to use two new colors. You apply Web swatches to the logo and then convert it to a button.

a. Open ID H-3.indd from the drive and folder where you store your Data Files, then save it as **button_ID-H**.

b. Click the Selection tool, then click one of the green objects to select the group of green objects.

c. Open the Swatches panel, click the Swatches Panel menu button, then click New Color Swatch.

d. Click the Color Type list arrow, click Spot, click the Color Mode list arrow, then click Web.

e. Choose a color in the list of Web swatches, then click OK to close the New Color Swatch dialog box.

f. Repeat Steps b-e to change the color of the yellow group to a Web color.

g. Select both color groups, then group them together.

h. Convert the logo to a button.

i. Change the event to On Click and the action to Go To URL.

j. Click after the // in the URL text box, then type **www.course.com**.

Advanced Challenge Exercise

- Select the button.
- Click Object on the Menu bar, point to Effects, then click Bevel and Emboss.
- Click the Style list arrow, then click Pillow Emboss.
- Close the Effects dialog box.

k. Save your work, compare your button to the sample shown in Figure H-19, then close the document.

FIGURE H-19

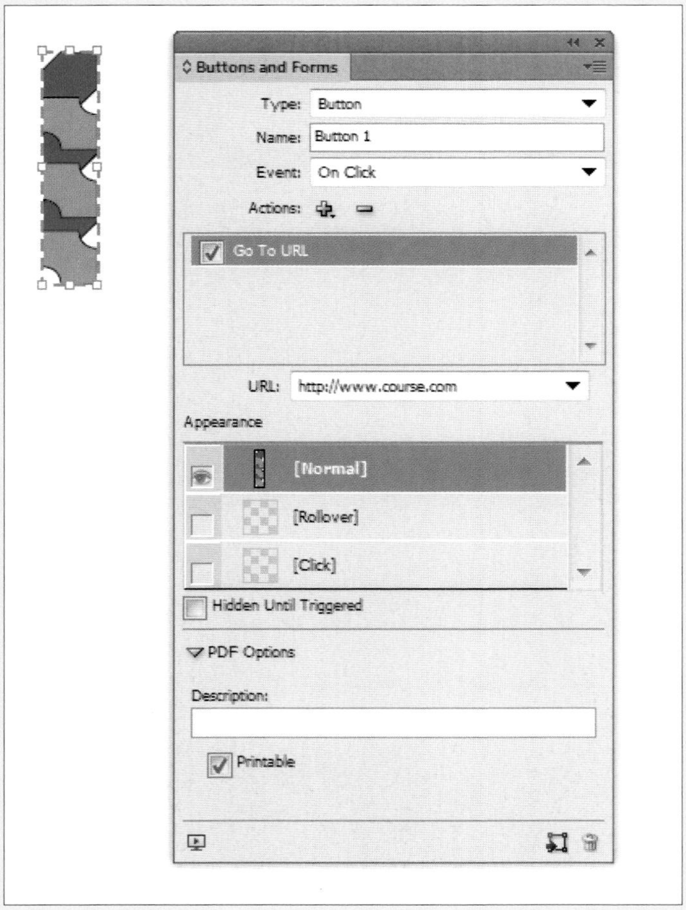

Independent Challenge 2

You've created a set of alphabet flash cards, and now you would like to promote them to an educational website. Before you send the prototype, you add interactivity to the set of cards and test out the idea in a browser.

   a. Open ID H-4.indd from the drive and folder where you store your Data Files, then save it as **web cards_ID-H**.

   b. Open the Pages panel, then double-click the A-Master to open it in the Document window.

   c. Create two buttons on the master page that viewers can click that will move to the next page be and the previous page. You can use anything as the buttons: text, small photos, or simple shapes.

   d. Name the buttons **Previous Page** and **Next Page** on the Buttons panel.

   e. For the Previous Page button, add an On Click event that will take viewers to the previous page.

   f. For the Next Page button, add an On Click event that will take viewers to the next page.

   g. Remove the Next Page button on page 26 (Z) and the Previous Page button on page 1 (A). (*Hint:* Open each page in the Document window, override all master items, then delete the respective buttons.)

   h. Save your work, then export the document as a Flash Player (SWF) file.

Advanced Challenge Exercise

- Select all of the pages in the Pages panel.
- Click the Page Panel menu button, point to Page Attributes, point to Page Transitions, then click Choose.
- Click the Uncover option button in the Page Transitions dialog box, then click OK.
- Save your work, then export the document as a Flash Player (SWF) file.
- Test your buttons and view the page transitions in the browser window.

   i. Test your buttons in the web browser, compare your screen to Figure H-20, then close the browser window.

FIGURE H-20

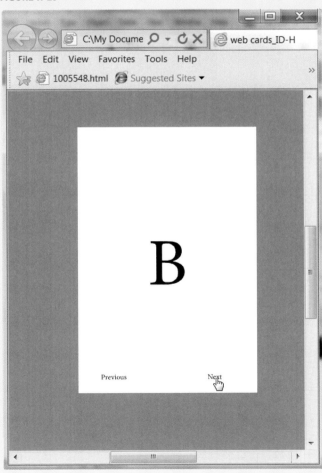

Integration

Independent Challenge 3

You volunteer each week at the local library, and each week you put together fun pages for the children's weekly story hour. The library is looking for new ideas to keep you busy, so you suggest putting the fun pages online so kids can play with them on the library website. You get to work by adding animation to the correct answers to the fun page questions.

a. Open ID H-5.indd from the drive and folder where you store your Data Files, then save it as **animation_ID-H**.

b. Select the lollipops image, then display the Animation panel.

c. Click the Preset list arrow, then click Disappear.

d. On the Animation panel, click the Event(s) list arrow, remove the check mark next to On Page Load, then choose On Roll Over (Self).

e. Click the Reverse on Roll Off check box.

f. Verify that the lollipops image is still selected, then convert the image into a button.

g. Name the button **Lollipops button**.

h. On the Buttons and Forms panel, add the On Roll Over event and then choose Animation as the action.

i. On the Buttons and Forms panel, verify that the Options setting is set to Play, then click the Reverse on Roll Off check box.

j. Export the file as a Flash Player (SWF) file, then test the button.

k. Compare your screen to Figure H-21, then close the browser window.

l. Save your work, then close animation_ID-H.indd.

FIGURE H-21

Point to the picture that does not belong with the rest of the group.

Lollipops image disappears

Original content sarsmis, Valentyn Volkov, Olena Mykhaylova, sgall, Africa Studio/Shutterstock.com

Real Life Independent Challenge

When you are planning a vacation, it is helpful to organize some of the trip's agenda so that your time is used wisely. Think of a place where you would like to go on your next vacation, and a friend or family member whom you would like to take with you. Identify four places or points of interest, or an event you'd like to attend while there. For example, if you were going to New York, you might want to attend a Broadway show, see the Empire State Building and the Statue of Liberty, or visit the Central Park Zoo. Use InDesign to create an interactive document with hyperlinks attached to the name of each point of interest. You'll then export the file as a PDF file so that you can send it to your traveling companion.

a. Start InDesign, create a new document using Letter – Half as the page size, then save it as **trip planner_ID-H** in the drive and folder where you store your Data Files.

b. Create a text box at the top of the page that includes the name of your destination.

c. Create four more text boxes below it that include the names of four points of interest.

d. Format the text to your liking.

e. Add an invisible hyperlink to each of the four text boxes that link to URLs for websites containing more information about the planned activity in the text box. (*Hint*: If you are not able to research the exact URLs for your points of interest, create made-up URLs to use in the hyperlinks.)

f. Test the hyperlinks using the Hyperlinks panel, if possible, then close any open browser windows and save your work.

g. Close trip planner_ID-H.indd, then exit InDesign.

Integration

Visual Workshop

Start InDesign, then create a new 800 px × 600 px web document. Save the document as **navigation_ID-H** in the drive and folder where you store your Data Files. Using Figure H-22 as a guide, create a 50 px × 50 px circle, then fill it with RGB Blue. Add a rollover appearance (RGB Red) and a click appearance (RGB Green). Convert the circle to a button that will play a sound when it is clicked. Compare your screen to Figure H-22, save your work, then exit InDesign.

FIGURE H-22

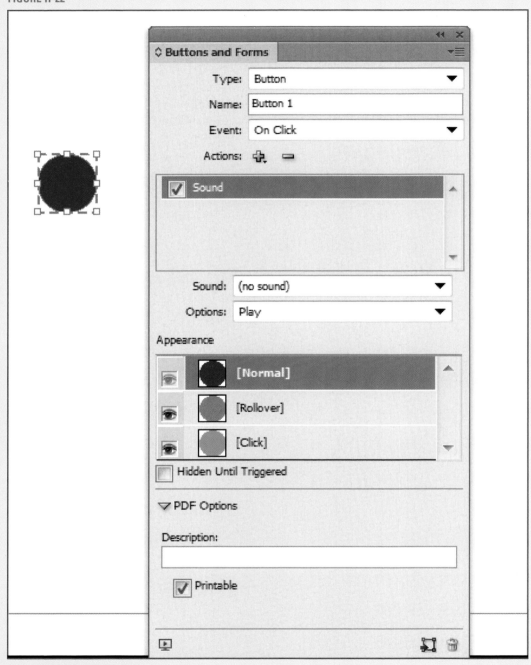

Data Files for InDesign CS6 Illustrated

To complete the lessons and practice exercises in this book, students need to use Data Files that are supplied by Cengage Learning. Below is a list of the Data Files that are supplied and the unit and practice exercise to which the files correspond. For information on how to obtain Data Files, please refer to the inside front cover of this book.

Data File Supplied	Student Creates File	Used In
UNIT A		
newsletter_ID-A.indd No Data File supplied	credit card flyer_ID-A.indd credit card flyer_ID-A.pdf	Lessons
boutique flyer_ID-A.indd No Data File supplied	cd cover_ID-A.indd cd cover_ID-A.pdf	Skills Review
No Data File supplied	postcard_ID-A.indd	Independent Challenge 1
No Data File supplied	sample_ID-A.indd sample ACE_ID-A.indd	Independent Challenge 2
ID A-1.indd	yard sale_ID-A.indd yard sale_ACE_ID-A.indd	Independent Challenge 3
No Data File supplied	n/a	Real Life IC
No Data File supplied	guides_ID-A.indd	Visual Workshop
UNIT B		
ID B-1.indd Letter.docx ID B-2.indd	november news_ID-B.indd december news_ID-B.indd	Lessons
ID B-3.indd Book News.docx ID B-4.indd	school news_ID-B.indd library news_ID-B.indd	Skills Review
Invitation Text.docx	party invitation_ID-B.indd	Independent Challenge 1
ID B-5.indd	greater outdoors_ID-B.indd greater outdoors_ACE_ID-B.indd	Independent Challenge 2
ID B-6.indd	daily specials_ID-B.indd daily specials_ACE_ID-B.indd	Independent Challenge 3
ID B-7.indd	moving sale_ID-B.indd moving sale_ACE_ID-B.indd	Real Life IC
ID B-8.indd	gingerbread house_ID-B.indd	Visual Workshop

Data File Supplied	Student Saves File As	Used In
UNIT C		
ID C-1.indd	ski trip_ID-C.indd	Lessons
ID C-2.indd	hang gliding_ID-C.indd	Skills Review
ID C-3.indd	color samples_ID-C.indd	Independent Challenge 1
ID C-4.indd	thank you_ID-C.indd thank you_ACE_ID-C.indd	Independent Challenge 2
No Data File supplied	services_ID-C.indd services_ACE_ID-C.indd	Independent Challenge 3
No Data File supplied	business card_ID-C.indd	Real Life Independent Challenge
No Data File supplied	bars_ID-C.indd	Visual Workshop
UNIT D		
ID D-1.indd ID D-2.indd pizza.psd sushi.psd sushi 2.psd	graphics_ID-D.indd specials_ID-D.indd	Lessons
ID D-3.indd ID D-4.indd green grapes.psd red grapes.psd oranges.psd	examples_ID-D.indd organic fruit_ID-D.indd	Skills Review
ID D-5.indd cat.psd	cat tree_ID-D.indd	Independent Challenge 1
ID D-6.indd watermelon.psd green grapes.psd citrus fruit.psd strawberries.psd lollipops.psd red grapes.psd	fun pages_ID-D.indd fun pages_ACE_ID-D.indd	Independent Challenge 2
ID D-7.indd watermelon.psd green grapes.psd citrus fruit.psd strawberries.psd oranges.psd red grapes.psd	smoothies_ID-D.indd cookbook images_ID-D.indl cookbook images_ACE_ID-D.indl	Independent Challenge 3
No Data File supplied tree.psd	cd cover_ID-D.indd	Real Life Independent Challenge
No Data File supplied horse.psd	horses_ID-D.indd	Visual Workshop

Data File Supplied	Student Saves File As	Used In
UNIT E		
No Data File supplied adventure.psd camp.psd computer.psd dance.psd canoe.psd sports.psd sewing.psd	camp booklet_ID-E.indd	Lessons
No Data File supplied apple pie.psd cupcakes.psd parfait.psd strawberry shortcake.psd chocolate cake.psd	desserts_ID-E.indd	Skills Review
No Data File supplied	flash cards_ID-E.indd	Independent Challenge 1
No Data File supplied	text samples_ID-E.indd text samples_ACE_ID-E.indd	Independent Challenge 2
No Data File supplied	quotes_ID-E.indd quotes_ACE_ID-E.indd	Independent Challenge 3
No Data File supplied red barn.psd canoe.psd landscape.psd flowers.psd mountains.psd building.psd	portfolio_ID-E.indd	Real Life Independent Challenge
No Data File supplied	master pages_ID-E.indd	Visual Workshop
UNIT F		
No Data File supplied USAmap.ai grand opening.ai Legend dots.ai	store locations_ID-F.indd	Lessons
No Data File supplied New York.tif Legend squares.ai Opening Soon.ai	new york coffee_ID-F.indd	Skills Review
ID F-1.indd snow boarder.tif	snowboard magazine_ID-F.indd	Independent Challenge 1
ID F-2.indd red grapes.psd	quick ad_ID-F.indd	Independent Challenge 2
ID F-3.indd watermelon.psd green grapes.psd citrus fruit.psd strawberries.psd lollipops.psd red grapes.psd	fun page layers_ID-F.indd	Independent Challenge 3

Data File Supplied	Student Saves File As	Used In
No Data File supplied mantel clock.tif vintage clock.tif	online sale_ID-F.indd	Real Life Independent Challenge
No Data File supplied	guide layers_ID-F.indd	Visual Workshop
UNIT G		
ID G-1.indd	apple cutouts_ID-G.indd	Lessons
ID G-2.indd	fall schedule_ID-G.indd	Skills Review
No Data File supplied	textbook colors_ID-G.indd	Independent Challenge 1
ID G-3.indd sports car.psd	car ad_ID-G.indd	Independent Challenge 2
No Data File supplied	lacrosse_ID-G.indd	Independent Challenge 3
No Data File supplied	weekly schedule_ID-G.indd	Real Life Independent Challenge
No Data File supplied	rainbow gradient_ID-G.indd	Visual Workshop
INTEGRATION UNIT		
ID H-1.indd amber.jpg citrus fruit.psd panda.psd Puppy Button.ai seafood.psd strawberries.psd strawberry shortcake.psd dog.psd	happy apple website_ID-H.indd	Lessons
ID H-2.indd canoers.tif adventure.psd camp.psd computer.psd sewing.psd sports.psd boy in grass.jpg Yoga Button.ai boy yoga.psd	happy camper website_ID-H.indd	Skills Review
ID H-3.indd	button_ID-H.indd	Independent Challenge 1
ID H-4.indd	web cards_ID-H.indd	Independent Challenge 2
ID H-5.indd watermelon.psd green grapes.psd citrus fruit.psd strawberries.psd lollipops.psd red grapes.psd	animation_ID-H.indd	Independent Challenge 3
No Data File supplied	trip planner_ID-H.indd	Real Life Independent Challenge
No Data File supplied	navigation_ID-H.indd	Visual Workshop

Glossary

Action A prewritten script attached to a button.

Align (objects) To position one or more selected objects in relation to each other, in relation to the margins of a document, or in relation to the boundaries of the page or spread.

Alignment (paragraph) The way a paragraph is horizontally spread out between the left and right sides of a text box.

Anchor points The small dots that connect straight or curved line segments of a path.

Baseline grid Type of grid that is useful for working with columns of text.

Bitmap graphic A graphic that is made up of pixels.

Bleed An item that extends one or more of the page borders. Bleed elements require an additional .25" size added to them to prevent white space appearing when the document is trimmed.

Bounding box A rectangle whose size matches the width and height of the selected object; includes eight selection handles that can be used to resize the object.

Bullets Small symbols, such as circles or squares, that appear before the beginning of a paragraph; typically used for lists of items.

Button An interactive, clickable item that becomes active when the document is exported as an interactive Portable Document Format (PDF) or as a Shockwave Flash file (SWF).

Cells Small rectangles laid out horizontally in rows and vertically in columns that make up a table.

Character style Formatting that can be applied consistently to text characters; enables you to control font, font size, and color.

CMYK (cyan, magenta, yellow, and black) Process inks; combinations of CMYK create process colors.

Color stop Icon below the Gradient Ramp that represents a color used in the gradient.

Content Indicator The content indicator, a donut-shaped icon, appears over a placed graphic when you move the Selection tool over the graphic. The content indicator allows you to move a graphic in a frame without moving the frame.

Column Vertical arrangement of cells in a table.

Control panel Panel that can be used to view or modify information about a selected object, such as the object's size or location on the page.

Crop To hide part of an image without permanently removing it.

Destination The place the source jumps to from a hyperlink.

Detach To convert a master item on a document page into a regular object so that the item is no longer associated with changes made to the corresponding master item on the master page.

Distribute To place equal space between three or more objects.

Document grid Type of grid that is useful for aligning objects.

Document tab Appears just above the horizontal ruler; includes the document name, the current magnification level of the document, and a Close button.

Document window In a workspace, the white space surrounded by a black border and drop shadow that represents the open InDesign document.

Effect Special feature that you add to an object to improve its appearance or to create a particular impression about the object.

Embed To make a file a permanent part of the InDesign file so that the embedded file cannot be affected by changes made to the original file outside of InDesign.

EPS (Encapsulated Postscript) A file format saved in the CMYK color mode that is ideal for print.

EPUB (Electronic Publication) An electronic book file format for ebooks that can be optimized and read on a variety of devices.

Event The activity that needs to take place for an action to occur, such as when the user clicks a button or moves the mouse pointer over a button.

Facing pages Left and right pages in a multiple-page document.

Fill The color that fills an object.

Font A set of characters based on a typeface using a specific size and style.

Gradient fill A type of fill in which two or more colors blend from one to another.

Grid Preset group of vertical and horizontal lines equidistant from each other in the Document window, much like traditional grid paper.

Group To select two or more objects and make them into one selectable object.

Guide Horizontal or vertical line that is used to create and position objects in the Document window.

Gutter The space between two columns.

Hanging indent A type of text indent in which the first line in each paragraph is positioned to the left of the remaining lines in the paragraph.

Hidden character A non-printing character, such as a space between words or a paragraph return.

Hyperlink Object that, when clicked, jumps to another location in the same document, to another document, or to a website.

IDML (InDesign Markup) An InDesign file format that allows you to open other versions of InDesign.

Indent A blank space between text and its margin or frame border.

Inset The amount of space between the top, bottom, right, and/or left sides of text and its table cell borders.

Island spread A spread whose pages remain together when pages are moved within a document.

JPEG (Joint Photographic Experts Group) Compressed graphic file format that is ideal for use on the web.

Justify To position text at specific horizontal locations within a text box or table cell.

Layers The designated levels within a document on which objects appear.

Leading The amount of space between the baselines of two lines of type.

Library A type of InDesign file used for storing often-used text, graphics, and InDesign pages.

Linear gradient A type of gradient fill that blends from one point to another, horizontally, vertically, or diagonally, depending on the angle of the gradient.

Link The connection between a placed graphic in a frame and the original graphic file on the hard drive.

Margin guide Colored horizontal or vertical line within a document that indicates a margin.

Master item Object placed on a master page; appears on every document page to which the master page is applied.

Master page Page design that can be applied consistently to multiple document pages.

Menu bar Bar that sits at the top of the InDesign workspace and includes several menu options.

Merge (cells) To combine table cells into one cell.

Merge (layers) To consolidate multiple layers into one single layer.

Normal mode The default view in InDesign; it displays all of the non-printing elements, such as frame borders, guides, grids, margin guides, and column guides.

Object Anything that can be selected, such as a text box, logo, picture, simple shape, line, or guide.

Override To "unlock" a master item on a document page in order to work with it.

Page guide Guide that appears on a single page and doesn't extend to other pages in a document.

Page item The name given to an item placed on a layer.

Page layout software Software that includes tools that allow you to easily position text and graphics on document pages.

Panel Small floating window that contains options for working with selected objects.

Paragraph style Formatting that can be applied consistently to paragraphs of text; enables you to control character formatting, indents, spacing before and after paragraphs, and alignment.

Paragraphs Lines of text that are separated by the space created when you press [Enter] (Win) or [return] (Mac).

Pasteboard Gray or white area surrounding the Document window.

PDF The file format used in Adobe Reader, a free software program that allows you to view documents created from other software programs without needing those programs installed on your computer.

Pixels Tiny color squares arranged in a grid that are used to display graphics shown on a monitor or television screen.

PNG (Portable Network Graphics) An ideal file format for use on the web that supports transparency.

Point of origin The point on an object from which the object is transformed.

Portable Document Format *See* PDF.

Preset A collection of document settings that is saved and stored with a descriptive name and is available for use in the New Document dialog box.

Preview A graphical representation of an original image file and not the file itself.

Preview mode InDesign view that hides all of the non-printing elements.

Process color A color that is made from using the four process inks (CMYK).

Process ink Ink used for color printing; different percentages of one or more process inks (CMYK) combine to create process colors.

Process match A combination of process inks (CMYK) that is the closest possible match to a spot color.

Proportion The original relationship between an object's width and height.

Radial gradient A type of gradient fill that blends from the center outward to the border(s) of the object.

RGB Stands for Red, Green, Blue. RGB is the color system for graphics displayed on a monitor.

Resolution The number of pixels per inch (ppi) used to display computer graphics on a monitor.

Row Horizontal arrangement of cells in a table.

Screen resolution *See* Resolution.

Selection color The color of the bounding box that appears around selected objects on a specific layer in a document.

Shuffle To change the order and location of pages by moving one or more pages within a document.

Smart Guides Smart guides are guides that appear automatically as you position objects on a page. Smart guides are visual clues that let you know when the object you are positioning is touching a side or the center of another object, a margin guide, or the center of the page.

Snap To exactly align with something, such as a guide.

Source A hyperlink that, when clicked, goes to a destination location, document, or website.

Split To break a table cell into smaller cells.

Spot color Color that is manufactured by a company and must be purchased when used in a publication that will be professionally printed.

Spread A set of left and right pages in a multiple-page document.

Spread guide Guide that extends to the pasteboard and appears on all of the pages in a spread.

State A different appearance for the same object. States are created on the Object States panel.

Status bar A bar along the bottom of the Document window. It shows the status of the document, such as the active page.

Story All of the text in one text box or all of the text in linked text boxes.

Stroke The color that outlines an object; similar to a border or an edge.

Swatch Color sample available on the Swatches panel.

SWF (Shockwave Flash) Scalable and compact file format that is popular for online animation and games; can be viewed by anyone with Flash Player installed on his or her computer.

Tab stop Ruler setting that works together with the [Tab] key to enable you to position, or justify, text at specific horizontal locations within a text box or table cell.

Table A rectangular object that is made of up rows and columns of smaller rectangles called cells.

Text box Object that is a container for text; also called a text frame.

Text frame *See* Text box.

Thread To flow text into linked text boxes.

Tools panel Panel that contains all available InDesign tools, such as those for creating objects, transforming objects, changing the page view, and navigating the workspace.

Typeface A design created for a set of characters including the alphabet, numbers, and some symbols.

Uniform scale A type of scale in which an object is scaled both horizontally and vertically by the same percentage.

URL (Uniform Resource Locator) Address of a website on the Internet.

Vector graphic A graphic that is made up of straight or curved line segments connected by anchor points.

Weight The thickness of a stroke; measured in points.

XML XML stands for **eXtensible Markup Language** and is a file format that InDesign documents can be saved as. XML files store and transport data in a format accessible by other programs. The XML format allows others to build, modify, and collaborate on projects using shared files by adding tags that describe the data.

Index

bitmap and vector, 78–79

capabilities, 2

content indicator, 82–83

embedding, 88–89

frames, 80–85

Links panel, 86–87

replacing linked images, 88–89

grids, 15

grouping objects, 60, 62–63, Int:8

guides, 14–15

gutter, 26

H

H (Height) text box, 56–57

hand pointer, 82–83

help feature, 10

hidden characters, 32

hidden tools, 6

hiding layers, 130–131

High Quality Display, 122

horizontal ruler, 6

HTML (Hypertext Markup Language) format, 16

hyperlinks, Int:2–5

Hyperlinks panel, Int:2–5

Hypertext Markup Language (HTML) format, 16

I

IDML (InDesign Markup Language) format, 16

Illustrator, Adobe, using colors from, 156

images, linked, 88–89

indents, 34

InDesign Markup Language (IDML) format, 16

.indl extension, 2

inserting

cells in tables, 158–159

rows into tables, 158

Insert Pages dialog box, 100

inset value, for cells, 154

interactive documents

animations, Int:10–11

buttons, 2, Int:6–7, Int:12–13

exporting as Flash Player file, Int:14–15

hyperlinks, Int:2–5

Rollover and Click appearances, Int:8–9

Inverse Rounded button, Corner Options dialog box, 66–67

island spreads, 113

J

JPEG (Joint Photographic Experts Group) format, 16

justifying text, in tables, 160

K

kerning, 31

L

Lab color mode, 148

Landscape button, Pages panel, 100–101

layers

arranging, 125

changing options, 124–125

changing order, 134–144

description, 121–122

duplicating, 126, 128–129

hiding all except one, 130

locking and hiding, 130–131

merging, 132

moving objects to another, 132–133

new, 126–127

pasting into document, 134

placing objects on, 122–123

selecting all objects in, 126

selection color of, 124

targeting, 124

leading, 32

libraries, 2, 90–98

linear gradients, 150

line segments, 78–79

linked documents, 4, 77

linked files, 91

linked images, 88–89

Link Info section, Links panel, 86–87

Links panel, 86–89

Link to list arrow, Int:2–3

liquid guides, 15

Live Distribute feature, 62–63

local overrides, 105

Lock command, 58–59

locking

layers, 130–131

objects, 58–59

looping animations, Int:10

M

Make all settings the same button, Corner Options dialog box, 66–67

manual text flow, 29